JEWISH ETHICS AND HALAKHAH FOR OUR TIME

Sources and Commentary

Volume II

THE LIBRARY OF JEWISH LAW AND ETHICS
VOLUME XVII
EDITED BY NORMAN LAMM

Jakob and Erna Michael professor of Jewish philosophy
Yeshiva University

JEWISH ETHICS AND HALAKHAH FOR OUR TIME

Sources and Commentary

Volume II

by

BASIL F. HERRING

KTAV PUBLISHING HOUSE, INC.
HOBOKEN, NEW JERSEY
YESHIVA UNIVERSITY PRESS
NEW YORK

Library of Congress Cataloging-in-Publication Data
(Revised for volume 2)

Herring, Basil.
Jewish ethics and Halakhah for our time.

(The Library of Jewish law and ethics ; v. 11)
"Sources" (32 p.) in pocket of v. 1.
Includes bibliographical references.
1. Ethics, Jewish. 2. Jewish law. 3. Orthodox
Judaism. I. Title. II. Series: Library of Jewish law
and ethics ; v.11, etc.
BJ1285.H38 1984 296.3′85 84-5699
ISBN 0-88125-044-9 v. 1.
ISBN 0-88125-045-7 pbk. : pbk.)

Manufactured in the United States of America

To Ari, Aliza, David, and Yael,
Who bring joy and fulfillment to our lives.
May they always walk before God
To enjoy His blessings
Together.

Contents

Editor's Foreword

To the surprise of almost everyone, Halakhah has entered a phase of burgeoning activity both in Israel and in the United States. Talmudic scholars, educated in more and larger yeshivot than existed even in Polish Jewry at its zenith, are not only continuing the theoretical and exegetical literature of the past in a variety of methodologies, but they are also applying themselves to contemporary problems. These problems are usually technological in nature, but they also extend to the ethical realm, where changing conceptions as well as improved technologies and scientific discoveries create unprecedented ethical dilemmas.

The fact that Halakhists are now more self-confident and aggressive in confronting such problems is not only of cultural significance but, far more, it is an indication both of the eternal validity of Halakhah in times of vast changes and the creativity of scholars of Torah.

This increasing intellectual activity of contemporary halakhic scholars is reflected in the fact that a mere five years have passed since we published Rabbi Basil F. Herring's first volume on *Jewish Ethics and Halakhah for Our Times: Sources and Commentary*, and we are now presenting this second volume, filled with new and engaging material, as part of our Library of Jewish Law and Ethics.

The reading public found that Dr. Herring's method of presentation felicitously succeeded in making the intracacies of Halakhah, otherwise seemingly impenetrable to the non-specialist, accessible to the "intelligent layman" (that fortunate though anonymous person for whom so much literature has been created for so many years in so many disciplines and with so much care!)

without sacrificing the substance of the argumentation by a patronizing over-simplification.

The present volume continues the same method innovated in the first one and, I hope, will prove at least as successful and thus lead to many others to come.

NORMAN LAMM
Editor

July 4, 1989

Preface

Jewish law, or Halakhah, is the system of principles, laws, enactments, and opinions that together attempt to regulate the daily life of the traditional Jew. This body of law covers vastly more than the ceremonial and narrowly "religious" realms. In reality it aspires to govern practically every aspect of communal and private endeavor, so as to render them fully consistent with the values, priorities, and practices of the rabbinic tradition as handed down through the ages.

Thus it is that Jewish law can be said to embrace the ethical dimension. For the Jew concerned to live in accordance with the dictates of that code, no ethical or moral concern is considered beyond the reach of Halakhah. And as that Jew grapples with the moral dilemmas that he confronts, be it as a functioning member of modern society or as a sensitive and thinking individual concerned to know right from wrong, he must perforce consider the view, or views, encountered in the halakhic literature, as he goes through the process of formulating his own response to the ethical challenges before him.

Of course ethics is a matter of conscience and personal judgment. Yet Jewish law insists that for the Jew such ethical decisions must be preceded by a thorough knowledge of the parameters of the Halakhah on the given issue.

Accordingly, this book attempts to present in detail most of the rabbinic sources, views, and responses on six somewhat representative topics in Jewish law and ethics. Within each broad chapter heading, a number of related, yet tangential, topics are also touched upon. I have tried to trace the development of the respective principles, arguments, and conclusions, without either prejudging their validity or imposing any particular perspective. It will be seen that while the various halakhists share many talmudic assumptions, their conclusions are far from unanimous, and sometimes even lacking in consensus. On certain points they might be said to be diametrically opposed. Nonetheless, armed with this information, an individual can proceed to formulate his or her own response to the issues herein addressed.

I trust that it will be readily apparent that the Halakhah, as projected by the rabbinic writings here encountered, does in fact address many of the current social and ethical issues that confront the modern Jew. Clichés and superficialities notwithstanding, the halakhic process is not a dry, ossified body of ancient, static law—but is, and has always been, a living, growing, expanding, dynamic, and repercussive entity. Many, whether on the so-called left or right of the religious spectrum, prefer to see the Halakhah as monolithic and homogeneous, free of inner tension and flexibility. Yet even a casual reading of this volume will show that, in practically every age since talmudic times, up to and including our own, the halakhic process has been characterized by discussion and debate, as well as disagreement and dissent, among halakhists of even the highest stature. It will also be apparent from these pages that Jewish law has never been a closed system, but has rather attempted to embrace the best insights, lessons, and experiences of each succeeding generation, albeit with exceeding care, precision, and at its own considered pace.

In recent years a number of the halakhic authorities who led our generation subsequent to the Second World War, and who were responsible in many ways for the revival and consolidation of traditional Jewish life and the Halakhah since that time, have themselves either aged markedly or died. Thus Jewish law currently finds itself in a period of transition, as we await the emergence of a new generation of scholars and recognized authorities to face the ever more complex issues and challenges posed by the rapidly changing society in which we find ourselves.

It cannot be gainsaid that there is a genuine interest, even on the part of those who may not themselves be committed to the Halakhah, to know what Jewish law has to say regarding many of the ethical problems generated by modern society. Unfortunately much of the halakhic material, both classic and modern, remains inaccessible to most laymen who have neither the background nor the time to study the literature on the subject. The response within the Jewish community to the first volume of *Jewish Ethics and Halakhah for Our Time*, which appeared a few years ago, prompted the current effort.

The present volume takes the same format as the first. I have chosen to deal with fewer issues, but in considerably more depth. One could say that each issue is dealt with in the classic responsa style, i.e., we begin with a question that describes a "real" situation and the dilemmas entailed therein, and we end each issue with a "ruling" that prescribes a course of action. To focus the discussion, each treatment of the topic is preceded by a rather comprehensive listing of the primary sources, in translation, germane to the give-and-take that follows among later authorities. For convenience, "primary" is defined as anything written until the codification of the *Shulḥan Arukh* and its accompanying commentary by R. Moses Isserles (the Rema) in the sixteenth century. I have tried to keep the notes short and to the point. Nonetheless some readers might feel that the many authorities and viewpoints that are cited in the course of the discussion are somewhat burdensome to follow in detail. I can only hope that the presentation of these discussions will be sufficiently interesting so as to enable the average reader to gain maximum benefit from the effort involved. In any case, each chapter does conclude with a broad summary of the preceding material.

Included too in the front of the book is an alphabetical listing of most of the halakhic authorities cited in the text and notes, together with some essential data (where available) as to their full names, time, place, and major works, to facilitate easy reference to the various personalities and works encountered in the course of the discussions. A more comprehensive description of the history of Halakhah, together with a discussion of the relationship between Jewish law and ethics, can be found in the introduction to volume 1 of *Jewish Ethics and Halakhah for Our Time.*

I do hope that the material found herein will be helpful to both professionals and laymen, rabbis and congregants, teachers and students, as well as thoughtful individuals of every stripe and persuasion, so as to stimulate further insight, consideration, discussion, as well as appreciation of the multifaceted diamond that is the rabbinic tradition.

Table of Authorities Cited

This alphabetized list consists of generally recognized authorities whose names are found in the chapters and discussions that follow. It provides in each case a few facts relative to their name(s), time, place, and major halakhic publications, without referring to their nonhalakhic works, but including, where applicable, any well-known teachers or students that they might have had.

Abu Zimrah. See *Radbaz*.
Abulafia, Ḥayyim b. David. 1700–1775. Smyrna, Turkey. Codifier.
Abulafia, Meir ha-Levi. See *Ramah*.
Adret. See *Rashba*.
Agudat Ezov. See *Maharam Zev*.
Aḥi'ezer. Ḥayyim Ozer Grodzinski. 1863–1940. Vilna. Responsa.
Alfasi. See *Rif*.
Alshikh, Moses. d. after 1593. Safed, Israel. Bible commentaries. Student of Joseph Karo.
Arukh la-Ner. See *Ettlinger, Jacob*.
Arukh ha-Shulḥan. Yeḥiel Mikhel ha-Levi Epstein. 1829–1908. Russia. Novellae and rulings to *Shulḥan Arukh*.
Asheri. See *Rosh*.
Avodat ha-Leviyyim. See *Jonathan b. David of Lunel*.
Avodat ha-Melekh. Menaḥem Krakowski. 1870–1929. Commentary to Maimonides' *Mishneh Torah*.
Azulai. See *Ḥida*.
Babad. See *Minḥat Ḥinukh*.
Baḥ. Joel Sirkes. 1561–1640. Poland. Commentary on the *Tur* (the *Bayit Ḥadash*, acronym "Baḥ"). Responsa (*Bayit Ḥadash*). Teacher and father-in-law of the Taz.

Baḥya b. Asher, Rabbeinu. 13th century. Saragossa, Spain. Commentary to Torah. Student of Rashba.

Baumol, Yehoshua. 1879–1947. Russia and New York. Responsa (*Emek Halakhah*).

Beit Ya'akov. Jacob b. Samuel of Zausmer. 17th century. Responsa.

Beit David. Joseph David. 1667–1736. Salonika. Responsa.

Benveniste. See *Knesset ha-Gedolah*.

Berlin. See *Neẓiv*.

Binyan Ẓion. See *Ettlinger, Jacob*.

Bleich, J. David. Contemporary. New York. Essays, articles, reviews.

Braun, Shelomoh Zalman. Contemporary. New York. Commentary/compendium on *Kiẓur Shulḥan Arukh* (*She'arim ha-Meẓuyyanim be'Halakhah*).

Chayes, Ẓvi Hirsch (Mahariẓ Chayes). 1805–1855. Galicia. Responsa (*Mahariẓ Chayes*), various studies on halakhic topics.

Darkhei Noam. Mordecai b. Judah ha-Levi. d. 1684. Cairo. Responsa.

Divrei Malki'el. Malki'el Ẓvi ha-Levi Tannenbaum. 19th century. Lomza, Lithuania. Responsa (publ. 1891–1901).

Duran. See *Tashbaẓ*.

Efrati, Shimon b. Yekutiel. 1909–. Poland and Israel. Responsa (*me-Emek ha-Bakha, mi-Gei ha-Harigah*).

Eibeschutz, Jonathan. 1690–1764. Prague. Commentaries on the *Shulḥan Arukh* (incl. *Kreiti u-Fleiti*).

Eiger, Akiva b. Moses. 1761–1837. Posen, Germany. Talmudic commentaries (incl. *Gilyon ha-Shas*) and glosses to *Shulḥan Arukh*.

Eiger, Solomon. 1786–1852. Germany. Talmudic commentaries (incl. *Gilyon Maharsha*). Son of R. Akiva Eiger.

Elberg, Simḥah. Contemporary. Warsaw and New York. Commentaries and novellae (*Shalmei Simḥah*).

Eliezer b. Samuel of Metz. 1115–1198. France. Tosafist, compendium and elaboration of *miẓvot* (*Sefer Yerayim*). Student of Rabbeinu Tam and Rashbam.

Elijah of Vilna, the Gra. 1720–1797. Commentaries and glosses to the Talmud, the *Shulḥan Arukh* (incl. *Be'ur ha-Gra*), Scripture, Midrash, and others.

Emden, Jacob b. Ẓvi, Yaveẓ. 1697–1776. Altona, Germany.

Responsa (incl. *She'elat Yaveẓ*). His father and teacher was the Ḥakham Ẓvi.

Emek Halakhah. See *Baumol, Yehoshua*.

Epstein, Barukh ha-Levi. See *Torah Temimah*.

Epstein, Moshe Mordecai. 1866–1933. Lithuania and Israel. Talmudic discussions (*Levush Mordecai*).

Epstein, Yeḥiel Mikhel ha-Levi. See *Arukh ha-Shulḥan*.

Ettlinger, Jacob. 1798–1871. Altona, Germany. Talmudic commentaries (incl. *Arukh la-Ner*) and responsa (*Binyan Ẓion*).

Falk, Joshua ha-Kohen. See *Sema*.

Feinstein, Moshe. 1895–1986. Luban, Russia, and New York. Responsa (*Iggerot Moshe*) and talmudic commentaries.

Gershom b. Judah Me'or ha-Golah, Rabbeinu. 960–1028. Mainz, Germany. Commentaries to Talmud, responsa. Taught the teachers of Rashi.

Gershuni, Yehudah. Contemporary. New York and Israel. Essays and articles (included in *Kol Ẓofayikh*).

Gesher ha-Ḥayyim. See *Tucatzinsky, Yeḥiel*.

Gombiner, Abraham. See *Magen Avraham*.

Goren, Shelomoh. Contemporary. Israel. Essays, articles, monographs.

Gra. See *Elijah of Vilna*.

Greenwald, Yekutiel. 1889–1955. Columbus, Ohio. Compendium of Laws of Mourning (*Kolbo al Aveilut*).

Grodzinski, Ḥayyim Ozer. See *Aḥi'ezer*.

Grossnass, A. L. Contemporary. England. Essays and articles.

Gulevsky, Ḥayyim Dubber. Contemporary. New York. Essays and articles.

ha-Meiri. See *Meiri*.

ha-Rah. Aaron ha-Levi. 1235–1300. Barcelona, Spain. Talmudic commentaries.

Hadaya, Ovadiah. 1891–1969. Jerusalem. Responsa (*Yaskil Avdi*).

Ḥafeẓ Ḥayyim. Israel Meir ha-Kohen Kagan. 1838–1933. Radun, Poland. Commentary to *Shulḥan Arukh* (*Mishnah Berurah*); ethical treatises.

Hagahot Maimoniyyot. R. Meir ha-Kohen. 13th century. Rothenburg, Germany. Maimonidean commentator, with additional responsa (*Teshuvot Maimoniyyot*). Student of Maharam Rothenburg.

Hai b. Sherira Gaon. 939–1038. Pumbedita. Various halakhic treatises, most particularly *Sefer ha-Mekaḥ ve'ha-Memkar.*

Ḥakham Ẓvi. Ẓvi Hirsch b. Jacob. 1660–1718. Altona, Germany. Responsa. Father of Jacob Emden.

Ḥananel b. Ḥushi'el, Rabbeinu. d. 1055. Kairouan. Talmudic commentary.

Ḥatam Sofer. Moses Sofer (Schreiber). 1762–1839. Pressburg, Hungary. Responsa (*Ḥatam Sofer*), Talmudic commentaries. Son-in-law of Akiva Eiger.

Ḥavvot Yair, Yair Ḥayyim Bachrach. 1638–1702. Germany. Responsa

Ḥayyim ha-Levi Soloveichik. 1853–1918. Volozhin, Russia. Novellae on the Talmud and Maimonides.

Ḥazon Ish. Avraham Yeshayahu Karelitz. 1878–1953. Vilna and Bnei Brak. Commentary on *Shulḥan Arukh.*

Heller, Ḥayyim. 1878–1960. Poland, Berlin, and New York. Author of studies in Scripture, Targumim, Peshitta, and Maimonides' *Sefer ha-Miẓvot.*

Heller, Yomtov Lipman. 1579–1654. Prague, Nikolsburg, and Poland. Commentary on Mishnah (*Tosafot Yomtov*), responsa.

Henkin, Yosef Eliyahu. 1880–1973. Responsa.

Ḥida. Ḥayyim Joseph David Azulai. 1724–1806. Jerusalem. Glosses to *Shulḥan Arukh.*

Ḥeshek Shelomoh, Solomon b. Mordecai. 1269–1340. Smyrna, Turkey. Commentary to the *Tur.*

Hubner, Shmuel. Contemporary. Israel. Responsa (*Nimmukei Shmuel*).

Ibn Ezra, Abraham. 1089–1164. Spain and Rome. Biblical commentator, poet, grammarian, philosopher.

Ibn Migash, Joseph b. Meir ha-Levi. 1077–1141. Spain. Talmudic commentaries. Student of Alfasi and teacher of Maimonides' father.

Iggerot Moshe. See *Feinstein, Moshe.*

Isaac b. Joseph of Corbeil. See *Semak.*

Isaac of Molena. Died before 1580. Spain and Cairo, Egypt. Responsa.

Israel Meir ha-Kohen Kagan. See *Ḥafeẓ Ḥayyim.*

Isserles, Moses. See *Rema.*

Jacob b. Asher. See *Tur.*

Jacob of Orleans. d. 1189. England. One of the authorities among the Tosafot. Student of Rabbeinu Tam.

Jaffe, Mordecai b. Abraham. See *Levush*.

Jakobovits, Immanuel. Contemporary. London. Essays and articles.

Jonathan b. David ha-Kohen of Lunel. 12th century. Commentary to Rif (*Avodat ha-Leviyyim*). Student of Ravad.

Joshua b. Abraham Maimoni, ha-Naggid. 1310–1355. Cairo. Responsa. Descendant of Maimonides.

Judah he-Ḥasid. See *Sefer Ḥasidim*.

Judah b. ha-Rosh. 1270–1349. Toledo, Spain. Responsa (*Zikhron Yehudah*).

Karelitz, Avraham Yeshayahu. See *Ḥazon Ish*.

Karo. See *Shulḥan Arukh*.

Kasher, Menaḥem. 1895–1983. Poland, New York, and Israel. Compendium/commentary on the Torah (*Torah Sheleimah*), essays and articles.

Klein, Menasheh. See *Mishneh Halakhot*.

Kluger, Solomon (Maharshak). 1785–1869. Brody, Poland. Responsa (incl. *Tuv Ta'am ve'Da'at*).

Knesset ha-Gedolah. Ḥayyim b. Israel Benveniste. 1603–1673. Smyrna, Turkey. Commentator and codifier. Student of Maharit.

Kolbo. See *Greenwald, Yekutiel*.

Kook, Abraham Isaac ha-Kohen. 1865–1935. Latvia and Israel. Halakhic monographs related to Israel and redemption.

Krakowski. See *Avodat ha-Melekh*.

Lamm, Norman. Contemporary. New York. Essays and articles.

Landau, Ezekiel b. Judah. See *Noda bi-Yehudah*.

Landsofer, Jonah b. Elijah. 1678–1712. Prague. Responsa (*Me'il Ẓedakah*).

Leḥem Mishneh. Abraham b. Moses di Boton. 1545–1588. Salonika, Greece. Maimonidean commentator. Student of Maharashdam.

Levush. Mordecai b. Abraham Jaffe. 1535–1612. Poland. Commentary on codes (the *Levushim*). Student of Maharshal and Rema.

Lieberman, Saul. 1898–1983. Poland, Jerusalem, and New York. Studies on Tosefta, Jerusalem Talmud, and history of halakhic literature.

Liebes, Yiẓḥak. Contemporary. New York. Responsa (*Beit Avi*).

Lipshutz, Israel. See *Tiferet Yisrael*.

Lorberbaum, Jacob b. Moses. 1760–1832. Poland. Commentaries on *Shulḥan Arukh*, Scripture (*Netivot ha-Mishpat*).

Luria, Solomon. See *Maharshal*.

Mabit, Moses b. Joseph. 1500–1580. Safed. Responsa (*Mabit*). Father of Maharit.

Magen Avraham. Abraham Gombiner. 1637–1683. Poland. Commentary to *Shulḥan Arukh*.

Maggid Mishnah. Vidal Yomtov of Tolosa. Late 14th century. Spain. Commentary on Maimonides' *Mishneh Torah*.

Maharam Zev. Zev Naḥum Bernstein. 1839–1910. Biale, Poland. Talmudic commentary (*Agudat Ezov*).

Maharam Schick. Moses b. Joseph. 1807–1879. Hungary. Responsa. Student of Ḥatam Sofer.

Maharam Padua. Meir b. Isaac Katzenellenbogen. 1473–1565. Italy. Responsa.

Maharam Lublin. Meir. b. Gedaliah. 1558–1616. Poland. Talmudic commentaries and responsa (*Manhir Einei Ḥakhamim*).

Maharam Rothenburg. Meir b. Barukh. 1215–1293. Germany. Talmudic commentaries, responsa. Students were Rosh, Mordecai, Hagahot Maimoniyyot, Tashbaẓ.

Maharashdam. Samuel b. Moses de Medini. 1506–1589. Salonika. Responsa (*Maharashdam*).

Mahari ben Lev. See *Maharival*.

Maharit Ẓahalon. Yomtov b. Moses. 1559–1620. Safed. Responsa, Talmudic commentaries. Student of Joseph Karo.

Maharit. Joseph b. Moses Trani. 1568–1639. Safed and Turkey. Talmudic commentaries and responsa (*Maharit*). Son of Mabit.

Mahariv. Jacob Weil. d. before 1456. Germany. Responsa (*Mahariv*); manual on laws of slaughtering.

Maharival. Joseph b. David Ibn Lev. 1505–1580. Salonika. Responsa.

Mahariẓ Chayes. See *Chayes*.

Maharsha. Samuel Adels. 1555–1631. Poland. Commentary to Talmud.

Maharshak. See *Kluger, Solomon*.

Maharshal. Solomon b. Yeḥiel Luria. 1510–1574. Poland. Talmudic commentaries (*Yam shel Shelomoh, Ḥokhmat Shelomoh*). Teacher of Levush and Sema.

Maharsham. Shalom Mordecai b. Moses Shvadron. 1835–1911. Galicia. Responsa.

Maimonides. Moses b. Maimon. 1135–1204. Fostat, Egypt. Codifier and author of *Mishneh Torah*, responsa, *Sefer ha-Miẓvot*, Commentary on Mishnah.

Mareh ha-Panim. Moses b. Simon Margaliyot. Died 1781. Lithuania. Commentaries on Jerusalem Talmud (*Mareh ha-Panim*, *Pnei Moshe*). Student was the young Elijah of Vilna.

Margaliyot, Moses. See *Mareh ha-Panim*.

Meir Simḥah ha-Kohen of Dvinsk. 1843–1926. Russia. Commentary to Maimonides and Talmud (*Or Sameaḥ*) and Torah (*Meshekh Ḥokhmah*), and responsa.

Meiri. Menaḥem b. Solomon. 1249–1316. Perpignan, France. Commentaries on Talmud (*Beit ha-Beḥirah*) and parts of Scripture.

Meisels, Ẓvi Hirsch. Contemporary. Poland and Chicago. Responsa (*Mekadeshei Hashem*).

Mekadeshei Hashem. See *Meisels, Ẓvi Hirsch*.

Minḥat Yiẓḥak. See *Weiss, Yiẓḥak Ya'akov*.

Minḥat Ḥinukh. Joseph b. Moses Babad. 1800–1875. Poland. Expositions and novellae to *Sefer ha-Ḥinukh*.

Mishneh la-Melekh. Judah b. Samuel Rosannes. 1657–1727. Turkey. Commentary on Maimonides' *Mishneh Torah*.

Mishneh Torah. See *Maimonides*.

Mishneh Halakhot. Menasheh Klein. Contemporary. New York. Responsa.

Mizraḥi, Elijah. 1450–1526. Turkey. Responsa, talmudic commentaries, supercommentary to Rashi on the Torah (the *Mizraḥi*).

Molena, Isaac of. See *Isaac of Molena*.

Mordecai b. Hillel ha-Kohen. Known as "the Mordecai." 1240–1298. Germany. Student of Maharam Rothenburg, brother-in-law of Hagahot Maimoniyyot. Compendium/commentary (the *Mordecai*).

Mordecai b. Judah ha-Levi. See *Darkhei Noam*.

Moses b. Isaac Lima. 1605–1658. Lithuania. Commentary on *Shulḥan Arukh* (*Ḥelkat Meḥokek*.) Student of Sema, colleague of Shakh.

Naḥmanides. Moses b. Naḥman. 1194–1270. Gerona, Spain.

Talmudic commentaries, responsa, monographs, glosses. First cousin of Rabbeinu Yonah and teacher of Rashba.

Nathanson Joseph Saul. 1810–1875. Lemberg, Poland. Responsa (*Sho'el u-Meshiv*) and commentaries (*Divrei Sha'ul*).

Netivot ha-Mishpat. See *Lorberbaum*.

Neẓiv. Naftali Ẓvi Yehudah Berlin. 1817–1893. Volozhin, Russia. Talmudic and biblical commentaries, responsa (*Ha'amek She'elah, Ha'amek Davar, Meishiv Davar*).

Nimmukei Yosef. Joseph Ibn Ḥabib. Early 15th century. Talmudic commentary.

Nissim b. Reuben Gerondi, Rabbeinu. Known as the Ran. 1310–1375. Spain. Talmudic commentaries (*Ḥiddushei ha-Ran*), ethical works (*Sha'arei Teshuvah*).

Noda bi-Yehudah. Ezekiel b. Judah Landau. 1713–1793. Prague. Responsa (*Noda bi-Yehudah*) and various commentaries.

Or ha-Meir. Judah Meir b. Jacob Shapiro. 1886–1934. Lublin. Responsa.

Or Zarua. Isaac b. Moses of Vienna. d. 1260. Compendium and commentary (*Or Zarua*). Responsa.

Oshry, Efraim. Kovno. Responsa (*mi-Ma'amakim*).

Ovadiah Yosef. Contemporary. Egypt, Israel. Responsa (*Yabia Omer, Yeḥaveh Da'at*).

Pick, Isaiah b. Judah Leib. 1725–1799. Breslau, Germany. Glosses and commentaries (incl. *Masoret ha-Shas*).

Pitḥei Teshuvah. Abraham b. Ẓvi Hirsch Eisenstadt. 1813–1868. Lithuania/Poland. Responsa digest in form of commentary to *Shulḥan Arukh*.

Preil, Eliezer Meir. d. 1934.

Rabbeinu Asher. See *Rosh*.

Rabbeinu Nissim. See *Nissim*.

Rabbeinu Tam. Jacob b. Meir. 1100–1171. Ramerupt, France. Responsa and talmudic commentaries (together in his *Sefer ha-Yashar*), also recorded in his pivotal position in Tosafot. Grandson of Rashi and teacher of (inter alia) Eliezer of Metz.

Radbaz. R. David b. Abu Zimra. 1479–1573. Alexandria and Cairo, Egypt. Responsa and talmudic/Maimonidean commentaries.

Ramah. Meir ha-Levi Abulafia. 1170–1244. Toledo, Spain. Commentaries to Talmud (*Yad Ramah*) and Maimonides.

Rambam. See *Maimonides*.

Ran. See *Nissim*.

Rashba. Solomon b. Abraham Adret. 1235–1310. Barcelona, Spain. Talmudic commentaries and responsa. Student of Rabbeinu Yonah of Gerondi.

Rashi. Solomon b. Isaac. 1040–1105. Troyes, France. Primary talmudic commentaries, responsa. Teacher of Rashbam and Rabbeinu Tam (his grandsons).

Ravad. Abraham b. David of Posquières. 1125–1198. Spain. Maimonidean critic. Commentaries and responsa. Student of Meshulam b. Jacob of Lunel.

Recanati, Menaḥem. Early 14th century. Italy. Commentary on Torah, halakhic compendium (*Piskei Halakhot*).

Reischer, Jacob b. Joseph. 1670–1733. Prague, Worms, Metz. Responsa (*Shevut Ya'akov*) and various commentaries.

Rema. Moses Isserles. 1530–1572. Cracow. Glosses to *Tur* and *Shulḥan Arukh*, responsa, and various commentaries.

Rif. Isaac b. Jacob Alfasi. 1013–1103. Fez. Talmudic codes, commentaries. Student of Rabbeinu Ḥananel.

Ritva. Yomtov b. Abraham Asbili. 1250–1330. Commentaries to the Talmud, responsa. Student of Aaron ha-Levi of Barcelona and Rashba.

Rivash. Isaac b. Sheshet Perfet. 1326–1408. Barcelona, Spain. Responsa (*Rivash*). Student of Nissim b. Reuven Gerondi.

Rosannes, Judah b. Samuel. See *Mishneh la-Melekh*.

Rosh. Asher b. Yeḥiel. 1250–1327. Worms, Germany, and Toledo, Spain. Talmudic commentaries, responsa. Student of Maharam Rothenburg.

Saadia b. Joseph Gaon. 882–942. Egypt, Israel, Babylon. Monographs on various topics, *Sefer ha-Miẓvot*, responsa.

Samuel b. Moses de Medini. See *Maharashdam*.

Schick, Maharam. See *Maharam Schick*.

Sdei Ḥemed. Ḥayyim Hezekiah b. Rephael. 1832–1904. Crimea. Halakhic compendium.

Sefer Yerayim. See *Eliezer b. Samuel of Metz*.

Sefer Ḥasidim, Judah he-Ḥasid. d. 1217. Regensburg, Germany. Compendium of ethical and halakhic teachings.

Sema. Joshua ha-Kohen Falk. 1555–1614. Poland. Commentaries on *Shulḥan Arukh* (*Sefer Me'irat Einayim*, *Perishah*, and *Derishah*). Student of Rema and Maharshal.

Semak. Isaac b. Joseph of Corbeil. d. 1280. French Tosafist. Compendium of contemporary Halakhah (*Sefer Miẓvot Katan*).

Seridei Esh. See *Weinberg, Yeḥiel*.

Sha'arei Teshuvah. See *Yonah b. Abraham of Gerondi*.

Shakh. Shabbetai b. Meir ha-Kohen. 1621–1662. Lithuania. Commentaries to *Shulḥan Arukh* (*Shakh, Nekkudot ha-Kesef*).

She'iltot. Aḥa of Shabḥa. 680–752. Pumbedita and Israel. Early collection of halakhic discussions.

Shevet mi-Yehudah. See *Unterman, Isser Yehudah*.

Shevut Ya'akov. See *Reischer, Jacob b. Joseph*.

Shivat Ẓion. Samuel b. Ezekiel Landau. d. 1834. Sudilkov, Poland. Responsa.

Shneur Zalman of Liadi. See *Shulḥan Arukh ha-Rav*.

Shternbuch, Moshe. Contemporary. South Africa and Israel. Responsa (*Teshuvot ve'Hanhagot*).

Shulḥan Arukh ha-Rav. Shneur Zalman of Liadi. 1745–1813. Code based on *Shulḥan Arukh*.

Shulḥan Arukh. Joseph b. Ephraim Karo. 1488–1575. Turkey, Greece, and Safed, Israel. Codifier (*Beit Yosef, Shulḥan Arukh*), Maimonidean commentator (*Kesef Mishnah*), and responsa.

Shvadron, Shalom Mordecai. See *Maharsham*.

Sirkes, Joel. See *Baḥ*.

Soloveichik, Ḥayyim ha-Levi. See *Ḥayyim ha-Levi Soloveichik*.

Soloveichik, Aaron. Contemporary. Lithuania, New York, and Chicago.

Soloveitchik, Joseph Dov (The Rav). Contemporary. New York and Boston. Student of his father, Moses Soloveitchik. Oral discourses and responsa.

Tam, Rabbeinu. See *Rabbeinu Tam*.

Tashbaẓ. Simon b. Ẓemaḥ Duran. 1361–1444. Majorca and Algiers. Responsa and commentaries to Talmud, Scripture, and others.

Taz. David b. Samuel ha-Levi. 1586–1667. Various communities in Poland. Commentary to *Shulḥan Arukh*. Son-in-law, and student, of Joel Sirkes.

Tendler, Moshe David. Contemporary. New York. Essays and articles. Son-in-law of Moshe Feinstein.

Teshuvot Maimoniyyot. See *Hagahot Maimoniyyot*.

Tiferet Ẓvi. Ẓvi Hirsch b. Benjamin Baschko. 1740–1807. Brod, Poland. Responsa.

Tiferet Yisrael. Israel Lipschutz. 1782–1860. Poland. Commentary on Mishnah (*Yakhin u-Boaz*).

Torah Temimah. Barukh ha-Levi Epstein. 1860–1942. Russia. Torah commentary. Student of his father (the *Arukh ha-Shulḥan*) and uncle (the *Neẓiv*).

Tosafot Yomtov. See *Heller, Yomtov Lipman.*

Tosafot. Collections, printed together with the Talmud itself, of comments and commentaries by French and German scholars in the 12th–14th century, arranged according to the order of talmudic discussions, usually reacting to Rashi.

Tucatzinsky, Yeḥiel. 1872–1955. Jerusalem. Responsa and compendium of Laws of Mourning (*Gesher ha-Ḥayyim*).

Tur. Jacob b. Asher, Ba'al ha-Turim. 1270–1340. Toledo, Spain. Codifier (the *Tur*), commentator on Torah. Son, and student, of the Rosh.

Tuv Ta'am ve'Da'at. See *Kluger, Solomon.*

Unterman, Isser Yehudah. 1886–1976. Lithuania and Israel. Responsa (*Shevet mi-Yehudah*).

Uziel, Ben Ẓion. 1880–1953. Jerusalem. Responsa (*Mishpetei Uziel*).

Vidal Yomtov of Tolosa. See *Maggid Mishnah.*

Vilna Gaon. See *Elijah of Vilna.*

Waldenberg, Eliezer. See *Ẓiẓ Eliezer.*

Weil, Jacob. See *Mahariv.*

Weinberg, Yeḥiel. 1885–1966. Lithuania, Berlin, Switzerland. Responsa (*Seridei Esh*), as well as studies and essays.

Weiss, Yiẓḥak Ya'akov. Contemporary. England and Jerusalem. Responsa (*Minḥat Yiẓḥak*).

Yad Eliyahu. Elijah Rogoler of Lublin. d. 1900.

Yaveẓ. See *Emden, Jacob.*

Yismaḥ Lev. Solomon Gagin. 19th century.

Yisraeli, Shaul. Contemporary. Jerusalem. Essays and articles.

Yomtov b. Abraham Asbili. See *Ritva.*

Yonah b. Abraham of Gerondi, Rabbeinu. 1200–1263. Spain. Ethical treatises (*Sha'arei Teshuvah*) and commentaries.

Yosef, Ovadiah. See *Ovadiah Yosef.*

Ẓahalon, Maharit. See *Maharit.*

Zevin, Shelomoh Yosef. 1890–1978. Encyclopedist (editor of *Encyclopedia Talmudit*), essayist, and reviewer.

Zimrah, Abu. See *Radbaz*.

Ẓiẓ Eliezer. Eliezer Yehudah b. Ya'akov Waldenberg. Contemporary. Jerusalem. Responsa.

1

Medical Practice, Research, and Self-Endangerment

Introduction

The ongoing success of modern medicine in combating disease and suffering has in large measure been the result of research and experimentation using human subjects. At present, hundreds of thousands of patients in the United States volunteer to be treated each year with experimental therapies in a wide range of clinical studies dealing with numerous serious illnesses. In recent years there has been increasing recognition of the need to formulate objective guidelines to establish what are, and are not, ethically acceptable practices in carrying out such investigations in the search for new cures, and dealing with the potentially negative consequences to the individuals involved.

On the one hand, there have come to light certain practices by the research community that appear to be highly questionable. On occasion even reputable investigators, with or without the informed consent of their subjects, have performed unnecessary surgery, injected cancer cells, or transplanted tumors, all to evaluate the effects of such procedures. Sometimes the subjects agreed to such practices under varying degrees of stress—as prison inmates, or soldiers, or patients and their families clutching at final straws. At other times such procedures were performed with the tacit agreement of leading research institutions—and governmental agencies. As a result of increased publicity, media attention, peer-review boards (themselves subject to criticism for often being ineffectual), and the rise of the field of medical ethics, many have called for critical scrutiny of the research process itself so as to prevent excesses and abuses such as these from taking place.

On the other hand, it is possible to stifle and inhibit researchers to the point where needed breakthroughs are put beyond reach. Experimentation, once considered a good thing, might well come to be viewed as a pejorative term. As Jonas Salk, developer of the first polio vaccine, has said, "It is much more difficult to do clinical investigations now than it was 30 years ago . . . we can reach the point where we regulate ourselves to the point of paralysis." Progress requires that risks be taken, risks that necessarily involve human subjects, for there are enough differences between animal and human physiology that there is no sure way to predict on the basis of animal studies alone what effects some drugs will have in man. And while it is also true that only thirty-six percent of published scientific articles are cited two or more times in subsequent research reports—indicating that almost two-thirds of such research is of negligible value to the scientific endeavor—who is to judge which will be the one to make a significant and lasting contribution to save the lives of thousands?

In addition, there are numerous specific ethical questions that medical research generates; e.g., what are morally acceptable criteria in choosing amongst volunteers? What are permissible parameters for eliciting informed consent? When must studies be discontinued? What are acceptable policies on media disclosure while safeguarding confidentiality?

More recently, the incidence and spread (through the exchange of body fluids) of the disease known as AIDS has posed a particularly difficult dilemma for physicians and other personnel who come into direct contact with such infectious patients, and thereby expose themselves in some small degree to the risk of acquiring this invariably fatal affliction. May a physician or caregiver refuse to treat such a patient, or withhold medical treatment, because of risk posed to the practitioner? Here too, what degree of risk is permissible, required, or forbidden?

Jewish law has been utilized in dealing with a number of these issues, applying analogous biblical, talmudic, and post-talmudic precedent wherever possible. Not surprisingly, within the corpus of halakhic works there is a substantial body of writings, both modern and premodern, that can be usefully brought to bear on some of the vexing issues at hand.

This chapter attempts to understand how Jewish law has balanced the conflicting claims of the needs of the individual versus the interests of others or the community at large: what is the nature of the obligation to bring healing or lessen suffering? what human costs are acceptable and what are not? When may one life be endangered to save another? What kind of risks and odds can be properly assumed? These are difficult questions, and the answers are far from straightforward or unanimous, but as we shall see, they are all addressed by the Halakhah, in one form or another.

The Question

A man is diagnosed as suffering from AIDS, a fatal disease that is spread through the exchange of body fluids. His doctors feel that he will not live more than six months at most, were he to rely upon conventional treatment. At the same time several of his physicians are deeply concerned for their own health and their own exposure to AIDS in the course of treating him, and others with the same diagnosis, through contact with specimens of infected blood and other fluids. They are considering the option of withdrawing from active participation in the further treatment of the patient.

The patient himself has his own dilemma. He is told that there is a new, experimental, and extremely toxic drug that is believed by some researchers to show promise in the treatment of AIDS. Indeed the drug has been effective in preliminary trials, but needs to be tested in humans. If the substance turns out to be safe and effective, it might not only lead to long-term survival for this subject himself, it will also save many other lives and ameliorate much human suffering. But if the clinical trial fails, the patient faces the possibility that his condition will deteriorate rapidly, leading to immediate death. He is asked to consent to be a volunteer in this research project.

The following questions are raised by this case:

1. What is the nature of the responsibility, whether upon laymen or medical personnel, to intervene to save the life of a person who is threatened by natural or unnatural causes?
2. What if there are risks to one's own health as a result of acting to save another's life, may one—must one—endanger one's health, or life, to that end?
3. To effect a cure or extended life-expectancy for himself, may a

dangerously ill patient agree to undergo treatment that might alleviate his condition and extend his life, but which, if unsuccessful, might also hasten his death significantly?

Sources

A. Leviticus 19:16

Thou shalt not go up and down as a talebearer among thy people; neither shalt thou stand idly by the blood of thy neighbor; I am the Lord.

B. Deuteronomy 22:1–2

Thou shalt not see thy brother's ox or his sheep driven away, and hide thyself from them; thou shalt surely bring them back to thy brother . . . and thou shalt restore it to him.

C. Leviticus 25:36

Take thou no interest of him or increase; but fear thy God, that thy brother may live with thee.

D. Kings 7:3 ff.

[Ben-hadad, king of Aram, laid siege to Samaria, causing great famine. Elisha the prophet foretold impending salvation, wherein food would be plentiful. But the king of Israel and his noblemen did not believe Elisha.] Now there were four leprous men at the entrance of the gate; and they said one to another: "Why sit we here until we die? If we say: We will enter into the city, then the famine is in the city, and we shall die there; and if we sit still here, we die also. Now therefore come, and let us fall unto the host of the Arameans; if they save us alive, we shall live, and if they kill us, we shall but die."

E. Sifra, Kedoshim 2:4

Whence do you know that if you see a man drowning in a river, or thugs or a wild animal attacking him, you are obligated to save him? Because it says, "neither shalt thou stand idly by the blood of thy neighbor" (A).

F. Bava Kamma 81b (as well as Sifri, Ki Teẓe 223)

Whence do we know that we are required to save the life of another? Because it says, "and thou shalt restore it unto him" (B).

G. Sanhedrin 73a

Whence do we know that a man who sees his fellow drowning in a river is obliged to save him? From the verse "neither shalt thou stand idly by the blood of thy neighbor" (A). But do we not derive this from "and thou shalt restore it unto him" (B), which teaches the obligation to save him? The answer is that from that verse one might think that one is merely obliged to save him with one's own body, but not to hire help, while this verse teaches that if necessary one must hire others as well.

H. Bava Meẓia 62a (as well as Torat Kohanim, Behar 5)

It is stated in the Beraita: If two men are traveling in a desert, and one of them has a container of water such that if he keeps it all for himself he will survive, but if he shares it with his fellow they will both die—Ben Petura says it is better for them both to drink rather than allow his fellow to die; but R. Akiva says "that thy brother may live with thee" (C) teaches that your life takes precedence over the life of your fellow.

I. Niddah 61a

Certain inhabitants of the Galil were rumored to have committed murder. They sought refuge [from the Roman authorities] with R. Tarfon. Said he to them: "What shall I do? If I do not hide you, you might be killed; but how can I hide you when I must be mindful of the statement of the Sages that even though a person should not believe rumor, one should take every precaution lest it be true! Go therefore, and hide somewhere else."

J. Jerusalem Talmud, Terumot 8:4

R. Imi was abducted and taken to certain death. When R. Yonatan was informed he said: "Let him prepare his death shroud [as we should not endanger ourselves to save him]." Said R. Simon b. Lakish: "I will go and save him, even if I have to kill or be killed." He went and placated the abductors, thus freeing R. Imi. He then said to the abductors: "Come with me to our Elder that he may pray for you." When they came before R. Yoḥanan he said: "May you suffer the same fate you intended for R. Imi." They left his presence, and prior to reaching Afifsirus they were all killed.

K. Avodah Zarah 27b

R. Yoḥanan: If a man is so sick that it is in doubt whether he will live or die [and the only physician available is a heathen], he should not turn to him for treatment (Rashi: . . . for such a doctor will certainly kill him, hence let him leave things be, as that way he might recover on his own). But if without medical help he will surely die, then he may avail himself of such a doctor (Rashi: . . . in any case he will die, whereas there is a possibility that the physician will cure him). But what of the limited time [*ḥayyei sha'ah*] that would have been his that he stands to lose if the physician kills him right away? The answer is that such limited duration of life can be disregarded. And whence do we know this? It is learnt from the story of the four lepers (D).

L. Maimonides, Commentary to the Mishnah, Nedarim 4:4
According to the law a physician is obliged to heal a sick Jew, as indicated by the Sages' interpretation of the verse "and thou shalt restore it unto him" (B). For they interpreted it to include restoring his body. Thus if a person is in danger and can be saved, one is obliged to save him, whether it is with one's body, one's possessions, or one's expertise.

M. Maimonides, M.T. Hilkhot Roẓeiaḥ 1:14
Whoever can save another but does not transgresses "neither shalt thou stand idly by the blood of thy neighbor" (A). Thus if you see your fellow drowning, or being attacked by ruffians or a wild animal, and you can save him by yourself or by paying someone else to do so, but you do not thus save him; or if you overhear idolaters or traitors conspiring to harm him or entrap him, but you do not alert him; or if you know of an idolater or aggressor about to attack him and you are in a position to placate them or prevent their act, but you do not do so—in all of these and similar cases you transgress the verse "neither shalt thou stand idly by the blood of thy neighbor" (A).

N. Maimonides, M.T. Hilkhot Roẓeiaḥ 7:8
A man who is exiled to a city of refuge for accidental homicide is not to leave there ever, even for the sake of a miẓvah, or to give evidence in monetary or capital cases, even to save the life of an accused by his evidence, or to save someone from an idolater, or from a river, a fire, or a collapsed structure. And even if all of Israel is in need of him, such as was the case with Joab ben Zeruiah, still he never leaves the refuge, until the High Priest dies. And if he leaves, he exposes himself to being killed.

O. Sefer Ḥasidim 674 (Bologna); 162 (Parma)

It is written "Neither shalt thou stand idly by the blood of thy neighbor." But if many are attacking him, one should not endanger oneself [in coming to his help]. . . . Thus if a man is drowning in a river, and he is heavy, one should not help him lest one be drowned with him.

Discussion

1. THE RESPONSIBILITY TO SAVE LIFE

The halakhic Midrash to Leviticus known as the *Sifra* (E) locates the responsibility to save an endangered life in the verse "neither shalt thou stand idly by the blood of thy neighbor" (A). The *Sifri* on Deuteronomy, reflected in a passage in *Bava Kamma* (E), finds a similar obligation in Deuteronomy 22:2 (B), which requires a person to "restore" the endangered goods of his fellow. As explained by Rashi, in his commentary to *Sanhedrin* 73a (G), the redundant *vav* at the end of the word *ve'hashevoto* gives the phrase the meaning "return his body to him," i.e., restore not only his possessions, but his life too.

Why require two such separate commandments, one positive and one negative? The Gemara in *Sanhedrin* (G) answers that Leviticus teaches specifically that if help is needed to save that life, the onlooker is obligated to make every effort to hire such assistance. One reason that has been offered is that the verse in Deuteronomy occurs in the context of the restoration of physical property, where no monetary outlay is required of an onlooker.[1] Hence the need for the verse in Leviticus requiring such expenditure.

Once such expenses have been incurred, who is responsible for payment? Can it be argued that once a person is obligated by the

1. *Shulḥan Arukh ha-Rav, Hil. Nizkei ha-Guf*, chap. 8. See, however, the questions raised by Rabbi Y. Liebes, *Beit Avi* (New York, 5736), p. 207, including the fact that even a commandment such as the one in Deuteronomy requires certain expenditures to be made. See also the *Minḥat Ḥinukh* 237, who takes the position, based on Deuteronomy (B), that one is not obligated to intervene and save the life of an attempted suicide, just as there is no obligation to save articles belonging to one's fellow that were deliberately discarded by him. Most authorities, however, do not agree with this argument; see N. Rakover, "Haẓalat Nefashot—Hebetim Mishpatiyim," *ha-Darom* 50 (Nissan 5740): 242, n. 5.

Torah to save his fellow's life, such obligation requires one to sacrifice of one's means in fulfilling God's command? *Bava Kamma* 81a lists as one of the decrees from the time of Joshua, that he who damages a farmer's crops while saving a life does not pay damages to the farmer. Likewise, the passage in *Sanhedrin* quoted earlier continues to state that if damages are incurred in saving a man from a pursuer (*rodef*), the intercessor is not liable, for "otherwise no man would save his fellow from a pursuer."[2] But does the victim himself, once saved, have to reimburse for expenses incurred? The thirteenth-century R. Meir Abulafia answers in the positive, arguing that the Gemara in *Sanhedrin* (G) pointedly requires the intercessor to expend the effort to hire help, but does not speak of him having to absorb such expense himself.[3] In similar vein, the Rosh requires the victim to repay all costs, assuming that he has the means to pay.[4] And while Maimonides and the *Shulḥan Arukh* do not codify this as law, Rema (R. Moses Isserles) in the sixteenth century specifically mandates reimbursement in cases where ransom was paid to save the life of an incarcerated Jew.[5]

What if the endangered party cannot reimburse the expenses, is there any limit to what the intercessor is required to expend of his own, or is he expected to spend everything he has? Several authorities in the twentieth century addressed this question. R. Abraham Isaac ha-Kohen Kook discussed the issue, but did not

---

2. Rakover, "Haẓalat Nefashot," n. 14. R. Ḥayyim Pelaggi (*Nishmat Kol Ḥai, H.M.* 48) is of the opinion that where the victim cannot reimburse for such damages, then the intercessor is indeed liable to pay. On the entire question of the pursuer, see below, chap. 4. Regarding the question of individual responsibility vs. communal responsibility to underwrite the cure for an individual, see Rabbi M. Hershler, *Halakhah u-Refuah* 3:45–50.

3. *Yad Ramah* to *Sanhedrin* 73a. A similar reading of this Gemara is found in *Responsa Mabit* 1:237.

4. *Piskei ha-Rosh, Sanhedrin* 8:2, as well as the *Responsa of the Rosh* 5:2, where the question involves payment of medical costs incurred without the express permission of the patient. The Rosh rules that the patient (for his estate) is nonetheless required to pay for such efforts where they were intended to save his life. A detailed discussion of this responsum is found in Rabbi Efraim Weinberger, "Shmirah al ha-Ḥayyim ve'ha-Beriyut be'Halakhah," *ha-Torah ve'ha-Medinah* 11–13 (5720–5722): 118 ff.

5. *Sh.A. Y.D.* 252:12. Likewise see *Responsa Beit Ya'akov* 148, as quoted in Rakover, "Haẓalat Nefashot," p. 246, n. 27. On this issue, see the article by Rabbi D. B. Wein, "be'Inyan Lo Ta'amod al Dam Re'ekha," *ha-Darom* 33:61–80, especially p. 69. See additional sources brought in the *Encyclopedia Talmudit*, s.v. "Haẓalat Nefashot," n. 31.

give a definitive answer.[6] Not so Rabbi Yeḥiel Weinberg: he has no doubt whatsoever that this talmudic passage requires total expenditure to save such a life—and in support of this position he quotes Rashi's formulation: "search out every possibility so that your fellow's blood not be spilled."[7]

What kind of situations are included in these obligations? *Sanhedrin* (G) mentions one who is in danger of drowning, and attacks by wild animals or by thugs. Others, as seen above, speak of perils related to being pursued or lost or imprisoned for ransom (on the assumption that noncompliance with the demand might well lead to the death of the prisoner). Maimonides, in codifying this passage into law (M), mentions these and adds several required instances of intercession by a third party even prior to an actual attack by homicidal conspirators. Furthermore, it would appear, it is not even necessary that death appear certain. Even where the fatal outcome is not certain, but only possible, then according to Rabbeinu Nissim,[8] an onlooker cannot remain passive, relying on good fortune to save that life, but is required to intervene actively.

In the context of medical intervention to save life, similar sentiments are encountered. Maimonides, in his *Commentary on the Mishnah* (L), applies the talmudic passage in *Sanhedrin* (G) to obligate a physician to save a patient if he is in a position to do so. Likewise the tosafist R. Jacob of Orleans derives the

6. *Mishpat Kohen* 144, pp. 342 ff.

7. *Yad Sha'ul, in Memory of R. Sha'ul Weingart* (Tel Aviv, 5713), pp. 371–395 (reprinted in *Responsa Seridei Esh*, vol. 1, *Ḥiddushim u-Biurim*, pp. 303 ff., esp. p. 313, no. 9). The opposite view was apparently espoused by R. Weinberg's interlocutor, R. Moshe Shternbuch. For a view similar to that of R. Weinberg, see R. Menaḥem ha-Meiri, *Beit ha-Beḥirah* to *Sanhedrin* 73a (G).

8. *Ḥiddushei ha-Ran* to *Sanhedrin* 73a. See the very comprehensive treatment of this topic in the *Encyclopedia Talmudit*, s.v. "Haẓalat Nefashot," n. 21. On the related issue of saving an individual who wishes to die, or has intentionally endangered himself, there is an extensive literature, involving two opposing opinions. On the one hand are those who do not require any intervention to save such a person. This includes *Minḥat Ḥinukh* 327, Rabbeinu Nissim, the *Yam shel Shelomoh*, and the *Responsa Shevut Ya'akov*. On the other hand is the view associated with Maharam Rothenburg that requires intervention irrespective of the wishes of the endangered party, a view accepted by R. Barukh ha-Levi Epstein, R. Eliezer Waldenberg, and Rabbi S. Y. Zevin. See the latter's discussion in his volume *le'Or ha-Halakhah* entitled "Mishpat Shylock," pp. 318–328, as well as his response to the contrary views expressed by Rabbi Yehudah Gershuni, "Ḥayyalei Yisrael ha-Mistaknim," *Or ha-Mizraḥ* 21:3–8. Also see Wein, "Lo Ta'amod," pp. 72–73.

physician's obligation to heal from the respective verses in Leviticus (A) and Deuteronomy (B).[9] Naḥmanides sees such an obligation in Leviticus 25:36 (C), as well as in the familiar exhortation to love one's fellow (Leviticus 19:18), which stipulate brotherly coexistence and responsibility.[10]

Yet it is in the context of such medical intervention that a more fundamental question is raised in the halakhic sources. Put simply, it is this: if we accept the notion that by Divine Providence our individual or collective destiny is foreordained through natural processes, what gives the physician the right to interfere with what could be considered "God's will"? Unlike the earlier cases of accidental peril or deliberate injury, should we not view disease as nature, with God's blessing, taking its proper course?

The Gemara in *Bava Kamma*, cognizant of this question, refers to the passage in Exodus regarding a fight in which a man is unjustly injured by his fellow. In this instance the Torah holds the aggressor responsible for all financial losses incurred, and in addition requires that he "shall cause him to be thoroughly healed" (Exod. 21:19). The Gemara quotes a Beraita that explains that "from here we derive that the physician is granted permission to cure," and the *Shulḥan Arukh* codifies this dispensation together with the obligation to save life[11]. Yet in spite of this specific passage in the Gemara, Maimonides in (L) and (M) does not refer to this verse at all as providing a warrant for medical intervention. An explanation of this glaring omission is offered in the twentieth century by R. Barukh ha-Levi Epstein, who explains that once Leviticus and Deuteronomy *obligate* medical intervention, as seen above, Maimonides sees no reason to quote a verse that would simply *allow* such intervention.[12]

---

9. *Sefer Berakhah Meshuleshet* (Jerusalem, 5728) to *Berakhot* 60a, in the name of *Tosafot ha-Rosh*, p. 40.

10. *Commentary of Naḥmanides to the Torah*, Lev. 25:36, as well as his *Torat ha-Adam*, *Kitvei ha-Ramban*, ed. C. B. Chavel, vol. 2, p. 48.

11. *Bava Kamma* 85a and *Berakhot* 60a, with the comments of Rashi, Tosafot, and the *Novellae of the Rashba* ad loc. See *Sh.A. Y.D.* 336:1.

12. *Torah Temimah* to Exod. 21:19, as well as the extended discussion by the same author in his *Tosefet Berakhah* ad loc. See J. David Bleich, "The Obligation to Heal in the Judaic Tradition: A Comparative Analysis," in *Jewish Bioethics*, ed. Fred Rosner and J. David Bleich (New York, 1983), pp. 1–44, especially n. 87. See also by the same author, *Judaism and Healing: Halakhic Perspectives* (New York, 1981), pp. 3 ff. A somewhat different interpretation of Maimonides is adopted by Rabbi I. Jakobovits, *Jewish Medical Ethics* (New York, 1975), p. 304, n. 8.

Those who accept this preponderant view point to the fact that talmudic literature is replete with positive references to the practice of medicine: e.g., a scholar should not live where there is no physician;[13] R. Yoḥanan b. Zakkai requested medical treatment for a colleague;[14] and R. Judah the Prince had a personal physician (being notably wealthy, he could apparently afford such exclusive attentions).[15] And in later periods Jewish history includes a long line of halakhists who practiced medicine, perhaps the most notable being Maimonides himself, who was a practitioner and the author of a number of medical treatises.[16]

At the same time, however, there was a minority that frowned on those who looked to the medical profession for cures from illness. Some, such as Ibn Ezra, noted that in Scripture King Asa was criticized for turning to a physician, instead of relying on God.[17] Naḥmanides likewise derives from that incident that "one who seeks God through a prophet does not seek physicians,"[18] for in his opinion, in a spiritually perfected world there is no need for physicians or their skills, as we would rely on God's healing, as it says "for I am the Lord your healer" (Lev. 26:11). Even so, Naḥmanides elsewhere condones, and even requires, recourse to the healing professions, until such time as the spiritual utopia will come to be, and "God will remove illness from their midst to the point that they will have no need of a physician and no need to safeguard themselves by any medical means whatsoever."[19]

Such minority opinions notwithstanding, the solid consensus of halakhic opinion enthusiastically supported medical healing wherever possible, even to the point of suspension of certain cardinal laws of Judaism in order to facilitate such ministrations. This included the desecration of the Sabbath as well as Yom

13. *Sanhedrin* 17b.
14. *Gittin* 56b.
15. *Bava Meẓia* 85b.
16. For an excellent historical and literary review of Jewish medical personalities, writings, attitudes, and practices, see Salo Wittmayer Baron, *A Religious and Cultural History of the Jews* (New York, 1971), 8:221–226 and notes thereon. See also the *Encyclopaedia Judaica*, s.v. "Maimonides," in the special section "As Physician," as well as the appended bibliography.
17. Abraham Ibn Ezra, *Commentary to the Torah*, Exod. 21:19, with reference to II Chronicles 16:12. See also the comments of Rabbeinu Baḥya ad loc.
18. See Naḥmanides' comments to Lev. 26:11.
19. See Bleich in *Jewish Bioethics*, pp. 24–28, and in *Judaism and Healing*, pp. 5 ff.

Kippur where there was any life-threatening sickness at hand.[20] So sensitive were these halakhists that they insisted that such desecration be performed neither by minors, nor by non-Jews, nor even through some change or subterfuge—but openly, deliberately, and by a sage, if at all possible.[21] All of this was intended to take every possible medical precaution to remove present or future danger to life.[22]

Illustrative of this attitude are the actions of the nineteenth-century rabbinic leader R. Ḥayyim Soloveichik. On more than one occasion he publicly suspended the laws of the Sabbath and Yom Kippur by reason of medical need. Once he forbade the synagogues in his town to recite the Kol Nidre prayer until cash was collected by his emissaries from each of the congregants on Yom Kippur itself, in order to effect the immediate release of five Jews who had been accused of a crime which might have led to their endangerment. As he explained his actions at the time, "It is not that I am lenient in suspending prohibitions of the Torah; on the contrary, I am strict in upholding the mandate to save life [*pikuaḥ nefesh*]."[23] On another occasion he insisted that his congregants eat and drink on Yom Kippur so as not to enfeeble themselves during a typhus outbreak that was raging in the city.

It is also significant in this context that the obligation to heal the sick is not limited to situations where the person's life is endangered. The term *ḥoleh* ("sick person"), on whose behalf one is bidden to act, is generally defined as any person who is weakened by sickness to the point that he is bedridden or cannot walk unaided.[24] Likewise, a person who is afflicted in even one limb or organ, but suffers to the point that his whole body is affected, is considered a *ḥoleh* whom one is obligated to heal.[25]

---

20. *Sh.A. O. H.* 328:3.

21. Maimonides, *M.T. Hil. Shabbat* 2:1; *Encyclopedia Talmudit*, s.v. "Ḥoleh," pp. 250–251.

22. Needless to say, the laws of healing regarding permissible and impermissible practices are complex and detailed. This is particularly true of such practice on the Sabbath and Yom Tov. It is beyond the scope of this study to examine those laws in detail.

23. Rabbi S. Y. Zevin, *Ishim ve'Shitot* (Tel Aviv, n.d.), pp. 64–65.

24. Maimonides, *M.T. Hil. Zekhiyah u-Matanah* 8–2; Naḥmanides, *Torat ha-Adam, Sh'ar ha-Meḥush; Sh.A. O.H.* 328:17. Such a definition is consistent with the biblical description of recovery as occurring when "he shall rise again and walk upon his staff" (Exod. 21:19).

25. Rema, *Sh.A. O.H.* 328:3, as well as the *Magen Avraham* ad loc. See *Encyclopedia Talmudit*, s.v. "Ḥoleh," n. 18.

Before leaving the question of the nature of the obligation to heal, there is one more issue that is of more than passing interest for the issue of medical malpractice and unsuccessful therapy. The question is this: does a physician who prescribes a course of therapy and treats a patient fulfill thereby his proper obligation whether or not the treatment is successful? Put somewhat differently: is the obligation to *cure* a patient, or to *treat* a patient? Does the fulfillment of obligation require a successful outcome of the therapy or procedure? The question in this form is asked by Rabbi Norman Lamm, and he answers by way of a historical analysis that demonstrates that indeed historically the Halakhah has been divided on this very point since the time of the early tannaim.[26]

Thus there are two divergent interpretations of the Beraita seen earlier that says "the physician is granted permission to cure." As we have seen, the preponderant view is that by this statement the physician need not be concerned that he is interfering with the Divine order; hence he is entitled to offer treatment. This is how Maimonides understands this particular verse (see above). But Naḥmanides goes further to perceive in this verse not merely permission but an actual obligation to intercede, irrespective of the eventual outcome, in that he should not hold back out of self-doubt or uncertainty. According to Naḥmanides the verse does not address the question of Providence at all, but rather self-doubt and the obligation to extend treatment.[27]

Rabbi Lamm traces this discussion, as reflected in subtle ways in opposing views found in the Mishnah and the Tosefta, in the context of medical manslaughter that should or should not require exile to a city of refuge. This is also true of one view among the tosafists which opposes Rashi's interpretation of (A), as to standing idly by the blood of one's neighbor. And in more recent times, the same dichotomy of views appears, in that the *Yad Avraham* agrees with Maimonides, whereas the *Arukh ha-Shulḥan* sides with Naḥmanides.

In short, there is certainly ample precedent for the view that

26. Rabbi N. Lamm, "Is it a Mitzvah to Administer Medical Therapy?" *Journal of Halakhah and Contemporary Society* 8 (Fall 1984): 5–13. A Hebrew version appeared in *Torah she'be'al Peh* 25 (5744): 140–143.

27. See Naḥmanides, *Torat ha-Adam, Sha'ar ha-Sakanah*, in *Kitvei ha-Ramban*, p. 41.

medical treatment per se, irrespective of outcome, is an act fulfilling a command of the Torah. Of course this is not to absolve the medical practitioner of all responsibility for the consequences of the treatment that he provides. But it does mean that, according to these sources at least, conscientious and reasonable medical care is in and of itself a positive and redeeming act in accordance with the Torah and Jewish law, even when the end result of the treatment is not successful.

We can conclude the discussion of the obligation to heal by referring to a responsum of the Rosh, in which he states that "every person should try to make available a cure for the sick, and whoever goes to great lengths for this purpose is to be praised."[28] He then adds that such effort and expense are proper in that "it is a known custom that when a man falls sick and cannot help himself, his relatives make every effort to find him a cure." Jewish law, apparently, considers us all "related," and hence under a similar obligation toward our fellow.

2. *RISKING ONE'S LIFE OR HEALTH*

We have seen that by most accounts there is a duty to make every effort to save the endangered life of a fellow human being. This includes making financial sacrifices if they are necessary at the time. But what if, in order to save a life, a person has to endanger his own?

Here it is helpful to distinguish between two situations. The first involves the certain or likely sacrifice of one's life that would result from helping one's fellow. The second involves the mere possibility of death to oneself—but not a probability.

Certain or Likely Self-Sacrifice

In the first situation, a pivotal text is found in *Bava Meẓia* (H), where two people are walking in a waterless desert, and only one has water. Were he alone to drink it he would survive and his fellow would die, but were he to share it with his fellow, both would perish. Ben Petura requires him to share; R. Akiva, quoting

28. *Responsa of the Rosh* 85:2. This is consistent with what we have already seen in the Rosh; see above n. 4.

Leviticus (C), does not, saying, "Your life comes before the life of your brother." It is the view of R. Akiva that is accepted by most subsequent authorities.[29]

This discussion bears further examination. Would Ben Petura insist on sharing the precious life-support irrespective of how much time they would both have to live? What if by sharing they would both die right away? Such a case would involve shipwrecked passengers where there is only one life-preserver, which, if shared, would lead to their almost immediate drowning. What of R. Akiva: is he saying that he *need* not share the water, or that he *must* not share it?

Rabbi I. Y. Unterman is certain that even Ben Petura would not counsel any sharing that would lead to immediate death.[30] The Ḥazon Ish agrees on this point.[31] Their reason is that Ben Petura is essentially concerned not to sacrifice the significant, if limited, time span (*ḥayyei sha'ah*) of the fellow-traveler in the interests of the long-term survival of the first party. But where there is no significant life-span, even as a result of their sharing (as in the case of the life-preserver), Ben Petura would agree with R. Akiva not to share. Accordingly, Ben Petura's statement that a person should not allow his fellow to die is not precise, for under certain circumstances he would in fact allow such a course of action.

But while Ben Petura would have them share the water, R. Akiva would disagree, as he sees no need for literal self-sacrifice to save another. But if the person wishes to share, may he do so? Here there are two interpretations. Rabbi Unterman says that a person is indeed obligated to save his own life, where the danger of death is certain or highly likely. And even where it is simply a matter of adding extra time to his own life, without any likelihood of long-term survival, still a person must preserve his life as long as possible; as R. Akiva says, "Your life takes precedence over the life of your fellow." The same view is held by Rabbi Moshe Feinstein, saying that no one can calculate the relative importance of

29. For certain historical and philosophical observations on this text, see Rabbi S. Lieberman, "How Much Greek in Jewish Palestine," *Biblical and Other Studies* (Cambridge, 1963), pp. 124 ff. See also S. Pines, "Shnayim She-hayu Holkhim Bamidbar," *Tarbiẓ* 16:238 ff. Those who explicitly accept the view of R. Akiva include the Meiri to *Bava Meẓia* 62a, as well as the *Ḥazon Ish, H. M. Likkutim* 20.

30. I. Y. Unterman, *Shevet mi-Yehudah* (Jerusalem, 1983), 1:8 (pp. 15–16).

31. Rabbi A. I. Karelitz, *Ḥazon Ish* (*Sanhedrin, Likkutim* 26).

different lives. Just as the Talmud forbids a man to kill another to save himself, saying, "Whence do you know that your blood is redder than his?" (*Pesaḥim* 25b), so in reverse might we say, "How do you know that his blood is redder than yours?" In such a case, a person should defer to providential design, so that whoever has the resource to survive should ensure his own life first.[32]

Others, however, disagree. Rabbi Yeḥiel Weinberg refers approvingly to R. Eliyahu of Prozin, who states than even R. Akiva does not forbid self-sacrifice to save another.[33] He argues that theoretically a Jew would be required to sacrifice his life for any of the commandments; but the verse "he shall live by them" (Lev. 18:5) teaches that it is permissible to preserve one's life, instead of sacrificing it. But permission is not an obligation. Hence someone who wishes to disregard the dispensation in order to fulfill another commandment (in this case "thou shalt not stand idly by"), may do so, and is considered praiseworthy.

The Mere Possibility of Self-Sacrifice

The second category involves the "mere" possibility, but not certainty or even probability, of the death of a person trying to save another from likely death. May a person undertake any mortal risk whatsoever? Here too there is a significant spectrum of opinion.

On the one hand is the view associated with the thirteenth-century *Hagahot Maimoniyyot.* This refers to the Jerusalem Talmud (J), wherein it is recorded that R. Simon b. Lakish endangered himself to rescue a colleague who had been abducted by well-known murderers. R. Joseph Karo, author of the *Shulḥan Arukh*, interpreted this action as follows: According to the Talmud, whoever saves one life is considered to have saved the entire world. The hostage was in certain danger, whereas his rescuer

32. Rabbi M. Feinstein, *Iggerot Moshe*, *Y.D.* 2:174 (4), p. 293. This raises the major topic concerning martyrdom in the face of forced transgression *(yehareg ve'al ya-avor)*—particularly when forced to commit murder. See in this connection Maimonides' *M.T. Hil. Yesodei ha-Torah*, chap. 5, and *Ḥiddushei R. Ḥayyim ha-Levi* ad loc. See also the detailed analysis by Hershler, in *ha-Darom* 46:42–47.

33. Rabbi Y. Weinberg, *Responsa Seridei Esh* (Jerusalem, 1977), 1:314–315, and a number of sources quoted there.

would be only in doubtful danger; under such circumstances, the obligation "do not stand idly by the blood of thy fellow" requires personal intervention.[34] This, as pointed out by R. Joel Sirkes (the Baḥ), was true even though he was not at all certain that his mission would be successful, and they might both be killed.[35]

Opposed to this view, stood a solid majority of early codifiers of Halakhah, including Alfasi, Maimonides, and the Rosh, all of whom pointedly omitted any reference to self-endangerment under such circumstances. Indeed, as the Baḥ noted, when Maimonides states (M) that you must act "when you can save him," it would seem that he requires foreknowledge of a successful outcome, i.e., where there is no self-endangerment. Similar sentiment is encountered in the *Sefer Ḥasidim* (O), which states that a person should not endanger himself to save someone who is attacked by many people, or for that matter to save a heavy drowning man whose weight might drag them both down.[36]

What of the contrary position espoused by the Jerusalem Talmud? The answer, according to the Maharam Zev (author of the *Agudat Ezov*) is that the Babylonian Talmud (the "Bavli") disagrees with the Talmud of Jerusalem (the "Yerushalmi").[37] There are three passages in the Bavli which he and others quote in support of this contention. The first involves R. Tarfon in *Niddah*

34. Bet Yosef to *Tur H.M.* 426:2, based on *Bava Batra* 11a and *Sanhedrin* 37a; also by the same author, the *Kesef Mishnah* to Maimonides, *M.T. Hil. Roẓeiaḥ* 1:14. As pointed out to me by Rabbi Norman Lamm, there are two versions of this oft-quoted rabbinic maxim ("whoever saves . . ."). While the Babylonian Talmud records the dictum in more restrictive fashion as referring to the saving of a single "Israelite" soul, the Jerusalem Talmud omits the specific reference to Jewish souls, and thereby leaves intact the more universalistic implication that saving *any* human life, whether Jew or Gentile, is the moral equivalent of saving the whole world.

35. *Hagahot ha-Baḥ* to *H.M.* there. The printed editions of the *Hagahot Maimoniyyot*, as found in the *Mishneh Torah*, lacks this passage, but it is found in the Constantinople editions. Later writers who accepted the view of the *Hagahot Maimoniyyot* as normative include the *Responsa Ḥavvot Yair* (no. 146), R. Ḥayyim David Abulafia in *Responsa Nishmat Ḥayyim* 11a, as well as the Moharaf, as mentioned in the *Sdei Ḥemed, Ma'arekhet Lamed* 144. See also the *Torah Temimah* to Lev. 19:16.

36. *Sefer Ḥasidim* 674. See also R. Joseph Babad, *Minḥat Ḥinukh* 296. Others who forbid self-endangerment to save another include the *Responsa Radbaz* 627 (see, however, below n. 57), and the Me'iri to *Sanhedrin* 73a (G), as well as Rabbeinu Yonah in the *Sefer Issur ve'Heter* 59:38. A comprehensive listing of such sources is found in Rabbi Ovadiah Yosef, *Yeḥaveh Da'at*, 3:84.

37. The *Agudat Ezov* is mentioned in the *Pitḥei Teshuvah* to *Sh.A. H.M.* 426.

(I), who refused to grant refuge to fellow Jews suspected by the Roman authorities of committing murder. He explained that given the rumors of their guilt, he had to take every precaution. Apparently he refused to endanger his own life at the hands of the authorities, even though their lives were at stake. The second passage is the one we have seen in *Sanhedrin* (G). There the Gemara explains the need for the verse in Leviticus ("neither shalt thou stand idly by") as necessary to teach the obligation to hire help in saving another. But if the Bavli agrees with the Yerushalmi, it should have given a much stronger justification for this verse; i.e., that it teaches self-endangerment rather than standing idly by while another is in peril! Why settle for the "mere" obligation to hire help? It must therefore be concluded that according to the Bavli there is no such obligation at all.

The third passage in the Bavli is a Beraita found in *Nedarim* 81a, recording the proper disposition of water from a well located in one town that flows to a second town. If in time of drought the inhabitants of the first town wish to retain all of the precious resource for themselves, may they do so? The Beraita answers that if their lives depend on keeping all the water, then they may indeed deprive the second town (this would be consistent with the view of R. Akiva in [H]); if however there is more than enough for drinking, but they wish to keep the balance nonetheless for washing their clothes, then there are two views: the majority of tannaim forbid such washing, while R. Yossi permits it, on the grounds that the long-term use of unsanitary clothing could lead to mental, if not physical, perils. In considering this debate, R. Naftali Ẓvi Yehudah Berlin (the Neẓiv) says that at issue is the question of possible self-endangerment when faced with the likely death of another. The majority are in favor of such self-endangerment, whereas R. Yossi (whose view is accepted by the She'iltot) is opposed to any exposure whatsoever.[38] Indeed, according to the nineteenth-century R. Israel Lipschutz, the very reason that Alfasi, Maimonides, and the Rosh omit the ruling of the Yerushalmi is that they accept the view of R. Yossi here, i.e., one need not risk one's life at all for another.[39]

In examining these passages in the Bavli, subsequent authori-

38. *Responsa Ha'amek She'elah* 147:4.
39. Rabbi I. Lipschutz, *Tiferet Yisrael* to *Yoma* 8:7 (Boaz).

ties raised a number of questions. Starting with the narrative of R. Tarfon, several objections against the use of this text were made.

1. Rabbi Eliezer Waldenberg points out that while the She'iltot interprets the episode as explained by the *Agudat Ezov*, Rashi does not do so, but rather understands R. Tarfon to have acted on the grounds that the Torah itself forbids providing haven to a suspected murderer. According to this, R. Tarfon was not motivated by a concern for his safety at the hands of the Romans, but rather for a prohibition of the Torah.[40]

2. Even according to the She'iltot, however, the text clearly implies that R. Tarfon believed that they had other refuge available to them. Such a case, as noted by R. Unterman cannot be instructive for normal cases of endangerment where there are no similar alternatives.[41] In addition, says Rabbi Waldenberg, R. Tarfon's answer implied that had he known for sure that they were in fact not murderers, he would have been duty-bound to save them.

3. Rabbi Ḥayyim Heller, in his commentary to Maimonides' *Sefer ha-Miẓvot*, makes a salient argument against the use of this text, saying that R. Tarfon was motivated entirely by another consideration—the prohibition against thwarting the proper punishment due a murderer. As the thirteenth-century *Sefer Ḥasidim* put it, "if a murderer flees unto you do not shelter him, whether he be Jew or Gentile, as was the case with R. Tarfon in Niddah."[42] Thus again this text is disqualified in the case of pure self-endangerment.

The second proof of the *Agudat Ezov* (G) is generally accepted by subsequent authorities.[43] Indeed for Rabbi Waldenberg this passage is sufficient proof that the Bavli does differ with the Yerushalmi on this issue.[44] But two authorities remain unconvinced of such a dichotomy between the two Talmudim. One is R.

---

40. Rabbi E. Waldenberg, *Responsa Ẓiẓ Eliezer* 9:45 (p. 180) referring to the interpretation of Rashi found in the *Ḥavvot Yair* and the *She'elat Yaveẓ*.

41. *Shevet mi-Yehudah* 1:9 (p. 17). See also *Responsa Ẓiẓ Eliezer* p. 181. There is even a question as to the correct reading in the *She'iltot* itself; see *Ha'amek She'elah, Parshat Shelaḥ* 129.

42. Rabbi Ḥayyim Heller, Commentary to Maimonides' *Sefer ha-Miẓvot*, negative commandment 297, p. 175, with reference to *Sefer Ḥasidim* 683.

43. See *Responsa Ẓiẓ Eliezer* and Heller, with reference to the *Arukh la-Ner* and *Yad Eliyahu*.

44. Rabbi Heller does, however, reject this proof too.

Yair Ḥayyim Bachrach, known as the Ḥavvot Yair, who is of the opinion that R. Akiva in (H) requires a man to save himself exclusively only if it is certain that by sharing his water they will both die. But even R. Akiva admits that if there is a significant possibility that by sharing they might both survive, then he should indeed share with his fellow.[45] If this be the case, R. Akiva requires self-endangerment to save the life of another—in full agreement with the Yerushalmi.

The second halakhist who doubts that the Bavli disagrees is Rabbi Unterman. He too discounts the story of R. Tarfon as having any bearing on our case—and for the reasons outlined above. As to *Nedarim*, Rabbi Unterman says that it is inconceivable that R. Yossi would advocate or countenance one town using water for laundry that could be used to save the lives of the inhabitants of another town. Such profligacy is not the issue at all. He adopts instead an interpretation of this Beraita first found in the *Sefer Yiḥusei Tannaim ve'Amoraim Ben Peturin*,[46] that there is indeed other water available to the hapless second town, but only at a great distance and accessible only with great effort. Weighing the effort involved in procurement against the long-term effects of unsanitary clothing, R. Yossi permits the withholding of the water in question. Accordingly, this constitutes no evidence on the issue of self-endangerment when faced with the imminent death of another.[47] Thus, Rabbi Unterman concludes, an individual is required to undertake a modicum of dangerous exposure to save the life of another who is in immediate danger—as the Yerushalmi indicates.

Yet the predominant view among later authorities is to reject the position of the Yerushalmi. A good example of a contemporary formulation of this position is that of the eminent halakhist Rabbi Moshe Feinstein. At first he considers an outright ban on self-endangerment, arguing that if it is permissible (as it surely is) to desecrate the Sabbath, a cardinal principle of the Halakhah, in order to avoid any potential danger to life, how can we permit an individual to enter into a similar danger for the sake of upholding a conventional commandment, such as the one "not

45. *Responsa Ḥavvot Yair* 146.

46. This source is mentioned in the generally excellent entry in the *Encyclopedia Talmudit*, s.v. "Haẓalat Nefashot," at n. 80.

47. *Shevet mi-Yehudah*, pp. 17–18.

to stand idly by"? But then R. Moshe formulates a distinction between this commandment and others, saying that "after all a Jewish soul will be saved thereby." This he does on the strength of Rashi's explanation (in *Sanhedrin* 74a) of why one person may not kill another to save his own life: by killing the other there is both loss of life as well as the transgression of killing, whereas by submitting to be killed at least the transgression is avoided. Apparently such a calculus can be used to substitute one life for another. With this in mind he can countenance one Jew's facing his own possible death in order to prevent a fellow Jew's certain death. But this reasoning only goes so far as to permit self-endangerment; it certainly does not require it.[48]

Authorities such as these rely in addition on certain objections to the position associated with the Yerushalmi. In the first place the Yerushalmi itself records the fact that R. Yonatan pointedly would not endanger himself as did R. Simon b. Lakish. That being the case, how can we be certain that the Yerushalmi itself accepts the actions of R. Simon b. Lakish as normative? Secondly it is quite possible that even R. Simon b. Lakish did not intend his selflessness to be taken as an act required by law, but merely as done as a measure of special, voluntary, piety (*midat ḥasidut*). How can we legislate such activity as a normative requirement?[49]

In addition there is some question as to the literal meaning of the passage itself. Rabbi Heller provides an entirely different translation that reads as follows: "Said R. Simon b. Lakish: 'If I will do battle with them, they might kill me before I can kill them. Such an eventuality I am not obligated to face at all. It would be better for me to go and attempt to ransom him, and pay money for his freedom.'" Accordingly, says Rabbi Heller, this particular passage of the Yerushalmi has no bearing on the issue of self-endangerment at all; if anything it proves the opposite of what is purported. The *Hagahot Maimoniyyot* must, he says, have been

---

48. *Responsa Iggerot Moshe* ad loc. Rabbi I. Jakobovits, "Medical Experimentation on Humans in Jewish Law," in *Jewish Bioethics*, p. 382, states without substantiation that "hazardous experiments may be performed on humans only if they may be potentially helpful to the subject himself." It is difficult to justify this statement on the basis of the sources we have seen (except possibly R. Meir Simḥah of Dvinsk). See Bleich's critique of this point in "Experimentation on Human Subjects," *Jewish Bioethics*, pp. 384–385.

49. Both objections are found in the *Responsa Ẓiẓ Eliezer*, p. 181. See also *Responsa Yad Eliyahu* 43.

referring to another passage in the Yerushalmi, one which is presently missing from our printed editions, a not unusual state of affairs given the condition of the Yerushalmi.[50]

Thus there is a consensus of sorts that a person need not endanger himself to save another life. But there is one passage in which Maimonides (N) goes even further. Discussing the law in the Mishnah that a man who commits accidental homicide may find safety from vengeful relatives in one of the six cities of refuge mandated in the Torah, Maimonides says that such a man does not leave the city even to save the life of another person, even if "all of Israel is in need of him . . . and if he leaves he exposes himself to being killed." In commenting on this sweeping ruling of Maimonides, R. Meir Simḥah of Dvinsk interprets the final phrase as the rationale for the entire statement, i.e., the man is exempted from leaving the city as he might be killed by the still vengeful relatives of the man he killed. R. Meir Simḥah, in his commentary of the Torah, likewise points to God's charge to Moses to return to Egypt to save the Israelites, when God said, "for all the people are dead that sought thy life" (Exod. 4:19). Clearly, he explains, Moses was not expected to return prior to that time as long as his own life was being sought, even though all of Israel needed him, for he could not be expected to endanger his own life on their account.[51]

Others, again, disagree. Rabbi Unterman for one argues that the accidental killer is in a unique category: once he enters a city of refuge he ceases to have any responsibility toward the outside world; like a first-degree murderer who is put to death, he is "dead to the world," even exempt from commandments that would require him to travel outside his circumscribed existence. Accordingly R. Meir Simḥah is in error in extrapolating from the accidental murderer to issues of self-endangerment.[52] Rabbi Simḥah Elberg also disagrees with R. Meir Simḥah, saying that this law in Maimonides reflects the special requirement that there be no *kofer*, or substitution, that might in any way mitigate the punishment of such a person. Thus even allowing him to leave temporarily would contravene the express biblical prohibition against tak-

50. Heller, p. 175.

51. See *Or Sameaḥ* to *M.T. Hil. Roẓeiaḥ* 7:8; *Meshekh Ḥokhmah* to Exodus 4:19.

52. *Shevet mi-Yehudah*, pp. 19–21.

ing "ransom for he that is fled to the city of refuge" (Num. 35:32).[53] What of Maimonides' final statement that if he does leave he exposes himself to being killed—would that not indicate that his concern is indeed for his physical safety? Rabbi Elberg answers that Maimonides does not say "for if he leaves," but rather "and if he leaves"; i.e., this is not the reason for staying in the city, but an additional law that if he disregards the prohibition against leaving he can be killed with impunity by a vengeful blood-relative.

A third view is that of Rabbi Yeḥiel Weinberg. He finds no basis for Rabbi Unterman's distinction. As to Rabbi Elberg, Rabbi Weinberg finds it inconceivable, "something which neither the mind nor the heart can accept," that the Halakhah would insist on keeping a man incarcerated when to do so would prevent him from saving the lives of others, let alone all Israel.[54] The prohibition against ransom is rather to ensure that no man avoids his sentence completely through the payment of money (as would be the case with punishment for lesser bodily injuries). Where the intent is merely a temporary dispensation designed to save another life, surely that prohibition is irrelevant. Elsewhere Rabbi Weinberg takes issue with R. Meir Simḥah, saying that if the entire concern is safety, why not simply provide an armed escort, just as is done in case of accidental exit from the city?[55] In light of this, Rabbi Weinberg gives an entirely different twist to Maimonides' ruling. Quoting the *Ḥeshek Shelomoh*, he reads Maimonides to say that it is prohibited for the man to leave the city permanently, i.e., he may leave temporarily, but must return immediately after performing his life-saving task. Accordingly Maimonides' use of the term *le'olam* in this case does not mean "ever" but rather "forever."

That a Jew is free to endanger himself for the sake of corporate Israel is abundantly clear from others quarters too, says Rabbi Weinberg. They include the story of Queen Esther presenting herself to the king without being bidden, and numerous talmudic references to martyrs in differing places and times, often in doing battle to protect the lives of fellow Jews. A similar conclusion is

53. Rabbi Simḥah Elberg, *ha-Pardes* 33 (2): 22–27.
54. Rabbi Y. Weinberg, *ha-Pardes* 33 (4): 8–9.
55. *Responsa Seridei Esh*, ad loc.

encountered in the writings of Rabbi Abraham Isaac ha-Kohen Kook, as well as the above-quoted responsum of Rabbi Feinstein.[56]

The discussion thus far has dealt with a danger to life. But what if to save the life of another, a person contemplates endangering a limb, or a partial disfigurement? Is such a gesture required, permitted, or forbidden? This question can be deferred to the chapter on organ transplants, where one of the key issues relates to the donor of such an organ; i.e., may a person donate an organ, even where there is no immediate danger to life.?

There is one further question that should be addressed, and that relates to percentages. What kind of odds of success or failure, life or death, are assumed by these discussions? An important source on this question is found in the sixteenth century, in the writings of R. David b. Abu Zimra, known as the Radbaz. In one place he writes that a person should not enter possible danger to save his fellow, for one who does so is a proverbial "foolish saint" (*ḥasid shoteh*). But elsewhere he says that "if the risk is less than even, i.e., less than a *safek mukhra*, and the likelihood is that he can save him without losing his own life, then if he does not save him he has transgressed against the commandment 'do not stand idly by the blood of your neighbor.' " Thus if there is a fifty percent probability that a person will lose his life by attempting to save another, then such action should not be undertaken. Where the odds are anything less than this, and survival is probable, then a person may undertake to act, and put his faith in Providence.[57] As a matter of fact, the nineteenth-century R. Moses Schick understands the Yerushalmi itself to accept this distinction, whereby it is only if the peril is unlikely to lead to death that it is mandatory to act.[58] Likewise Rabbi Yeḥiel Epstein (author of the *Arukh ha-Shulḥan*), while accepting the view that a person should not endanger himself, adds that "it all depends on the circumstance, and a person should evaluate the situation in balanced fashion so as not to guard oneself

---

56. *Mishpat Kohen* 143; *Responsa Iggerot Moshe*, ad loc.

57. See the *Responsa Radbaz* 627, 218. The *Encyclopedia Talmudit* (s.v. "Haẓalat Nefashot," n. 74) also identifies this view with Tosafot, but the reference appears erroneous, and I am unable to locate such a view. Compare also the article by A. S. Avraham, "Nisyonot Refu'iyim be'Va'alei Ḥayyim u-Bivnei Adam," *Assia* 10:3, pp. 24–25.

58. See his glosses to *Miẓvot Hashem* 238, as well as his views in *Responsa Maharam Schick, Y.D.* 155.

overmuch . . . for whoever saves a Jewish soul is considered to have saved the whole world."[59] Implicit in this view is a requirement to act where the danger to oneself is highly unlikely.

Rabbi Unterman adopts a somewhat different measure, saying that it depends on the individual: where an individual would act to save his own possessions in spite of personal danger, that would likewise be considered a sufficient margin of safety for him to act on behalf of another. But where he would refuse to act even at the cost of losing his possessions, he is not expected to act on behalf of another either.[60]

3. *HAZARDOUS PROCEDURES TO SAVE ONE'S OWN LIFE*

Thus far we have dealt with self-endangerment to save another. But what if a person is himself endangered, and facing the imminent prospect of death, may he choose a course of action that might save his life, but might also shorten his life even further? A second question relates to self-endangerment, not to save one's life, but rather to secure relief from intense pain or suffering. May one volunteer to undergo risk for the sake of such improvement?

Risking Limited Life-span for Long Term Survival

As to the first question there is scriptural precedent for precisely such a dilemma. The Book of Kings (D) records the story of the four lepers, who were facing death by starvation as a result of a famine which precluded them from acquiring food in their isolated state. Reasoning that their life-expectancy was practically nil anyway, they chose to hand themselves over to the besieging Aramean enemy, who might execute them immediately—or take them captive and feed them. This incident took on decided significance for subsequent halakhists, in that tradition identified these lepers as halakhically knowledgeable in their own right (*giborim ba-torah*, "heroes in Torah"), namely, Gehazi, servant of the prophet Elisha, and his three sons.[61]

---

59. *Arukh ha-Shulḥan* to *Sh.A. H.M.* 426.

60. Unterman, op. cit., p. 21.

61. See Rashi's comments to II Kings 7, based on the Jerusalem Talmud, *Sanhedrin* 10:2.

Using this as source and precedent, R. Yoḥanan in *Avodah Zarah* (K) derives the fundamental principle that where life-expectancy is extremely limited anyway (the lepers' death by starvation was imminent), risky alternatives may be undertaken. And although the Halakhah in general values every moment of life as of infinite value, especially in the last moments of life,[62] here we invoke the principle that "such limited duration of life can be disregarded (*le'ḥayyei sha'ah lo ḥayshinan*). Apparently where the purpose is to save life, and not to end or shorten it, we may legitimately take a gamble, even where the currency is life itself. Based on this precedent, the Gemara extrapolates to the case of a Jew, mortally ill, whose only available medical assistance is a pagan physician, of the kind known on occasion to kill his Jewish patients. Here too, says the Gemara, the Jew should avoid such "help," for he might unexpectedly recover on his own anyway; but where death is imminent and practically certain, the Jew has nothing to lose, for what time he has left can be discounted, in the manner of the four lepers; hence he may consult that physician on the off-chance that he might just cure him, or extend his life indefinitely. As Tosafot explains, just as we desecrate the Sabbath itself when a wall of stones has fallen and buried a man under the debris, as long as there is a possibility that such action will extend his life even momentarily, so too here, since the patient will die for sure if he does not consult the physician, therefore we should take the chance, for "in both cases we choose doubtful life over certain death."[63]

The *Shulḥan Arukh* accepts this conclusion of the Gemara,[64] and a number of later authorities accordingly permit hazardous medical treatment for mortally ill patients, including R. Jacob Reischer, R. Solomon Eiger, R. Meir Posner, R. Jacob Ettlinger, and more recently, Rabbis Unterman and Waldenberg—and a number of others.[65] But at this point several other questions

62. For a detailed discussion of this matter, as it relates to the issue of euthanasia, see *Jewish Ethics and Halakhah for Our Time*, vol. 1, chap 3.

63. Tosafot to *Avodah Zarah* 27b, s.v. *leḥayyei*. Such disregard of a limited life-span is to be contrasted with Ben Peturah's view (see above) that the saving of even limited life of one's fellow indeed requires self-endangerment.

64. *Sh.A. Y.D.* 155:1.

65. *Responsa Shevut Ya'akov* 3:75; *Gilyon Maharsha* to *Sh.A. Y.D.* 155:1; *Responsa Beit Meir* to Sh.A. *Y.D.* 339; *Responsa Binyan Ẓion* 1:111; Unterman in *Noam* 13:5; Waldenberg, *Responsa Ẓiẓ Eliezer* 4:13. See also Rabbi S. Goren in

arise: Are there any minimum chances of success required? How long is "limited duration of life"? Who establishes these facts—physicians or rabbis?

On the first question, regarding the likelihood of success required, there are essentially two views. Rabbi Joseph Hochgelehrter, author of the *Mishnat Ḥakhamim*, requires at least a fifty percent chance of success, whereas R. Ḥayyim Ozer Grodzinski, known as Aḥi'ezer, accepts any significant chance of success as sufficient.[66] These two views are reflected in instructive fashion in two responsa by Rabbi Moshe Feinstein, in which this eminent contemporary rabbi first embraces the view of the Aḥi'ezer and then reverses himself to adopt the opposite position. In the first responsum, written in 1961, Rabbi Feinstein, with the concurrence of his colleague Rabbi Yosef Eliyahu Henkin, permits an individual facing certain death to undergo surgery that stands even a remote chance of success.[67] This is premised on a reading of the passage in *Avodah Zarah* that R. Yoḥanan would countenance any possible alternative to certain death, including an unlikely chance from a pagan physician, or (as in the case of Gehazi) the unlikely mercies of the Arameans. This reading of the Gemara follows the comments of Rashi, regarding which R. Feinstein says, "I have seen none who differ with him."

But in 1972 Rabbi Feinstein appears to have reversed himself. For in that year he penned a responsum regarding open-heart surgery that agreed substantially with the view of the *Mishnat Ḥakhamim*, and moreover attributed this view to Rashi and the above-mentioned Tosafot as well.[68] He argues that R. Yoḥanan in

---

Shanah be'Shanah, 5736, pp. 149–155. Some of these are mentioned by F. Rosner, "Jewish Ethical Issues in Hazardous Medical Therapy," *Tradition* 19 (1): 55–58. See also, from a religious scientist's perspective, the comments of K. Stern, "Experimentation on Human Subjects: A Search for Halakhic Guidelines," *Tradition* 17 (4): 41–52, as well as Dr. Jacob Levy in *Noam* 13:77–82.

66. *Responsa Aḥi'ezer* 2:16 (6). The *Responsa Beit David* permits odds of even one in a thousand. Conversely the *Tiferet Yisrael* (to *Yoma* 8:3) permits smallpox inoculation even where there is a one in a thousand chance of contracting the disease itself as a result of the inoculation. Rabbi Jakobovits (*Medical Experimentation*, pp. 380, 382) agrees with the *Aḥi'ezer* that even the remotest chance of success should be attempted, but he then goes on to say that "it is obligatory to apply to terminal patients even untried or uncertain cures." Some years later, however, he retreated from this problematic position. See his *Jewish Medical Ethics* (2nd edition, 1975, p. 292). In this regard see Bleich, *Healing*, p. 116.

67. *Responsa Iggerot Moshe, Y.D.* 2:58.

68. *Responsa Iggerot Moshe, Y.D.* 3:36. Both the *Ḥatam Sofer* (*Y.D.* 36) and the *Ẓiẓ Eliezer* (10:25 and 5:5) adopt similar views.

this passage permits recourse to hazardous practice only where there is a fifty-fifty chance of success. (As a matter of fact, he says, where the chances of success are more than fifty-fifty, a person is *obliged* to take the chance to achieve long-term, normal living.) In the case of the pagan physician recourse is permitted because we may assume that there are enough reliable physicians who will act with every intention of curing the patient. But this assumption only holds true where the physician is himself confident of the effectiveness of his therapy. Where the physician admits that the proposed therapy is unreliable to the extent that a majority of patients will die, then we cannot permit such recourse, and we cannot discount the momentary life at hand. Rabbi Feinstein accordingly reads the Gehazi narrative as a case of even risks; they could have been killed or they could equally have been taken captive. Thus where the outcome can go either way, a person can choose to wager all or nothing. It depends on the individual; he is not obligated one way or the other. Ultimately, says R. Feinstein, this case depends on the will of people at large (*da'at inshi*). For Gehazi was indeed not a halakhic authority, but a simple, in many ways errant man, and like him, most common people would choose normal life at the risk of immediate death—where the odds of success are even. But it depends on the individual—not everyone would agree with Gehazi.

As for his previously held view, R. Moshe appreciates that it too has its proponents—notably the Aḥi'ezer—and he therefore notes that one who relies on that view to accept a long-shot chance on complete recovery is not to be faulted.

These two responsa of Rabbi Feinstein, taken together, constitute a remarkable instance of halakhic openness and flexibility. On the one hand, far from dogmatic assertion of personal infallibility, we are witness to a readiness to reconsider a firmly held and widely shared opinion. On the other hand, we can recognize an openness to the possibility of personal predilection and choice, given R. Moshe's position that would allow individual discretion, irrespective of a majority, where the mathematical odds of survival are inconclusive.

There is a somewhat different formulation of acceptable and unacceptable risk under such circumstances, whereby a distinction can be drawn between a procedure or drug that has a proven therapeutic effect, albeit with a significant possibility of death resulting under certain circumstances, and a drug that is experimental in nature, its potential benefit unsubstantiated. This distinction was first made by R. Jacob Emden, using the terms *refuah bedukah* (the former case, a "proven therapy") and *she'einah bedukah* (the latter case, being unproven).[69] As explained by Rabbi J. David Bleich,[70] this means that while a patient is obliged to seek medical cure for his condition, he need accept therapy only where the proffered treatment is of the former kind, i.e., of proven benefit. But where the treatment is entirely experimental, its effectiveness not medically established, there exists no obligation, although one is free to try it, nonetheless. Where such experimental drugs or procedures are not merely unproven, but are actually dangerous, then according to R. Moshe Dov Welner such therapy is forbidden. It is only a proven efficacy that can counterbalance a downside risk to the life of the patient.[71] Thus, he argues, the *Sefer Ḥasidim* forbids the folk usage of certain herbs which either cured or killed their user, for their benefits were not medically proven, while their hazards were known to all.[72]

How long is the "momentary duration of life" which can be discounted or disregarded? The Aḥi'ezer, saying that it makes no difference whether it be a matter of hours or months, accepts a case wherein a six-month prognosis is offered by the physician, every day of which may be the patient's last. Rabbi Feinstein, as does R. Solomon Kluger,[73] sets the limit at twelve months of expected life. But he also adds that if the contemplated therapy or surgery merely promises to extend the life-span without eliminating the likelihood of death at any time, it should not be undertaken. In an additional comment, he notes that it would not be permissible to undergo such therapy if long-term survival can be achieved instead by remaining restricted to bed continuously. Such inconvenience is to be preferred over the dire risks otherwise posed.

Finally, as to the establishment of these facts, the accepted

---

69. *Mor u-Keẓia* to *Sh.A. O.H.* 328.
70. Bleich, *Bioethics*, p. 31.
71. Rabbi M. D. Welner, in *ha-Torah ve'ha-Medinah* 7–8 (1956–57): 314.
72. *Sefer Ḥasidim* 467.
73. *Darkhei Teshuvah* to *Sh.A. Y.D.* 155:6.

view seems to be that of the *Shevut Ya'akov*, who requires that each case be individually adjudicated, with the concurrence of the best medical opinion (by a majority of two to one) and the preeminent rabbinical authority of the city.[74]

Risking life to Avoid Unbearable Pain

Regarding this question, there are a number of relevant texts. Both Naḥmanides and Rabbeinu Nissim note that in every medical treatment there is an element of danger, whether through human error or unforeseen complications.[75] Nonetheless they accept that in the normal course of things one may have recourse to medical treatment, such potential dangers notwithstanding. Such a position is entirely consistent with the generalized mandate granted a physician to cure sickness, as discussed earlier. But where there is a heightened risk factor, such recourse needs justification. Indeed, it is the view of R. Jacob Emden that such heightened risk for the "mere" sake of alleviation of intense pain is not justifiable.[76] The case before him involved surgery to remove gallstones, a procedure which in his time occasionally led to early death. Yet others, notably the Meiri and R. Moses Isserles, implicitly permit hazardous procedures where the only purpose is the relief from great pain.[77] The comments of the latter occur in the context of the special prohibition against wounding one's parent. Isserles (the Rema) rules that it is permissible for a physician to perform surgery (that involves necessary cutting) "where there is no one else available who can do this, and the parent is in pain, the son can perform blood-letting and amputation, following parental consent." Amputation to relieve pain can certainly be classified as major surgery where there is no intent to save life (at the very least this would be true of the sixteenth century, when R. Isserles lived). Armed with such precedent, recent authorities have tended to adopt the lenient view, with permissive rulings

---

74. *Responsa Shevut Ya'akov* 3:75.

75. Naḥmanides, *Torat ha-Adam*, in *Kitvei ha-Ramban* 2:43; *Ḥiddushei ha-Ran, Sanhedrin* 84b. See Bleich, *Halakhic Problems*, 1:122. See also the *Responsa Ẓiẓ Eliezer* 10:15 (17,1).

76. *Mor u-Keẓia* to *Sh.A. O.H.* 328.

77. Meiri to *Sanhedrin* 84b; Rema to *Sh.A. Y.D.* 241:3. Both are quoted by R. Yeḥiel Ya'akov Breish, *Ḥelkat Ya'akov* 3:11.

offered by Rabbi Shelomoh Zalman Auerbach and Rabbi Shelomoh Zalman Braun.[78] What is the basis of such leniency in the face of possible death?

Both of the latter authors offer as a key rationale the fact that the therapy thus undertaken is done "for the sake of healing." Yet this should not lead one to conclude that armed with such a rationale they would permit any medical procedure or therapy. The cases which the pivotal passage of Isserles permitted involved well-established procedures, not experimental ones. Thus it is safe to say that the relief of pain justifies only medical treatment that is established, albeit with a due measure of risk to life. Put another way, we might say that a therapy or procedure which is proven and widely accepted, in spite of attendant risks, can indeed be administered. This approach is entirely consistent with the principle, seen elsewhere,[79] and articulated here by Rabbi Bleich, that Halakhah condones exposure to dangerous sources, if such exposure is commonly accepted in society at large. A person may rely on a measure of Divine Providence to protect him no less than the many who are safely delivered from such danger. As the Gemara *Shabbat* 129b puts it, "since the multitude are accustomed to doing this . . . it may be considered permissible, since 'the Lord preserveth the simple' [Ps. 116:6]." Once such an explanation is adopted, it becomes entirely possible that even Emden would not disagree, for in rejecting gallstone surgery he stated explicitly that "even though many have undergone this procedure and survived, many have also hastened their death as a result of this surgery"; i.e., the procedure in his time was indeed fraught with danger, with perhaps an equal number of patients succumbing as surviving the experience. Well might he agree to permit a more established procedure, with fewer, albeit real, attendant risks.[80]

78. See A. S. Avraham, "Nisyonot Refu'iyim," p. 24, reporting on correspondence with Rabbi Auerbach. See Rabbi Braun, *She'arim ha-Meẓuyyanim be'Halakhah* 190:4.

79. For a detailed discussion of this principle, as related to the hazards of cigarettes, alcohol, and nonmedical drugs, see *Jewish Ethics and Halakhah for Our Time*, vol. 1, pp. 221–243.

80. There is a connected—although separate—issue dealing with the permissibility of cosmetic plastic surgery, intended to deal with purely psychological pain or anguish related to physical deformities that are a source of social discomfort. May a person undergo such a procedure in spite of the risks inhering in every surgical situation? For a detailed review of sources, see Bleich, *Halakhic Problems*, 1:119–123.

SUMMARY AND CONCLUSIONS

We are now in a position to summarize our findings on the halakhic stance toward several issues involved in scientific research and hazardous practices involving human subjects and patients.

There is clearly an obligation to take direct action to save an endangered life—based on the prohibition against standing idle while another is imperiled. The duty extends to hiring others and undertaking the financial costs requisite to do the job (according to R. Meir Abulafia, Rosh, and Rema), but where the victim can afford it he is required to reimburse for all expenses incurred. According to R. Yeḥiel Weinberg there is no limit to monies properly spent in this cause.

Such intervention extends to every life-threatening situation, whether actual or only contemplated. Maimonides, as well as others, explicitly includes medical treatment in this obligation. There is, however, some debate of a philosophical nature as to the propriety of interfering with nature. While a minority (Ibn Ezra and Naḥmanides in particular) consider medical intervention a compromise of faith in Providence, the majority (based on numerous talmudic sources) consider the practice of and recourse to medicine to be in the best traditions of social and religious responsibility. Indeed under the rubric of *pikuaḥ nefesh*—the saving of life—cardinal principles of Judaism were set aside temporarily, including the Sabbath, major festivals, and kashrut. Such action extended even to situations of doubtful danger, where there was a less than certain threat to life.

But in the context of medical research, a more direct issue is that of self-endangerment. May a person allow him or herself to be exposed to hazardous conditions for the sake of saving another's life? Where a person wishes to volunteer for certain or probable death, most agree with the view of R. Akiva that there is no such obligation. Whether a person may volunteer if he so wishes is a matter of debate: Rabbi Unterman forbids such self-sacrifice, Rabbi Weinberg permits and even praises it. The minority view is that of Ben Petura, requiring self-sacrifice—but even there it is only where there is significant extension of life to be gained for the endangered party.

Where the contemplated action involves only a possible, but not probable prospect of death to the intercessor, there is further debate. Based on a passage in the Yerushalmi, a minority view (associated with the *Hagahot Maimoniyyot*) requires intervention. The majority sees no such obligation of self-endangerment, even where the victim faces certain death and the onlooker only possible death. This majority view, including Maimonides and the *Shulḥan Arukh*, argues that the Bavli differs with the Yerushalmi. This generated a debate over the interpretation of three key passages in the Bavli—as well as the Yerushalmi.

Consequently one could say that while all the talmudic passages are controversial, on balance the position of the Bavli, in its majority interpretation, won out. Thus one would not be obligated to face any peril whatsoever—but neither is one prohibited (where one's own death is unlikely to happen). There is one statement of Maimonides that is debated among modern halakhists, relating to the issue of saving many lives. One interpretation—put forward by R. Meir Simḥah of Dvinsk—would have Maimonides forbid self-endangerment even then, while others (notably Rabbis Unterman and Weinberg) reject such an interpretation.

This last issue has particular relevance for medical research, where a healthy person volunteers for some risk in order to save many endangered people. The majority view, it would appear, would permit such self-endangerment, even according to Maimonides. On the question of odds and degree of risk, a major source is the Radbaz, who writes that a person may entertain danger under such circumstances where the likelihood of his death is less than fifty–fifty. But where it could go either way (i.e., fifty–fifty), and certainly where death is likely or probable, such imperilment would be foolish and prohibited. The *Arukh ha-Shulḥan* counsels common sense and calculated risk, weighing the odds so as to act prudently without, however, being guilty of "just standing there doing nothing."

But what if the party facing imminent death is oneself? May one elect to risk even that limited life-span in the hope of finding long-term survival? Medically speaking, may a patient facing imminent death be treated in a manner that might cure him or kill him? Here there is ample scriptural precedent in the story of the four lepers who undertook precisely such a risk—and were saved. The Gemara quotes this instance to permit recourse to dangerous treatment where the only alternative is imminent death, saying that we may well disregard the limited life that remains. Apparently long-term survival, even if doubtful, is preferable to short-term life, even if certain. This position was accepted by all authorities.

But there was some debate over the odds involved. Some (including the Aḥi'ezer) would accept even the remotest of odds, as long as there was some chance of long-term survival. But most would stand by the requirement of at least even odds of survival with the contemplated treatment. Anything less than this is considered unacceptable. Rabbi Moshe Feinstein requires better than even odds of success; where it is fifty–fifty, he leaves room for some choice, for whereas most people would take such a risk, some might not—they may choose what they will. Anything less than even odds, however, R. Moshe forbids.

Another approach is that of R. Jacob Emden, who says that whatever the odds, there should be at least some proven therapeutic benefit associated with the contemplated treatment. A treatment which is entirely experimental and unproven to date need not be taken; but a patient nonetheless can, if so desired, choose such treatment, as long as it is not known to be dangerous.

One further question, the duration of "limited life," is also raised. Here the consensus (notably the Aḥi'ezer, R. Solomon Kluger, and R. Feinstein) appears to set the limit at twelve months of life where every day might be the patient's last. Anything beyond this is considered a normal life. In all such matters, says the Shevut Ya'akov, there should be a two to one majority of physicians in agreement over the efficacy of the steps to be taken—and also consultation with rabbinic authority in each case.

Finally, where the self-endangerment is not to save one's life, but rather to secure relief from enduring pain, the Meiri and the Rema both appear to permit hazardous therapy or surgery. And while R. Emden appears to forbid this, upon further examination it would appear that even he would permit such a course where the contemplated treatment is commonly practiced and the dangers widely assumed. In such cases, even though there is a possibility of immediate death, one may fall back on a measure of Providence to assume that one will be part of the clear majority who survive. This approach accords with the doctrine that "the Lord preserveth the simple."

To return to the case with which we began this excursus, several conclusions are indicated:

1. There is certainly an obligation to save the endangered life of another person, especially when one is in a position to act as a result of one's knowledge, training, or circumstance. This extends to the thwarting of "nature," or what some might call "God's will." Thus a physician is obliged to heal wherever he or she can.

2. Where fulfilling this obligation puts one at risk, several caveats apply: no one, not even a physician, is required to expose him or herself to certain or even probable death to save another person. Where the risk factor to the physician is only possible but not likely to cause death or disease, the majority and normative view would not require the physician to expose himself to such risk. The choice in this instance can be left to the individual. At the same time if the risk factor is as high as 50 percent, it would appear that the Halakhah would forbid such exposure. In the present case, where the likelihood of contamination is small, the choice can be left to the individual physicians, and their decisions are to be respected.

3. As to the question of experimental treatment that might shorten life: the patient may take the chance—but only if the physician feels that there is a good likelihood of a successful outcome. In the present case the odds are not sufficiently encouraging—it would seem that further testing not involving human subjects is called for. The patient, following the majority view, should not agree to the trial.

2

The Definition and Determination of Death

Introduction

Up until relatively recently, society generally had little difficulty in identifying the time, and the signs, of death. Before the advent of modern medical technology, laymen as well as the medical community assumed that death occurred upon cessation of breathing and blood circulation. But new technology has made it possible to artificially assist these cardio-pulmonary functions in a variety of ways, even in the absence of other conventional signs of life, such as normal brain activity traditionally associated with life.

Thus it has become necessary to reexamine traditional assumptions regarding the dividing line between life and death, and to determine more carefully precisely where life ends and death begins. The problem centers on the issue of the primary locus of life—is it to be found in the heart or the brain? Furthermore, does death occur at a given moment, or is it a process occurring over time, involving a variety of organs, cells, and functions? From a religious point of view, the issue is this: if death is the departure of the soul from the body, at which point can it be said that body and soul have separated?

These are not merely academic questions. They are of immense practical significance in a variety of situations. Large numbers of patients are found in hospitals and chronic-care institutions on varying degrees of artificial-support systems, at great expense to their families and the state. Many of them can remain in such conditions indefinitely. Given the finite human and economic resources available, how long should such support be maintained? What of the psychological impact on family members, or on medical personnel? What undetermined suffering is thereby imposed on the patients themselves? What likelihood of recovery or improvement should exist before such support is instituted?

These questions are given added urgency in light of the availability of life-saving organ-transplant surgery. Kidneys, lungs, hearts, livers, and other organs are increasingly removed from cadavers (the main, and sometimes only, source of such organs) for implantation in endangered recipients. But in order to be effective, these organs must be removed almost immediately upon the death of the donor body, for thereafter the organs begin to deteriorate. Hence it is vital that the determination of death be based on clear rulings and guidelines, so as to make the procedure effective, and eliminate legal complications.

Clearly such questions go beyond purely medical considerations, in that they raise all kinds of ethical, legal, religious, and philosophical issues as to the nature of life and the notion of death. And in recent years, a number of responses have been articulated.

One approach has been to formulate a comprehensive notion of "brain death." The most widely used attempt is that known as "The Ad Hoc Committee of the Harvard Medical School to Examine the Definition of Brain Death," as issued in 1968. Essentially this group identified criteria that would show that no brain function is present in a patient in deep coma, and that the condition is irreversible. The major criteria include a total unresponsiveness to external stimuli or inner need; complete absence of spontaneous movement or spontaneous breathing; no central nervous system reflexes whatsoever; and a flat electroencephalogram (EEG). Once these conditions are satisfied, complete brain death has occurred, and, it is argued, the patient may be removed from all support systems and further medical treatment. This holds true even though there might be ongoing heart function.

Others, however, stand opposed to such notions of brain death.

Thus the philosopher Hans Jonas argues that these criteria do not define death at all—they merely describe the conditions under which death is allowed to take place unopposed. He sees no sharp borderline between life and death, and disagrees with the idea that life requires spontaneous (i.e. unassisted) functioning. He and others deny the importance of central nervous system or brain function defining death. They further argue that such notions of brain death easily lead to premature declarations of death, and to the future possibility of any number of abuses practiced on such bodies once they are declared "dead," even though the heart continues to beat. They favor instead the traditional criteria, i.e., the cessation of cardio-pulmonary function.

On either side of these views are a number of others, some more extreme, some more moderate, in proposing or rejecting forms of brain death, as applied to different parts of the brain and their functions, the kinds of tests necessary to measure such functions, and the need for review and delay in making final determinations of life-and-death status.

For the Halakhah, it goes without saying that these issues are of cardinal significance, not merely in identifying the end of life, but also in a host of related issues, including inheritance, marital status, delayed burial, the permissibility of postmortem and transplants, culpability for homicide, and the question of withholding medical treatment. On the one hand, there is an absolute concern to safeguard human personality and life. On the other, there are considerations of speedy burial, mitigation of suffering in the dying, and opportunities to save endangered lives. These concerns need careful weighing and balancing, consistent with biblical and talmudic law and precedent, even while taking full cognizance of current medical practice and ethical concerns. Such complex factors have led to a significant halakhic debate and a variety of views among contemporary scholars, indicating, at the very least, that the halakhic process is alive and well.

The Question

A twenty-five-year-old man, critically injured in an automobile accident, is brought unconscious into the emergency room of a hospital. His heart continues to beat, but he cannot breathe unaided, and thus he is connected to a respirator. An EEG and brain scan both indicate that there is extensive brain damage, and apparently irreversible coma. The attending physician sees no possibility of recovery under these circumstances. He requests permission from the family to declare the patient brain dead, and thereafter to disconnect the respirator. What should the family do?

From a halakhic point of view, the following issues are raised by this case:

1. What is the classic halakhic determination of death, i.e., when, according to the Halakhah, does life end and death begin?
2. Is there any halakhic validity to the notion of brain death, or permanent loss of brain function, as an independent indicator that death has occurred?
3. Once a person is declared dead, is it permissible to delay burial out of concern that he may in spite of everything be alive, or somehow able to be resuscitated?

The Sources

A. Genesis 7:21–22

All flesh perished that moved upon the earth . . . all in whose nostrils was the breath of the spirit of life.

B. I Samuel 25:37

And it came to pass in the morning when the wine was gone out of Nabal, that his wife told him these things, and his heart died within him, and he became as a stone. And it came to pass about ten days later, after the Lord smote Nabal, that he died.

C. I Kings 17:17–22

And it came to pass after these things that the son of the woman [of Zarephath], the mistress of the house, fell sick; and his sickness was so sore that there was no soul [*neshamah*] left in him. . . . And Elijah stretched himself upon the child three times, and cried unto the Lord and said: "O my Lord I pray thee, let this child's soul come back into him." And the Lord harkened unto the voice of Elijah; and the soul of child came back into him, and he revived.

D. Mishnah Sanhedrin 6:7

Whoever delays a burial transgresses a negative commandment [that commands "His body shall not remain all night upon the tree, but thou shalt surely bury him the same day," Deut. 21:23]. But if the delay is in order to honor the dead, such as to arrange the casket or shrouds, there is no transgression.

E. Mishnah Ohalot 1:6

And likewise cattle and wild beasts . . . if their heads have been severed, they impart the impurity of death [as carcasses], even if they move convulsively like the tail of a lizard that twitches [after it has been severed from the body].

F. Beraita Semaḥot 8:1

It is proper to visit the cemetery up till three days after burial to check on the dead, without concern for appearing to act in accordance with "the ways of the Emori." It once happened that a person was found to be alive, and lived a further twenty-five years, bearing five children before he died.

G. Mishnah Yoma 8:7

If on the Sabbath a person is buried under debris and it is doubtful whether he is alive or dead . . . the debris is to be removed from over him [even though this act violates the Sabbath]. If when he is found he is alive, one should continue to remove the debris. But if he is dead one should leave the body in its place [until after the Sabbath].

H. Yoma 85a

The tannaim have said: "In removing the debris one uncovers as far as the victim's nose (*Rashi:* 'where he appears to be dead and there is no movement'). But there are those who say that one uncovers as far as the chest." Let us say that these views correspond to the following tannaitic views: "From whence is a newborn created? One opinion is that it is from his head, but Abba Shaul says that it is from his navel." But it is possible that even Abba Shaul agrees that in saving life, essential life is found at the nose, as (A) teaches.

I. Jerusalem Talmud, Yoma 8:5

How far does one check for signs of life? There are two amoraic views: one requires an examination of the nose, the other an examination of the navel. The first view is that life is sustained by breathing, while the second is that life begins at the navel [through the umbilical cord].

J. Maimonides, Commentary On The Mishnah 8:7

When one uncovers the nose and can detect no breathing, it is forbidden to remove any further debris on the Sabbath, for that person is certainly dead.

K. Maimonides, M.T. Hil. Shabbat 2:19

If one examines the nose and does not find life therein, one should leave him there, for he has already died.

L. Maimonides, M.T. Hil. Avel 4:5

Whoever closes the eyes of a person just as he is dying is considered to have spilled his blood. One should instead wait a while, for perhaps it is a fainting spell [and not death itself].

M. Maimonides, Guide Of The Perplexed 1:42

Similarly "death" [*mavet*] is a term denoting both death and severe illness. Thus "and Nabal's heart died within him and he became as a stone" (B) refers to the severity of his illness. On this account Scripture makes it clear with regard to the son of the woman of Zarephath that "his sickness was so sore that there was no soul left in him" (C), for if it had said "and he died," it would have possible to interpret this as meaning that it was a case of severe illness. In such a case the individual is near death, as Nabal was when he heard the news. Some of the men of Andalusia interpret the verse as meaning that his breath was suspended so that no breath at all could be perceived in him—as happens to people struck with apoplexy or with asphyxia deriving from the womb, so that it is not known if the one in question is dead or alive, and the doubt remains a day or two.

N. Rabbeinu Baḥya, Deuteronomy 6:5

And because the heart is the first organ in the creation of man, and the last among the organs of the body to die, therefore Scripture says, "you shall love the Lord your God with all your heart," i.e., until the last moment of life.

O. Shulḥan Arukh, Oraḥ Ḥayyim 330:5

If a woman dies in childbirth on the Sabbath, a knife may even be brought from the public domain, to cut open the womb and remove the fetus, in case it is still alive.

REMA: But the reason that we do not permit this nowadays, even on days other than the Sabbath, is because we are unable to determine the time of death of the mother with sufficient precision to save the life of the fetus.

Discussion

1. CLASSIC HALAKHIC DEFINITIONS OF DEATH

Nowhere in Scripture is there a clear or categorical statement as to the exact moment, or time span, during which death occurs. It was left to the talmudic tradition to clarify the traditional criteria for the determination of death. Even within the Talmud itself there is no consistent attempt to determine the moment of death per se. This is not to say that there is no discussion of the matter, but merely to indicate that the issue was always tied to other concerns of the law, e.g., the laws of impurity, of marital status, of Sabbath desecration, or of timely burial. But it was precisely because of these many ramifications that the question of determining the precise moment of death became rather important.

The pivotal discussion of the issue occurs in the context of Sabbath observance. The Mishnah in *Yoma* (G) permits suspension of Sabbath prohibitions in order to save the life of a person buried beneath collapsed debris, but such suspension is not permitted once it is ascertained that the victim is already dead. The Gemara (H), in discussing this, attempts to clarify how one establishes that such a person is already dead. Two anonymous tannaitic views are recorded: the first takes the position that the moment the victim's nose is uncovered, and no breathing can be detected, the victim is to be pronounced dead. The prooftext quoted in support of such a definition occurs in the great flood recounted in Genesis, where it is recorded that death came to all "in whose nostrils was the breath of the spirit of life" (A). The second view, as understood by the amora Rav Pappa, differs from the first by accepting a determination of death based on an examination of the chest, i.e., the heart, even without reference to nasal breathing. According to this explanation, both agree that where the nose is uncovered first, the determination may be made from the nose. Where they differ is when it is the chest that is first accessible, and the question becomes whether or not it is necessary, or permissible on the Sabbath, to uncover and check as far as the nose.

A parallel discussion in the Jerusalem Talmud (I) likewise mentions two views, but records the second of them as referring to the navel or stomach area as indicative of life. In addition a number of later authorities had a variant reading in the Babylonian Talmud itself, whereby it is the navel and not the chest that is to be examined for signs of life.[1] Such a reading is also reflected in a passage in *Sotah* 45b, where the navel is mentioned as a criterion of life and death.[2] Nonetheless it was the version of *Yoma* as printed in our present Talmud that was generally accepted by Rashi and several later authorities.

In practical terms, however, such variant readings made little difference, in view of the fact that virtually all of the major codifiers, starting with Maimonides (K), accepted the first view as law—i.e., it is the nose which indicates life or death by the presence or absence of detectable breathing.[3] Indeed Maimonides is entirely unambiguous in his commentary to this Mishnah when he says "for that person is certainly dead [where there is no detectable breathing]" (J). Such a conclusion is entirely in line with the reasoning of Abba Shaul (H) that asserts that essential life is found at the nose (*ikkar ḥiyyuta be'appei hu*). The only early authority who follows the second view in *Yoma*, i.e., that it is heartbeat that is synonymous with life, is Rabbeinu Baḥya ben Asher, who considers the heart to be the last organ to die (N).

And yet this discussion itself raises a key question. In establishing that it is the nasal breathing that counts, does this view mean to say that it is the breathing itself that represents life, while the absence of breathing represents death? Or is the intent simply to say that continued breathing is the best indicator or external sign that critical organs continue to function and bestow life on the victim. In other words, is it possible that breath is not

1. Those who have such a reading include Alfasi, Rabbeinu Ḥananel, Rabbeinu Nissim, and the Rosh.

2. In this regard see the comments in the comprehensive article by Dr. Abraham Steinberg, "Keviat Rega ha-Mavet," *Noam* 19 (1977): 222–224.

3. Besides Maimonides, see *Tur/Sh. A. O. H.* 329:4.

synonymous with life itself, but simply a sufficiently reliable indicator of continued life?

It is the commentary of Rashi that sheds some light on this critical issue. For in explaining the first, normative, view, he adds that the nose is to be examined where the person appears to be dead, "and there is no movement" (H). This implies that even if there is no breathing, death cannot be considered to have taken place as long as there is some other bodily movement. In other words, if it can be ascertained that other organs in the body continue to function, such that there is some detectable movement, then death cannot fairly be said to have taken place. In a second comment, Rashi similarly says that underlying this first view is the assumption that life will sometimes only be "detected at the nose" (H). This seems to be saying that only detection of life occurs at the nose, but life itself may well be centered elsewhere, e.g., at the heart. According to this, there is no argument as to where life "resides," for all can agree that life resides in the chest, as Rashi puts it. Where there is debate is whether an examination of the chest is sufficiently reliable—and to this question the dominant view answers in the negative.

If this be Rashi's intention, then the absence of breathing is not by itself sufficient to determine death. Put otherwise, one could say that lack of breathing is a necessary but not sufficient indication of death. Essentially lack of breathing establishes a conclusive presumption that other bodily functions are absent too. However, if this presumption is contradicted by other signs that other life functions continue, then surely life persists. In point of fact, a number of prominent halakhists subsequently understood Rashi, and the talmudic debate, as leading precisely to such a conclusion. We will return to their views later.

There is, however, a different way of understanding the discussion in *Yoma*, at least as explained by Rabbi Aaron Soloveichik.[4] Maimonides in the *Mishneh Torah* (L) asserts that it is necessary to wait a while after a person appears to have died before declaring him dead, because he might only be in a fainting spell. Apparently the cessation of breathing can lead on occasion to an erroneous

4. Rabbi Aaron Soloveichik, "The Halakhic Definition of Death," *Jewish Bioethics*, pp. 296–302.

belief that death has occurred.[5] If so, Maimonides believes that life might continue for some time after breathing has stopped, in that the absence of respiration does not in itself constitute death. In his *Commentary to the Mishnah* (E) Maimonides makes a similar statement, implying strongly that where there is some movement originating in a controlling center of the body (such as the brain or central nervous system), then life remains.[6] The problem with these Maimonidean statements is that they appear to be contradicted by his clear ruling, based on *Yoma*, that where the victim's nose is examined and no breathing is detectable "they are to leave him there, for he has already died" (K). This apparently accepts the lack of breathing as a sufficient proof that death has occurred. How do we reconcile these passages?

To answer this question, Rabbi Soloveichik proposes that Maimonides believes (together with the *Tur* and *Shulḥan Arukh*) that as a rule death does not occur in one moment, but rather is a process taking place over a period of time. It begins the moment spontaneous breathing ceases, and ends only when all major organs, including the brain, have ceased functioning. During this process the person is neither fully alive nor fully dead; he may not be handled or treated as if dead already, and if there are any means of resuscitation they must be employed wherever possible. The one limitation occurs on the Sabbath: because of the gravity of the Sabbath it may be desecrated only to the prevent the death of one fully alive; but once the process of death has begun, i.e., there is no breathing, the Sabbath may not be suspended on his behalf. Rabbi Soloveichik does add, however, that where there is "even the remotest possibility of resuscitation, one is obliged to desecrate the Sabbath." Thus Maimonides rules one way on the Sabbath and another on weekdays.

Elsewhere Maimonides discusses the occurrence of death, but in a manner that is unclear and problematical. In his *Guide of the Perplexed* (M), while discussing ambiguous terms in Scrip-

5. See Rabbi Eliezer Waldenburg, *Ẓiẓ Eliezer* 9:45 (2), who has a similar understanding of this passage in Maimonides.

6. Maimonides, *Commentary to the Mishnah, Ohalot* 1:6, where he states that spasmodic movement of a limb following decapitation does not indicate life, because such movement does not originate in one center but is the result of spontaneous nerve activity in various parts of the body. See Soloveichik, pp. 297–298.

ture, he explains the term *mavet*. It is his contention that the term usually means "death," but on occasion conveys the notion of severe illness that precedes death. He refers to the death of Nabal, whose heart "died within him" some ten days before his actual demise. He also to refers to the child of the Zarephite woman, who, as related in the Book of Kings (C), fell mortally sick until "there was no soul left in him."[7] Maimonides says that this verse deliberately does not say "he died," because that would leave open the possibility that he was not yet dead, as the term *mavet* can imply. By using this formulation, Scripture conveys that he in fact died, prior to his miraculous resuscitation by Elijah.

Thus far in this passage Maimonides seems to take the term *neshamah* as referring to the soul that leaves the body when death occurs. But then he goes on to quote an Andalusian (i.e., Spanish) tradition which understood this verse to be referring not to the soul (*neshamah*) but rather to the related and almost similar term *neshimah*, which is usually translated as "breathing." Thus it is their view that the child had not died, but rather had stopped breathing, "as happens to people struck with apoplexy." Such a condition, says Maimonides (evidently talking from his experience as a renowned physician) may persist for one or two days before death actually occurs.

Does he agree with the Spanish view? Subsequent commentators are divided on this question.[8] If he does agree with the view he attributes to them, it would be quite consistent with his statement (L) in the *Mishneh Torah* that accepts that even after

---

7. I translate the Hebrew word in the text as "soul," even though the Jewish Publication Society translation reads "breath." "Soul" is certainly the more literal intent of the verse, given our present concerns. Likewise I translate Maimonides in the *Guide* as "soul," even though the authoritative translation of Pines has "breath."

8. Abravanel in his commentary to the *Guide* 1:42 is certain that Maimonides disagrees with the Spaniards and affirms that the young man actually died and was brought back to life. On the other hand, Narboni, Shemtov, and Ibn Kaspi ascribe the Spanish view to Maimonides himself. See their respective commentaries to this passage in the *Guide*, particularly in Ibn Kaspi's commentary entitled *Maskiyyot Kesef*, in *Sheloshah Kadmonei Mefarshei ha-Moreh* (Jerusalem, 1961). It would appear that the approach taken in interpreting this Maimonidean passage is a function of how one views Maimonides' views of miracles in general. Thus those who take a more naturalistic approach downplay the likelihood of the boy's death, and therefore see a congruence between Maimonides and the Andalusians. In this regard, see my *Joseph Ibn Kaspi's "Gevia Kesef"* (New York, 1982), pp. 99–122, 274.

breathing has stopped life may continue for some time. But it appears that he cannot openly embrace their view for another, doctrinal, reason: it would imply that he denies the philosophically controversial miracle performed by Elijah. This, it appears, he does not want to do. In any case, his formulation of their position would confirm, if he is in agreement with it, that it is his belief that life can persist for some time even after breathing has ceased.

Leaving Maimonides aside for the moment, we encounter an important statement on the time of death in the comments of R. Moses Isserles, the Rema. The *Shulḥan Arukh* had ruled (O) that where a woman dies while in labor (presumably indicated by the lack of breathing), every effort is to be made to save the unborn fetus. This includes desecration of the Sabbath to bring any implements necessary to open her abdomen and remove the baby. Isserles, however, explains that in his time (he died in 1572 in Poland) such a procedure should not be performed even on weekdays "for we are unable to determine the time of death of the mother with sufficient precision." It would appear that his reasoning is as follows: given the urgency to save the baby, there might be a premature decision to incise the mother's abdomen before death has actually occurred; such an action might well hasten the mother's actual death if it had not yet occurred. Given the choice, Isserles cannot permit the possible hastening of the mother's death in order to save the unborn life of her fetus. Apparently this is true even though the mother has already stopped breathing. It would appear that Rema understands the discussion in *Yoma* to yield the conclusion that where breathing has stopped or is not discernible, life may yet be present. As explained by Rabbi Soloveichik, it is possible that even after breathing has stopped, she is not yet completely dead, hence Isserles forbids any action that might snuff out the final vestiges of life before their naturally occurring time.

The question of determination of death came up again a century later as part of a celebrated controversy. In the early eighteenth century R. Ẓvi Ashkenazi, popularly known as the Ḥakham Ẓvi, wrote several responsa defending his viewpoint that it is quite impossible for man or animal to live without a functioning heart. He ruled, therefore, in a case brought before him, that where a chicken is opened and no heart is found, and it is alleged to be unkosher because of this defect, we must conclude that the chicken is kosher, in that it must have had a heart that was misplaced in the interim (or witnesses attesting that no heart was found were either mistaken or lying).[9] The issue was taken up by other contemporary authorities, notably R. Jonathan Eibeschutz.[10] The latter asserted that it was quite conceivable that there was no heart to start with, and that other organs might well have fulfilled the functions of the heart. Hence, lacking a heart, the chicken in question was defective, and is not kosher.

In the course of his responsum, the Ḥakham Ẓvi discusses at length the possibility of life persisting in the absence of a functioning heart. Quoting the Zohar extensively, he asserts that the soul resides in the heart; that all the organs depend absolutely on the continued functioning of the heart; and that it is the heart which is the last organ of the body to die. This view, he says, is shared by all branches of the rabbinic tradition, i.e., the halakhic, the philosophic, and the pietistic/mystical. Among the former he quotes Rashi, Maimonides, and the *Shulḥan Arukh* in their discussions of *treifot*, i.e., defective animal carcasses. Among the latter he quotes the writings of Saadia Gaon, Judah ha-Levi, Abraham Ibn Ezra, Maimonides' *Guide* (1:39), and Isaac Luria. He concludes that

> Rashi agrees with us that the soul resides in the heart. Sometimes, however, even though the soul is still within the heart, a heartbeat cannot be detected from above. This is attributable to the weakness of the heartbeat and the location of the heart within the chest. . . . But breathing that emanates from the heart via the lungs is [easily] detectable as long as the heart beats. It is clear that there can only be breathing while there is life in the heart. For breathing derives from, and makes possible, the functioning of the heart.

It is apparent that the Ḥakham Ẓvi considers life to terminate only with the death of the heart. Any movement that is visible once the heart ceases to function (or is removed) does not indicate

9. *Responsa Ḥakham Ẓvi* 77. Other responsa in which he takes up the issue are nos. 74, 76.

10. See his commentary to *Sh.A. Y.D.*, *Kreiti u-Pleiti* 40:4.

life at all—but rather is the result of local nerve activity that causes a variety of movements (i.e., *pirkhus*). Indeed, says Ḥakham Ẓvi, even those who agree with the ancient physician Galen, who argued that movement originates in the brain, agree that life is to be identified with the heart.

This last point of the Ḥakham Ẓvi, however, is debatable. For as we have seen, Rashi (H) accepts the lack of breathing as indicative of death only "where there is no movement." Can one not conclude therefrom that Rashi does not classify all movement subsequent to cessation of breathing as mere *pirkhus?* If so, Rashi's view cannot be said to agree with Ḥakham Ẓvi on this key point. As a matter of fact, such a reading of Rashi seems to be the basis of a responsum written a century later, in a landmark ruling by the leader of nineteenth-century Hungarian Jewry, R. Moses Sofer, popularly known as the Ḥatam Sofer.[11]

In this responsum the Ḥatam Sofer initially states that Jewish law accepts that "everything depends on breathing in the nose." This, he explains, is based on one of two sources: either a tradition taken over from ancient medical authorities (*ba'alei tiviyyim ha-rishonim*) on which much of the sages' scientific assumptions was based; or else a tradition handed down by Moses from Sinai, possibly associated with the verse "all in whose nostrils was the breath of the spirit of life" (A). The Ḥatam Sofer then refers to Maimonides' statement (L) that when a person is dying some time must pass before death can be pronounced definitively. Curiously, says Ḥatam Sofer, Maimonides' formulation here does not specify the point at which death occurs. The explanation, he says, is that this ruling must be taken in conjunction with the Maimonidean statement (K) that if life is not found at the nose, then death must be assumed. Together they state that once breathing is absent for some time (the length is not specified), one may safely assume that death has indeed occurred.

Ḥatam Sofer then goes on to quote Maimonides' *Guide*. He sides with those commentators who understand Maimonides to differ with the Spanish tradition by asserting that the son of the Zarephite woman did indeed die. He also refers to the *Responsa Radbaz* (in the sixteenth century), which cogently disproves the

11. *Responsa Ḥatam Sofer, Y.D.* 338.

Spanish position.[12] Consequently the Ḥatam Sofer formulates the criteria for death as follows: "Wherever he lies motionless as a stone, and he has no heartbeat and afterwards his breathing stops, we can but rely on the words of the Holy Torah that he has died."

Clearly this posits three criteria: no movement, no heartbeat, and no breathing. Apparently his view is that all three must be present before death can be certified. Where either movement (i.e., reflex activity emanating from the central nervous system), or heartbeat (i.e., pulse or blood circulation), or breathing persists, life must be said to prevail, even if only for the moment. The question is, whence does the Ḥatam Sofer draw this triple test? In the ensuing discussion he indicates that these three criteria are well known to those, like members of the *Ḥevra Kadisha*, the burial society, who have received a tradition in these matters handed down since time immemorial. Experts such as these, he writes, can carefully distinguish between states that precede death and those that constitute death. Yet the Ḥatam Sofer himself does not make clear what are the talmudic sources for these three criteria. Hence they must be inferred.

Clearly the Ḥatam Sofer considers his position to be consistent with the discussion in *Yoma*. There, as we have seen, the preponderance of authorities accept the tannaitic view that it is breathing detected at the nose that signifies life. But as for heartbeat and movement the truth is that the major early codifiers do not explicitly mention these criteria, for the Talmud itself clearly accepts the view that it is breathing, and not chest activity, that is the correct determinant (H). Hence this responsum of the Ḥatam Sofer must be seen as a turning point in the history of the question.[13] To justify the Ḥatam Sofer's position, several contemporary halakhists point to the comments of Rashi, seen earlier, that contains the seeds of the view that movement signifies ongoing life.[14] It would appear that the Ḥatam Sofer accepts this reading of Rashi.

As to the matter of heartbeat, there are a number of possible

---

12. *Responsa Radbaz* 5:2203.

13. Rabbi S. Goren, in *Shanah be'Shanah*, 5734, pp. 125–130. This view is in contrast to that of Rabbi J. David Bleich in *ha-Pardes* 51, no. 4, (5732): 17, who says that "it is universally agreed that (continued) heartbeat is a sign of life."

14. Bleich, *ha-Pardes*, p. 16.

sources. One is the passage in Maimonides' *Guide* (M), apparently accepting the notion that heartbeat (and life) can continue after breathing has ceased.[15] This is true whether or not Maimonides accepts the Spanish interpretation of the passage in Kings. Thus, in order to prevent a contradiction between this passage in the *Guide* and those in the *Mishneh Torah* that do not mention heartbeat at all, the Ḥatam Sofer must assume that residual heartbeat signifies ongoing life.[16] Besides Maimonides, there are others, such as Rabbeinu Baḥya, and other nonhalakhic authorities referred to by the Ḥakham Ẓvi, who consider the heart to be the ultimate abode of life in the body, hence the last to cease functioning.

The Ḥatam Sofer then considers the possibility that the criteria in *Yoma* apply only to cases similar to those under discussion in *Yoma*, i.e., unexpected, accidental death. Is it possible, he asks, that other criteria apply under other circumstances, such as when death follows protracted illness and a general breakdown of the body's organs? The answer is in the negative. He explains that it is only in cases of violent death, such as that in *Yoma*, that one can err by misdiagnosing a victim who has gone into shock—and erroneously declare him dead because of a temporary lack of vital signs. Yet the Gemara accepts these signs as sufficient to establish death. Certainly therefore, such criteria are to be invoked where shock is not at issue, as when these vital signs are absent after a lingering illness. Thus, he concludes, these signs are valid in all cases.

This responsum of the Ḥatam Sofer was widely quoted and accepted subsequent to its publication. It was the basis for other, similar, responsa, notably one authored by R. Joseph Saul Nathanson.[17]

The next stage in the history of the problem occured in the late nineteenth century with a responsum written by Rabbi Shalom Mordecai Shvadron, popularly known as the Maharsham, a noted leader of Galician Jewry.[18] Written in response to a query that

15. Ibid., p. 15.

16. See Steinberg, "Keviat Rega ha-Mavet," pp. 234–235.

17. *Responsa Divrei Shaul, Y.D.* 394. This responsum is quoted at some length by Rabbi Waldenberg, together with similar sentiments found in *Tiferet Yisrael* (*Niddah* 10:17), *Responsa Mahariẓ Chayes* 52, *Responsa Ḥayyim She'al* 2:25, and others.

18. *Responsa Maharsham* 6:124.

arose in Hungary, he picked up where the Ḥatam Sofer had left off. The case involved a man found unconscious, not breathing, and according to all but one witness present, without pulse or movement. Administered medical treatment, he failed to respond, was declared dead, and was shortly thereafter buried. The question arose when it was disclosed that prior to burial certain gasping noises were heard emanating from the body, noises which according to several physicians were caused by residual gases escaping from the cadaver. The question as posed was thus: was the man properly pronounced dead, in view of the contradictory facts that he had no vital signs, yet these unusual noises persisted, possibly indicating ongoing life?

The Maharsham first quotes *Yoma* (H) to prove that the absence of breathing indicates that death has occurred. This, however,

> is true only where there is no indication to the contrary, so that we may rely on an examination for breath. For an absolute majority die when there is no discernible breathing. . . . But if we discern some sign of life elsewhere in the body, then the rule of majority cases is invalid, and we should not rely on the absence of breath to declare him dead.

On the basis of this reasoning, he rules that the person in question should not have been declared dead at the time, certainly not as long as such noises continued.

Here it is evident that the Maharsham goes beyond the position of the Ḥatam Sofer, to say that under certain circumstances even the three criteria are insufficient. This is apparent from the fact that in the case under discussion the three criteria were clearly all present. Indeed it is to be noted that the question came from Hungary, and involved a Hungarian *Ḥevra Kadisha* who had heard these noises but decided to go ahead with the burial anyway. Apparently they were following the directives of the Ḥatam Sofer, as an early authority for Hungarian Jewry. Interestingly, the Ḥatam Sofer in his responsum had made explicit reference to the expertise of the members of the *Ḥevra Kadisha* in recognizing the proper dividing line between life and death. In any case it is Maharsham's view that any unusual symptoms that might indicate life are cause for a careful reexamination of the status of one in whom the criteria enumerated by the Ḥatam Sofer are already present.[19]

Rabbi Eliezer Waldenberg utilizes the position adopted by these authorities to rule that extreme care must be taken even where these criteria of death are present. This is especially true in cases of sudden death and following heavy sedation or drug use, where it is quite possible that the signs are misleading and are reversible. It is for this reason, he writes, that Maimonides did not specify an exact time required to wait after apparent death. Where death is expected and medication is not a factor, one may declare death after a few minutes are past; where shock or other medical factors figure, greater caution is in order.[20]

Indeed, given the realities of modern medicine, it is sometimes possible to resuscitate patients, even after all movement, heartbeat, and breathing have disappeared. As a result, a number of leading contemporary authorities, such as Rabbi M. Shternbuch, Rabbi Shelomoh Zalman Auerbach, Rabbi Isser Yehudah Unterman, as well as Rabbi Waldenberg, all require that every effort be made to resuscitate such patients, wherever possible. In so doing they appear to hold the position that death per se does not occur upon cessation of these vital signs. It is only when all efforts to revive the patient fail that it can be said that death has occurred retroactively.[21] Rabbi Auerbach specifically mandates setting aside the Sabbath laws, even after the vital signs are absent. He is apparently of the opinion that the discussion in *Yoma* that forbids desecration of the Sabbath once breathing is not detectable does not apply when it is possible to resuscitate a victim by some means or another. In talmudic times, he says, there were no respirators, hence there was no realistic chance of restoring life. This is not the case today.[22]

---

19. Rabbi Waldenberg (*Ẓiẓ Eliezer* 9:45 [6]) sees no distinction between the Ḥatam Sofer and Maharsham, implying that even the former accepts any sign of life as reason to delay burial. This, however, is difficult to reconcile with the text of the Ḥatam Sofer and his insistence on these specific criteria.

20. *Responsa Ẓiẓ Eliezer* 9:45 (2).

21. See Rabbi M. Shternbuch, *Kuntres Ba'ayot ha-Zeman be'Hashkafat ha-Torah*, p. 9; Rabbi Auerbach is quoted in G. Kraus, *ha-Ma'ayan* 9 (5729): 20; Rabbi Unterman, *Torah she-be'Al Peh* 11 (5729): 13, with slight changes in his *Shevet mi-Yehudah*, p. 369. See also *Noam* 3 (5730). As to Rabbi Waldenberg, see *Ẓiẓ Eliezer* 10:25 (5). See A. Steinberg, "Keviat Rega ha-Mavet," nn. 62, 117.

22. See Kraus, op. cit.

Rabbi Waldenberg is further of the opinion that where resuscitation is successful, this does not contradict the validity of the criteria of the Ḥatam Sofer, but simply indicates that the measurement of the vital signs "was not precise," and some organ function had been present all along, albeit undetected. Accordingly he rules that where a physician has any diagnostic means whatsoever to detect such hidden life, he is obliged to invoke and if possible to resuscitate the patient. Rabbi Waldenberg has similar recourse to the position of the Rema seen earlier. The latter, it will be recalled, had forbidden any abdominal incision to remove the fetus from a mother who had died in childbirth, because time of death could not be ascertained with sufficient precision. Does this imply, as Rabbi Soloveichik had explained, that the Rema does not accept the lack of breathing as proof of death?

Rabbi Waldenberg disagrees with Rabbi Soloveichik, and says that according to the Rema we are simply no longer capable of determining what is or is not a lack of breathing. This, he says, is especially true of those who are not expert in such matters, who might for lack of experience be incapable of detecting extremely faint breathing. Indeed the Ḥatam Sofer had mentioned this possibility, in contrasting the expert knowledge of the *Ḥevra Kadisha*. Thus, to Rabbi Waldenberg, the key criterion remains the presence or absence of breathing.

R. Moshe Feinstein too attempted to resolve the problems posed by this statement of Isserles. In a responsum written in 1968,[23] he asks why it is that Isserles has a doubt as to the exact moment of death. "After all," he says, "we too are capable of recognizing when nasal breathing has ceased, whereas prior to the stoppage of breathing he is certainly alive, even in the time of the Gemara." Rabbi Feinstein answers that lack of breathing for a short time does not mean that death has occurred. It sometimes happens that the extremely ill can stop breathing, as if in a faint, and then resume after a few moments. It is only when breathing has been absent for a number of minutes that we can be sure that this is indeed death. This, says R. Moshe, is the intent in Maimonides (L), in requiring such a waiting period. And apparently Isserles concurs, to say that it is necessary to exercise extreme caution during these initial few minutes to ensure that there has in fact

23. *Responsa Iggerot Moshe, Y.D.* 2:174 (2).

been no momentary breathing. Such caution requires a measure of expertise that may have been lost to later generations (by the time of Maimonides lost to the masses, and by the time of Isserles lost altogether). Thus Isserles requires a hiatus of several minutes to be certain—but by this time the fetus would surely have died.

In a second responsum, written in 1970, Rabbi Feinstein takes up the question again, attempting to clarify the exact relationship of the heart, breathing, and life.[24] Thus he states that while lack of breathing is the conventional criterion for establishing death, nonetheless if an individual who has no breathing or pulse undergoes an electrocardiogram that indicates some kind of heart function still remaining, that individual cannot be considered to have died. As long as there is any sign of life remaining in the heart, it cannot be disregarded, and every effort must be made to prolong life even on the Sabbath.[25] On this latter point, another contemporary halakhist, Rabbi Ḥayyim Dubber Gulevsky, goes even further, to say that even if both breathing and heartbeat are absent, still the Sabbath is to be desecrated in order to restore life if at all possible. This he relates to the talmudic injunction to "desecrate on his behalf one Sabbath, so that he can subsequently observe many Sabbaths."[26]

Rabbi Feinstein continues to explain that the Gemara in *Yoma* does not mean to say that it is breathing that maintains life. For all authorities are in agreement that it is the brain and heart that maintain ongoing life—breathing merely indicates continued

---

24. Ibid., *Y.D.* 2:146.

25. This is true even though, as Rabbi Feinstein points out, the Halakhah generally disregards substances and measurements that are not visible to the naked eye, whether it be microscopically detected blood, tefilin measurements, or ingested microbes and other organisms. The Halakhah as a rule is concerned only with data accessible to the five senses through conventional means.

26. See Rabbi Ḥayyim Dubber Gulevsky, in *ha-Maor* 21, no. 3 (1969): 11–12. He refers to correspondence with Rabbi Feinstein. A position seemingly diametrically opposed to Rabbi Gulevsky is found in Y. Levy, "Be'Inyan Hashtalat Evarim me-ha-Met," *Noam* 12 (1969): 301 ff. In this article he argues that the Gemara in *Yoma* does not intend to establish a uniform criterion of "physical death," but merely what is to be considered "halakhic death," i.e., the point beyond which it is not permissible to desecrate the Sabbath in order to reverse the loss of life. He goes on to argue that at times other than the Sabbath the two other criteria (heartbeat and movement) are added to determine when "physical death" occurs. Levy is of the view that the Ḥatam Sofer subscribes to this distinction. But such a reading is not clear from the Gemara or later authorities. See Steinberg, "Keviat Rega ha-Mavet," p. 225.

heart function. As a matter of fact, he says, heart function is not restricted to heartbeat or the circulation of blood, for even after heartbeat has ceased other functions remain for some time. Such functions make breathing possible for some time. Thus it is only when breathing has stopped that it is evident that all heart function has ended. Hence an EKG that indicates some heart function can be said to measure such residual activity indicating life.

With this explanation, Rabbi Feinstein can dispense with the rationale of the Ḥakham Ẓvi, seen earlier, as to why breathing is the major criterion: it is not that the heart is hidden deep in the chest and any faint heartbeat is not easily discernible; it is rather that it is not heartbeat per se which indicates life or death. This also explains the passage in the *Guide* where Maimonides considers Nabal's heart to have "died," even though the rest of his body continued to function. What Maimonides means, apparently, is that his heart stopped beating but its supplementary functions continued for some time to maintain vestiges of life. In any case, the practical consequence of Rabbi Feinstein's distinction is that death cannot be determined with a stethoscope alone, without reference to breathing or the lack thereof. It is the absence of both heartbeat and breathing for some time that is the litmus test of life.

And yet, even though the absence of breathing for an extended period is conclusive proof that all heart function has ceased, R. Moshe does not rule out entirely the possibility that life may continue for some time even after breathing and heart function have ceased. This he does on the basis of two talmudic passages, the one occurring in *Yevamot* 121a, where it is recounted that an individual was submerged for three days and emerged alive. Rabbi Feinstein appreciates that such an outcome is surely contradicted by common experience; nonetheless he cannot deny the historical account completely.[27] The second passage, which we will examine

27. While survival for such extended periods without breathing has no current scientific parallel, there are documented cases of survival following drowning and submersion for periods of up to one hour. This phenomenon, known as the mammalian diving reflex, usually involves a young person, in that the young retain the unexplained ability to survive during this time without any intake of oxygen, by redirecting all available oxygen to the organs most in need of them, i.e., the brain and the heart.

later, occurs in *Semaḥot* (F), where it is recorded that a man was buried, only to emerge alive some time later, i.e., after a protracted time without breathing. On the basis of these passages he concludes that one whose heart has stopped totally, only to be resuscitated by artificial means—or for that matter been removed and replaced with a transplanted one—retains the status of a living person, and cannot be said to have died simply because he did not have a functional heart in the interim.

Yet, such extraordinary circumstances aside, this responsum affirms that the litmus test for life and death is the presence or absence of both spontaneous breathing and heartbeat, over a period of time, by which it can be determined whether the heart continues its life-support functions.

In 1976 Rabbi Feinstein returned to the topic with a short but critical responsum.[28] He starts out by reaffirming that it is the absence of breathing for a protracted period that establishes death, to be determined by repeated examinations of the nasal area with a feather or light paper. But then he adds that this does not apply to those patients who are in a coma and unable to breathe unaided, and continue to breathe only with the aid of a respirator. Such patients, he says, continue to breathe with such assistance even after they have died, such breathing not being an indicator of life. Nonetheless it is forbidden to disconnect the respirator as long as it continues to function, for it is quite possible that the patient still lives (i.e., is still capable of temporary unaided breathing). But if the respirator requires servicing, so that the patient is momentarily disconnected, then it is proper to wait approximately fifteen minutes to see if there is spontaneous breathing. If such breathing is not present, it is clear that death has already occurred. If, however, there is some breathing activity, albeit with great difficulty, the respirator must be reconnected. This procedure should be repeated "many times."[29]

R. Moshe makes it clear that this distinction applies only to

28. *Responsa Iggerot Moshe, Y.D.* 3:132.

29. It should perhaps be added that newer respirators currently in use do not require such servicing, thus this particular recommendation of Rabbi Feinstein is no longer feasible. On the other hand, there are ongoing improvements in the utilization of diagnostic techniques (e.g., intravenous subtraction angiography) to determine with a high degree of reliability that brain death has occurred conclusively, eliminating any possibility of autonomous breathing by the patient.

patients hovering near death as a result of protracted illness. Those who are connected to a respirator as a result of accident or drug overdose, either of which can cause temporary, reversible suspension of breathing functions, are not to be considered dead, for they might well regain that ability in time. This is true even though they may display no other signs of life. He adds one further requirement: a blood-flow test. This procedure, known as radio-isotope scanning, is used to show that the brain is effectively cut off from blood circulation. Only if such a test proves positive, i.e., there is no blood flow to the brain, may the respirator be left disconnected, and the patient be pronounced dead. If the test is negative, the respirator must be reconnected for an indefinite period. In any case, this responsum takes the position that while the respirator continues to function in aiding the patient's own breathing, it may not be removed so as to lead to immediate death.

This last proviso of Rabbi Feinstein impacts directly on the issue of brain death, and has been subsequently debated and interpreted in a number of ways. We will return to it in the next section. Putting this particular issue aside, the responsum is also notable for its attitude towards respirator-aided breathing. For it can be understood to say that a patient who depends entirely on a respirator for steady, consistent breathing is not to be considered "breathing" as the term is used in halakhic literature as a criterion of life or death. Does this mean that the ongoing heart function of such a patient is of no consequence, i.e., is the patient to be considered already dead even though the heart continues to beat unaided as long as the respirator provides it with oxygen?

On the one hand it is possible to understand Rabbi Feinstein to say no. For the responsum does not mention heart function at all, and it could well be that he assumes that the heart too is incapable of independent function. Where the heart can continue to beat unaided, it might be argued that Rabbi Feinstein would never permit disconnecting the respirator. Indeed he explicitly states that this is to be done only where "there are no other recognizable signs of life, and he does not respond at all to pinpricks, as in the case of one who is in coma." In other words, the heart (heartbeat is surely "a sign of life") too is incapable of independent function. This is the interpretation of Rabbi A.

Abraham.[30] Yet most halakhists understand Rabbi Feinstein in this responsum to be taking a new position, quite inconsistent with his earlier ruling. They understand him here to accept the lack of unaided breathing as sufficient by itself to confirm the death of the person involved, irrespective of ongoing heartbeat. Such is the view of R. Moshe's son-in-law, Rabbi Moshe Tendler.[31]

This reading of R. Moshe is widespread. Thus Rabbi Eliezer Waldenberg poses several questions regarding this responsum. If indeed there are no such recognizable signs of life in the brain, he asks, why not disconnect the respirator immediately and permanently? Why does Rabbi Feinstein insist on the tentative steps as outlined by him? It must be that these other signs, or their absence, have been inconclusive; but if they are indeed conclusive, then Rabbi Feinstein should permit disconnecting the machine in a forthright manner, something which he obviously does not do. This, says Rabbi Waldenberg, is difficult to reconcile. He further questions the distinction made by Rabbi Feinstein between patients dying of natural causes ("at the hands of heaven") and those who are the victims of a critical accident (which he considers "at the hands of man"). After all, he argues, the case in *Yoma* (H) involves precisely the latter rather than the former, and if so why consider a car accident more "at the hands of man" than is an accidentally collapsed building?[32] Thus he concludes that as long as the heart continues to beat unaided, life must be said to continue unabated, in accordance with the traditional criteria as found in the Ḥatam Sofer.

Another contemporary rabbi, J. David Bleich, likewise interprets R. Moshe to be saying that independent heartbeat does not signify continued life. In a number of articles, Rabbi Bleich takes strong exception to Rabbi Feinstein's position.[33] He finds this latter responsum to be in contradiction to the earlier responsum that had made heartbeat a sign of continued life, whether or not independent breathing is present. He also questions the permis-

30. *Nishmat Avraham*, *Y.D.* 339.

31. See, for instance, Rabbi Tendler's views in M. Tendler, et al., "Brain Death: A Status Report of Medical and Ethical Considerations," *Journal of the American Medical Association* 238 (October 10, 1977): 1653–1654.

32. *Responsa Ẓiẓ Eliezer* 13:89 (12).

33. Bleich, "Simmanei Mittah," *ha-Pardes* 51, no. 4 (1977): 15–18; idem, "Establishing Criteria of Death," reprinted and expanded in *Jewish Bioethics*, pp. 277–296. See also his "Neurological Criteria," Ibid., pp. 304 ff.

sibility of temporarily deferring the reconnection to the respirator, for he feels that withholding oxygen in this manner can be compared to denying basic sustenance to a seriously ill patient to shorten his life, an act which is clearly forbidden.[34] Certainly, Rabbi Bleich argues, it would be imperative to reconnect the machine immediately in order to avoid any "psychological stress which may hasten death [and] is the result of human action." But the fundamental objection of Rabbi Bleich is the fact that Rabbi Feinstein appears to have accepted the absence of breathing as sufficient grounds for declaring death, even if the heart continues to beat unaided. Rabbi Bleich adduces the many authorities that we have encountered to prove that the heart is indeed central to any such determination.

Of course it is a matter of interpretation. For if one understands Rabbi Feinstein to be assuming that there is also no independent heart function, as the former view has it, then these objections are by and large removed. The difference could well be in whether one assumes the responsum to be talking of a heart-lung machine (which supports both organs when they are nonfunctional) or a respirator (which assists only breathing).[35] If indeed Rabbi Fein-

34. For a discussion of some of the issues involved in euthanasia, especially relative to withholding natural sustenance, see *Jewish Ethics and Halakhah*, Vol. 1, pp. 84–86.

35. In his discussion of the position of the Ḥatam Sofer, Rabbi Bleich states that it is the view of this authority that "death is synonymous with the cessation of respiration." While he allows that the Ḥatam Sofer may have amended this definition of death to include the absence of both pulse and respiration (why an amendment is necessary within one and the same responsum is problematic), Rabbi Bleich remains of the opinion that according to the Ḥatam Sofer it is breathing which signifies life, and it is "accepted as the sole operational definition, because in the vast majority of cases it is indicative of prior cardiac arrest." This interpretation of the Ḥatam Sofer is open to question, in that, as we have seen, and as Rabbi Bleich himself notes, the Ḥatam Sofer requires a triple test (absence of breathing, heartbeat, and movement) to declare death. This would suggest that death is not congruent with any one of them alone, but only with all three together, so that the absence of breathing still always requires the additional confirmation of the two other signs. This is indeed the understanding of Rabbi Shternbuch, "Ba'ayot ha-Zeman," p. 10. See also Steinberg, "Keviat Rega ha-Mavet," n. 58. It is also interesting that Rabbi Shelomoh Goren, in attempting to demonstrate that brain death is an acceptable definition of death for the Halakhah, starts out with the same understanding of the Ḥatam Sofer (i.e., breathing alone is the key criterion), but comes to the very opposite conclusion, i.e., that neither heartbeat nor movement is a significant index of ongoing life, for only brain death by itself is of crucial significance, in that it is the brain stem that controls all breathing. See his article in the Israeli newspaper *ha-Ẓofeh*, October 31, 1986.

stein has in mind the heart-lung machine, then it would be consistent with and buttressed by his earlier position that forbade the artificial prolongation of the life of a patient, where the patient is on a heart-lung machine in order to maintain his organs for transplantation. This R. Moshe derived from the position of the Rema, who had permitted the removal of external factors artificially prolonging and complicating the natural demise of a patient.[36] Similar reasoning is offered by Rabbi Moshe Munk and Rabbi Barukh Rabinowitz.[37] On the other hand, it is not beyond Rabbi Feinstein to move beyond an earlier position to embrace an opposing view, as we have seen in chapter 1. Thus each responsum must be understood on its own terms.

We can conclude this section by returning once more to the comment of Rema (O), to ask the question, does his restriction still apply? Rabbi Waldenberg feels that indeed, given the reality of medical knowledge today, we can revert to the position of the *Shulḥan Arukh* to permit procedures immediately following determination of maternal death. He quotes the *Koret ha-Brit*, who points out that the language of R. Isserles does not indicate disagreement, but merely changed circumstances. In addition he quotes the view of the *Yismaḥ Lev*, which explains the restriction of Rema to be motivated by doubts as to the viability and term of the fetus anyway; hence where it is known that it is a full-term baby, and there are no medical counterindications, even Rema might have been more lenient. Accordingly, Rabbi Waldenberg rules that once medical opinion can clearly establish the absence of breathing and heartbeat, death can be certified without further delay.[38] In section 3 we will take up the matter of delayed confirmation of death.

Dr. Ya'akov Levy, a physician and author of numerous halakhic articles, is also of the opinion that medical knowledge in our time can establish beyond reasonable doubt that there is no breathing or blood pressure, by the use of the sphygmomanometer, and the

---

36. *Responsa Iggerot Moshe, Y.D.* 2:174 (3). On this subject, see *Jewish Ethics and Halakhah*, Vol. 1, p. 84.

37. Rabbi M. Munk, in *She'arim* 24 (1966); Rabbi B. Rabinowitz in *Assia* 3 (1971). See also Y. Levy, *Noam* 16 (1973): 61, who in posing the question for resolution by leading halakhic authorities, raises several considerations, pro and con. See also his article in *Noam* 12 (1969).

38. *Responsa Ẓiẓ Eliezer* 10:25 (4).

EKG. Consequently he too argues for reinstating the original view of the *Shulḥan Arukh.*[39]

2. THE HALAKHIC STATUS OF BRAIN DEATH

In 1970 Rabbi Gedalyah Rabinowitz and Dr. M. Konigsberg authored an article in which they argued in favor of brain death as a halakhically acceptable definition of death.[40] From Rashi's comments in *Yoma* (and the corresponding formulations of the Ḥatam Sofer and the Maharsham) they derived that the absence of breathing does not by itself constitute death, but is rather an external sign that death has occurred. They quote the Mishnah in *Ohalot* (E) that says that a decapitated animal is considered dead even though there are still convulsive movements, and they conclude from this that even though as a rule bodily movements are a sign of continued life, where the head has been severed such movements are of no consequence, and death can be said to have occurred.

Maimonides' commentary to this Mishnah says that such convulsive movements occur "when the moving force is not spread throughout all the limbs by originating in one initial starting point, but rather takes place independently throughout the body." As explained by these authors, certain involuntary movements (which in the Mishnah are referred to as *pirkhus*) are controlled by parts of the nervous system other than the brain or brain stem. But the brain is the organ responsible for integrated or coordinated bodily movement, and consequently must be considered the "center of life" of the body. All other functions, such as breathing or eating, merely provide support systems that allow the brain to function. Accordingly they conclude that where the brain itself is dead, all integrated movement becomes impossible. And when the Gemara in *Yoma* speaks of the absence of breathing as the sign of death, it is because without breathing, the brain will necessarily die within minutes. For the same reason, Mai-

39. Levy, *ha-Ma'ayan*, Tammuz 1971. See Bleich, *Or ha-Mizraḥ* 21 (1972) and *Bioethics*, p. 283.

40. G. A. Rabinowitz and M. Konigsberg, "Hagdarat ha-Mavet u-Keviat Zemano lefi ha-Halakhah," *ha-Darom* 34 (Tishri 1970): 59–76. Rabbi Rabinowitz repeated and expanded somewhat upon these remarks in an essay published in 1983 in *Halakhah u-Refuah* 3 (5743): 106–110.

monides (L) requires a few minutes to lapse after breathing has ceased; for by then the brain will certainly have died, unless breathing starts again.

They further argue—and this is crucial to their view—that heart function is not controlled by the brain, and is therefore not to be taken as a sign of ongoing life. They explain that the heart can continue to beat, albeit erratically, even after decapitation or the removal of the heart from the body. Thus where the Halakhah requires that it is breathing that indicates life, it is only in order to ascertain whether or not the brain has died. But where brain death can be independently established (i.e., a complete absence of coordinated bodily movement, plus a flat electroencephalogram reading over a period of some time, and where drug overdose is not a possible cause of these symptoms), then artificially supported breathing becomes redundant, in that the patient is already dead. This is true even where the heart continues to beat unaided. This, they argue, is certainly the case where the attending physicians consider the patient to be in an irreversible coma.

This article, as might be expected, met with heated discussion. Dr. Ya'akov Levy disagrees on both medical and halakhic grounds. He argues that many medical authorities do not accept the notion of brain death as sufficient by itself to establish death. They require in addition the complete absence of blood circulation and breathing. Dr. Levy further faults Rabinowitz and Konigsberg for their readiness to accept the finality and irreversibility of the condition of such a patient, whose heart continues to beat unaided. He argues that there is always the possibility of erroneous diagnosis, of unexplained recovery, or of medical breakthroughs in the future that might assist such a patient. He also is at a loss to justify their stated readiness to withhold basic sustenance; he finds this the equivalent of homicide, and quite incomparable with the Rema's permission to withhold "artificial" life support, arguing that food, even intravenous feeding, cannot be considered extraordinary maintenance.[41]

Such criticisms, however, are themselves debatable. As Dr. Avraham Steinberg points out,[42] the possibility of clinical error exists no matter what criteria are adopted, including those of the

41. Y. Levy, in *ha-Ma'ayan*, Tishri 5730, Nissan 5732, and in *Noam* 16 (5733).
42. Steinberg, pp. 236–237.

Ḥatam Sofer himself. On the question of future breakthroughs, the Halakhah always accepts the means and methods current in the age at hand in the determination of the status of physical realities. Thus, halakhic determinations cannot be made on the basis of some future anticipated possibilities. Nonetheless, Steinberg cannot accept the position of Rabinowitz and Konigsberg, in the absence of any convincing proof in their article that heartbeat is of little importance in the determination of death—given the fact that all the authorities dealing with the issue require the absence of heartbeat. In addition he takes philosophical issue with the idea of brain death as an exclusive criterion of death; human life, he argues, is more than intellect, it also embraces moral, animal, and vegetative dimensions that might persist in the absence of consciousness or purposive movement. Thus he favors the more holistic and integrative criteria encountered in the traditional formulae.

Rabbi Barukh Rabinowitz also takes issue in similar terms with those who would advocate an exclusive brain-death approach.[43] He points out that the classic halakhic definition of death (the absence of heartbeat, breathing, and brain-directed movement) is in fact very much in line with modern psychology and philosophy that rejects the Cartesian view of man as purely a thinking animal. Man, in current thinking, is rather a combination of thought and feeling, instinct as well as intellect. To wit: a baby born without a brain, as sometimes happens, is not only human, but entitled to life, and to whatever elemental pleasures, feelings, or instincts are available to it, irrespective of the inability of other humans to experience similar things. The existence of a fundamental, irreducible "humanness" could well be called the "image of God" with which every human being is endowed.[44]

So too, says Rabbi Rabinowitz, the Halakhah views human life as an integrated whole, inclusive of mental, instinctive, and physiological functions. This integrative approach is reflected in

---

43. *Assia*, 5739, pp. 190–198. This paper was part of a medical-rabbinic symposium dedicated to the problems of transplants and time of death. The same issue of the journal contains other contributions to the topic.

44. On the question of what precisely separates man from animal, and what constitutes man's unique identity, see my "Speaking of Man and Beast," *Judaism* 28, no. 2 (Spring 1979): 169–176, especially Maimonides' perspective on the possibility of animal communication and mental capacity.

the Mishnah in *Ohalot* (E), that shows that as long as the body remains physically intact, and the head in place, any and all movements are to be taken as definitive signs of life, even if there is no hope of recovery whatsoever. And yet a distinction is to be made between two states that precede death: the state of being fully alive, and the state of *gesisah*, i.e., moribund life. The former requires every active intervention to preserve and extend life indefinitely—including, according to some authorities, self-endangerment by a third party.[45] But the latter is a state in which the death process has already begun, and in which, according to other authorities, it is not necessary to preserve or extend the life in question.[46] This state of *goses*, says Rabbi Rabinowitz, can be said to begin when a person's life depends entirely on external life-support systems, providing for both heart and lung functions. When this stage is reached, and presumably there is no discernible brain activity, these support systems may indeed be disconnected. But as long as there is either independent heart or pulmonary function in evidence, the patient is not deceased, nor to be left to die.

Rabbi G. Blidstein also questions the conclusions of Rabinowitz and Konigsberg. Specifically he addresses their understanding of the Mishnah in *Ohalot* (E), and he argues that although it states that decapitated animals are "impure," it should not be assumed that this means that they are dead. Elsewhere the Mishnah (*Ḥullin* 117b) distinguishes between decapitation and death, to state that where there is any movement whatsoever, death has not occurred. Put differently, even though the animal has attained the status of *neveilah* ("carcass") and imparts the impurity of death, it is a "living carcass" (*neveilah me-ḥayyim*). It is important, he argues, that such fine distinctions be applied to the varying circumstances and purposes surrounding death.[47]

Yet others, more recently, have come to adopt views closely resembling that of Rabinowitz and Konigsberg.[48] Rabbi Shelomoh Goren comes to the conclusion that indeed brain death is a sufficient independent criterion of death in the Halakhah. Start-

---

45. See above in chap. 1.
46. On this topic see *Jewish Ethics and Halakhah*, vol. 1, pp. 59 ff.
47. See G. Blidstein, *ha-Darom* 37 (Nissan 5734): 73–75.
48. Rabbi S. Goren, "Hashtalat Kaved le'Or ha-Halakhah," *ha-Zofeh* October 31, 1986, and November 7, 1986.

ing with the discussion in *Yoma*, he identifies breathing or its absence as the sole operative indicator of life. All breathing, he explains, is the exclusive function of the brain (or more precisely the brain stem or "medulla"). Thus when Maimonides (K) and the *Shulḥan Arukh* codify that the absence of breathing establishes death, that is an implicit acceptance of brain death. But what of ongoing heart function? Rabbi Goren distinguishes between the biological heart and the functional heart. The former is an organ that pumps blood; the latter provides oxygenated blood to the entire body, and most particularly to the brain, for it is the brain that determines human identity. The moment the heart ceases to provide this facility of supporting the brain, it is no longer a functional heart, and its activity may be disregarded, i.e., it is as if there is no further relevant heart function, other than mere *pirkhus*, or local organ reflex action.

Rabbi Goren goes one step further: faced with the pivotal responsum of the Ḥatam Sofer with its tripartite criteria of death, he claims that the Ḥatam Sofer himself merely added the criteria of heart and movement as optional corroborating factors, not required or integral to the essential definition of death as received from Sinai (*"le'ravḥa de'milta"*). For they are not mentioned in *Yoma* at all, and the major codes do not include them either. He buttresses his argument further by referring to the Mishnah in *Ohalot* (E), where residual organ movement does not affect the determination of death, and Maimonides' consequent view that where the brain stem is functionally cut off from the rest of the body (*nishberah mafrakto ve'rov basar imo*) death can be said to have occurred.[49] On this basis, he argues that even though local movement and pulse may be present, death has occurred once all brain function has been lost, as indicated by the total lack of independent breathing.[50]

Clearly this position accepts without reservation that brain death is compatible with the Halakhah, much as do Rabinowitz

49. Maimonides, *M. T. Hil. Tumat Met* 1:16. He refers also to Naḥmanides' *Novellae* to *Ḥullin* 21a for similar conclusions.

50. Rabbi Goren is so certain of his position that he cannot understand how others differ with it. He sees no possibility of interpreting the Ḥatam Sofer any other way, and he considers the contrary position of his successors in the Israeli Chief Rabbinate to be "in total contradiction to the Halakhah." See also his remarks in the *Jerusalem Post*, October 31, 1986.

and Konigsberg. It refuses to countenance the view that heartbeat per se is of importance to the determination of death, and considers any assertion to the contrary quite mistaken, indeed those who do not declare death at that point are regarded as guilty of needlessly endangering the lives of those patients who could benefit from the use of the cadaver's organs. Yet it is difficult to accept the notion that the Ḥatam Sofer himself would agree to this position, for his responsum is quite clear, if not categorical, on the equal and mutually reinforcing character of all three criteria.

A conclusion essentially similar to that of Rabbi Goren is found in a second article by Dr. Steinberg,[51] written in 1986. He too focuses on *Yoma*, and infers therefrom that the key is the absence of breathing. He also examines Maimonides' position on residual movement, and finds it consistent with the notion of life residing in the breathing center, i.e., the brain stem. He points out that nowhere in the Talmud is breathing attributed to the heart, nor do any early halakhic authorities insist on heart failure as an indispensable determinant of death. And while it is true that neither is there mention of the brain as fulfilling this function, the state of current knowledge allows us to assert that it is the brain that controls breathing. On this basis, Dr. Steinberg can dismiss the position of the Ḥakham Ẓvi as based on the mistaken assumption that breathing originates in and is controlled by the heart—something which we know today to be simply not true. As to the Ḥatam Sofer, he postulates that even this authority might agree with his position. For the Ḥatam Sofer was dealing with death precipitated by heart-failure in the first place—but where it is the loss of breathing capability, such a case might correspond to the son of the Zarephite woman whom Maimonides (according to the Ḥatam Sofer) considered (M) to have died in the absence of breathing. He also dismisses the position of Rabbi Waldenberg, saying that it is quite clear from a medical standpoint that breathing is not a function dependent on the heart. And from a halakhic point of view he denies that there are grounds to reject brain death, given the teachings of the Talmud that emphasize continued breathing as the critical consideration.

What is the position of Rabbi Feinstein on the matter of brain

51. At present unpublished.

death? Several months before the appearance of the Rabinowitz-Konigsberg article, Rabbi Feinstein addressed the issue directly.[52] He pointed out that nowhere in the Talmud or early authorities is brain-function identified with life itself. Consequently, he says, "it is the brain and the heart which give life to a person." As we saw earlier, in this responsum he goes to great lengths to show that as long as the heart continues any function whatsoever (even beyond heart beat per se), life must be said to persist. It would appear that Rabbi Feinstein is saying that death does not occur the moment the brain ceases to function, but rather that it will follow some minutes after both brain and heart functions are lost. Prior to that point the patient is to be considered alive. This is equally true when breathing or pulse are not detected, for they might conceivably start up again. The only exception that he allows, it would appear, is where there is an actual decapitation, by which the head is actually severed from the body. This is indeed the upshot of an explicit eighteenth-century ruling by Rabbi Jacob Reischer in a case involving a pregnant woman who was decapitated on the Sabbath. He ruled that it was entirely permissible to open her abdomen immediately in order to save the fetus. Likewise Rabbi Akiva Eiger was of the opinion that cases of decapitation are not included in the ruling of the Rema.[53]

In his responsum of 1976, examined above, R. Moshe takes up the issue again. Here he no longer speaks explicitly of heart function, but only of breathing. He states that it is the absence of breathing which determines death—but then qualifies this by saying that those who can breathe only with the help of a respirator, and who have no independent respiratory function at all, are strictly speaking not breathing at all. We are simply inflating their lungs mechanically, and they are to be considered dead already, subject to confirmation by blood-flow and other tests to remove all doubt that the brain is irreversibly "dead." Conversely, where the test indicates some circulation in the brain, all other signs to the contrary, life yet persists.[54]

As noted earlier, this responsum has been interpreted in several ways, depending on whether one considers Rabbi Feinstein to

52. *Responsa Iggerot Moshe, Y.D.* 2:146. Cf. at n. 24 above.

53. *Responsa Shevut Ya'akov* 1:13; and Rabbi Akiva Eiger's gloss to the Rema, ad loc. See Y. Levy, *Noam* 12 (1969):304.

54. *Responsa Iggerot Moshe, Y.D.* 3:132.

have retained the lack of independent heart-function as a necessary component of death. On balance it would appear that Rabbi Feinstein accepts the arguments of those favoring brain death as the exclusive determinant of death. Thus he insists on checking for the absence of breathing, "and if it is seen that he is not breathing, this is reliable confirmation of death, without further doubt." In embracing their view, he appears to be swayed by the medical evidence pointing to the direct causative connection between the brain stem and breathing activity, as well as the lack of any definitive statement in talmudic literature that the heart is the locus of life. Instead it is the concept of decapitation that becomes the functional model for declaring the brain-dead patient devoid of all life. Thus in the same responsum he writes:

> There is now a test used by leading physicians whereby they inject a liquid into the arteries to determine if the brain has lost its connection to the rest of the body . . . and accordingly does not belong to the rest of the body, the brain having already decomposed, such a state being the equivalent of death by decapitation.

Here Rabbi Feinstein accepts the argument for brain death (or more accurately death of the brain stem) as analogous to decapitation. It is not necessary, apparently, for the head to be physically removed, as long as the brain function is irrevocably destroyed. Moreover this is true whether or not the heart continues to function, such function being independent of the brain itself. Thus it is that under such circumstances Rabbi Feinstein permits the respirator to be removed (or more accurately not to be reconnected), death having occurred.

It was this responsum that subsequently served as a major fulcrum in the current debate over the determination of death, leading a number of halakhists to endorse the notion of brain death as consistent with the Halakhah. By the end of 1986 his views received the imprimatur of the Chief Rabbinate of Israel, which took an official position supporting brain death under carefully circumscribed circumstances. Thus Chief Rabbi Mordecai Eliyahu issued a statement explaining the talmudic background to this decision.[55] From *Yoma* he concludes that it is indeed the absence of breathing that suffices to establish death—any persistent heartbeat to be viewed as mere postmortem fluttering (*pirpur)* of the heart muscle. He furthermore agrees with Rabbi Goren's view that identifies brain death with the talmudic category of functional separation of the brain stem from the body (*nishberah mafrakto*). And he quotes Maimonides' position that one can rely upon informed medical opinion in such matters.[56] Consequently he (and his colleagues), after lengthy consultations and review, permitted the removal of respirators from brain-dead patients, once various accompanying confirmatory tests and safeguards had been satisfied in each individual case.[57]

Yet in spite of these decisions, the acceptance of brain-death criteria remains far from universal halakhic adoption. Opponents, including those cited above, remain unconvinced as to the halakhic validity of such "noncardiac" definitions of death. One example of such steadfast opposition to brain death is found in the lone dissenting opinion of Rabbi J. David Bleich, who in 1986 stood opposed, on halakhic grounds, to the adoption by New York State of brain-death criteria in determining the time of death.[58]

On balance, therefore, we encounter a significant divide in the matter of brain death, one which is characterized by flux and movement in some positions, but consistency and a resolve to resist change in others.

3. *REVIVING THE DEAD AND DELAYED BURIAL*

The final question to be dealt with is as follows: once all criteria of death have been satisfied, and no vital or other signs whatso-

55. Rabbi M. Eliyahu, "Hashtalat Evarim al Pi ha-Halakhah," *Barkai* 4 (Spring 5747): 18–31.

56. Maimonides, *M. T. Hil. Roẓeiaḥ* 2:8.

57. Another description of the background leading to the ruling of the Chief Rabbinate was provided by Rabbi S. Israeli, "be'Heter Hashtalat Lev ka-Yom," *Barkai* 4 (Spring 5747): 32–41. Rabbi Israeli attempts to show, inter alia, that Rabbi Feinstein's view all along supported the brain death definition—and furthermore that even the Ḥatam Sofer is fully in agreement that it is lack of breathing by itself that determines death. But such attributions are subject to question, in light of what we have seen of these two halakhists.

58. See New York State Task Force on Life and the Law, *The Determination of Death*, pp. 25–41.

ever are present, may extraordinary steps be taken in the hope that somehow life may yet remain undetected, or that life may be restored by medical or other means? An examination of the literature on this question must deal with two separate areas: one is the first hour following death, the other is the time beyond an hour, stretching over a day or two.

The First Hour

In dealing with the first hour, our earlier discussion makes it quite clear that all authorities agree that resuscitation should be attempted wherever possible. Rabbi Waldenberg in particular requires extreme care in pronouncing death, especially cases of sudden or accidental demise. And practically all contemporary authorities recognize the proficiency of modern medicine in resuscitating patients heretofore given up for dead. This applies equally on the Sabbath, which is to be set aside according to most authorities.[59] While there is some question within the talmudic literature on whether there is a halakhic obligation to resurrect the dead—as in the case of the prophet Elijah and the lad whom he brought back to life (C)—such theoretical considerations do not affect the question of medical intervention to resuscitate by conventional means.[60] Indeed such resuscitation falls squarely within the parameters of the obligation on a third party to save human life whenever and wherever possible—as we saw in an earlier chapter.

Where there is significant rabbinic innovation is where successful resuscitation would result in extended suffering for the patient. Both Rabbis Feinstein and Waldenberg believe that it is wrong to artificially prolong a life beyond the point of natural death, if doing so results in extreme pain and suffering for the patient facing imminent death.[61] For this reason, Rabbi Feinstein forbids the practice of maintaining a patient on life-support systems purely in order to keep his organs fresh for transplantation. For even if the patient is in a coma, there is no way that

59. See above at nn. 18–26.
60. See Bleich, *Bioethics*, pp. 289–290.
61. See *Responsa Iggerot Moshe, Y.D.* 2:174 (3); *Responsa Ẓiẓ Eliezer* 13:89 (11). See also Rabbi Feinstein's article in *Moria* (Ellul 1984), p. 52, and his comments as quoted in *Halakhah u-Refuah*, vol. 4:102–103.

others can know whether that patient experiences pain or suffering. Of course, in light of Rabbi Feinstein's later pronouncement that a brain-dead patient is in fact deceased (as discussed above), where such artificial support is provided nonetheless, it follows that there is no pain or suffering at that time, hence such "maintenance" might be permissible in order to save another's life. Rabbi Waldenberg writes that even though a patient on a life-support system is to be considered fully alive (as seen above), nonetheless "if it becomes apparent afterwards that he suffers greatly because of this support it is permissible (and possibly even required) to remove it from him . . . for this provisional life that is given him is merely the result of man's action, and extending his life in this fashion can be said to go against God's will."

While neither of these authorities say so specifically, it would seem that the same reasoning applies even more where all vital signs are already absent, and it is a matter of resuscitation to restore a life of pain and suffering. They would not only not require such resuscitation, they would even prohibit it![62] This matter is directly related to the issues raised by the hospital procedure known as DNR ("Do Not Resuscitate"), sometimes invoked where terminal patients in great pain suffer life-threatening complications, and the hospital staff is instructed to withhold treatment. Rabbis Feinstein and Waldenberg would appear to endorse the principle behind such action (or more accurately, inaction), although not necessarily the manner and terms by which it is implemented in actual medical practice.[63]

There is some disagreement as to precisely how long it is necessary to wait, or to attempt resuscitation, before all hope of revitalization is set aside. Rabbi Yeḥiel Tucatzinsky indicates that in Jerusalem it is customary not to remove the body from the deathbed for a period of twenty minutes. Others record the custom in Jerusalem of waiting thirty minutes, with the maximum required period being one hour.[64] Rabbi Feinstein refers to "a

62. See *Nishmat Avraham, Y.D.* 339:4.

63. See, however, the view expressed in Rabbi Levi Meier, "Code and No-Code: A Psychological Analysis and the Viewpoint of Jewish Law," *Jewish Values in Bioethics* (New York 1986), pp. 35–45, esp. p. 43.

64. *Gesher ha-Ḥayyim* 1:3, p. 48; *Responsa Yismaḥ Lev, Y.D.* 9.

short time, about a quarter of an hour."[65] Rabbi Shternbuch makes the point that in spite of this waiting period, the actual time of death must be fixed retroactively as occurring at the moment breathing ceased.[66] These authorities do not quote any particular source for these times, as it would appear that the question is an entirely empirical one: what is the minimum time that must pass before the cessation of all vital signs can be considered irreversible?

Beyond the First Hour

In this area, there is an interesting history of debate and discussion as to whether burial might be delayed pending absolute confirmation of death.

In 1772, the Duke of the German city of Schwerin prohibited Jews from carrying out any burials on the day on which death occurred, the ostensible reason being to ensure that no living person was mistakenly buried. Thus the Jews of the city were required to wait a full three days before burial. Confronted with this edict, they sought the guidance of two contemporary Jewish personages: Moses Mendelssohn and Rabbi Jacob Emden. Mendelssohn was highly regarded in many Jewish and Gentile circles, known to be respectful of Jewish law, while Emden (known as Yaveẓ) was the leading halakhic authority of the day.[67]

The fundamental issue involved the scriptural requirement (Deut. 21:23) that an executed criminal be buried on the day of his death, saying, "his body shall not remain all night upon the tree, but thou shalt surely bury him the same day." The Mishnah in *Sanhedrin* 46a (D) derives from this verse that improper delay of burial of any corpse infringes a negative commandment of the Torah. Subsequent authorities, including Maimonides, accepted

---

65. *Responsa Iggerot Moshe, Y.D.* 3:132.

66. Rabbi M. Shternbuch, *Ba'ayot ha-Zeman* 1:9.

67. The controversy is well documented. See, for instance, Alexander Altmann, *Moses Mendelssohn* (Philadelphia, 1973), pp. 288–295, and the notes thereon. The original materials were collected in *Bikkurei ha-Ittim* (1824), pp. 219–238. See also Silberstein's article in *Zeitschrift für die Juden in Deutschland* 1 (1929):233–244, 278–286. See also, at some length, the analysis of the affair by Rabbi Waldenberg, *Ẓiẓ Eliezer* 9:46, who adds that the correspondent to whom the Ḥatam Sofer addressed his responsum was R. Ẓvi Hirsch Chayes (known as the Mahariẓ Chayes), whose response is also preserved.

this as one of the 613 commandments.[68] Now the Mishnah itself, as well as the *Sifri* to this verse, indicates that this prohibition is suspended where the delay is necessary to preserve "the honor of the dead." This, says the Mishnah, includes proper funeral arrangements, the arrival of distant relatives (according to the tractate *Semaḥot*), or a dignified eulogy (according to *Sanhedrin* 47a).

Mendelssohn, in a written response to the question before him, quoted the Mishnah and its exemption in cases where the honor of the deceased is at stake. From this he concluded that the rabbinic intent was likewise to exclude a case where there was a possible doubt that death had actually occurred and the possible saving of a life was involved. What, he asked, could possibly be more "honor" than possibly saving his life? He further quotes two talmudic passages in support of his contention that such delayed burial is allowed. One occurs in *Semaḥot* (F), where it is recorded that it is permissible to check on the dead up to three days after interment in a crypt, given the possibility that life might have persisted unnoticed. Indeed this Beraita quotes precisely such a case of mistaken pronouncement of death to buttress its point, and Mendelssohn concludes that crypt-burial in an underground vault was specifically intended to save such undetected life. He also refers to the passage in *Niddah* 69b, which he takes as delaying pronouncement of death for similar reasons.

This response touched off a sharp dissent by Emden. In the first place he rejected any suggestion by Mendelssohn that burial in crypts was intended to avoid mistaken death; the preferred burial was always below ground. Furthermore, he argued that the Halakhah does not legislate its laws based on extremely unlikely and miraculous instances such as the one in *Semaḥot*. The conventional rabbinic criteria of death, he writes, can be relied upon to establish death beyond any and all reasonable doubts. He also rejected Mendelssohn's interpretation of *Niddah* as completely erroneous, and chided him for being too quick to exchange time-honored Jewish customs for Gentile ones, as in the present instance.

This exchange did not lead to any resolution of their differ-

---

68. For a detailed description of the laws of delayed burial, see *Encyclopedia Talmudit* 9:434 ff.

ences. Mendelssohn and his followers favored and practiced delayed burial, whereas the traditional community stood opposed to the practice. Nonetheless the latter had no choice but to conform to the civic laws that demanded such delay. And with the passage of time, many Jews were led to believe that Jewish law itself favored such delay. It was left to the Ḥatam Sofer to correct this impression many years later, in the responsum which was examined at length earlier in this chapter. Indeed the entire responsum can be seen as an attempt to set the record straight in the wake of the Mendelssohn/Emden affair. The Ḥatam Sofer rejects any suggestion that there was ever a concern for mistaken diagnosis once all the classic signs of death are present, saying, "The truth will have its way, for such events (as in *Semaḥot*) are extremely rare, occurring perhaps once in a thousand years, involving less than a minority of a minority, hence not covered by the principle that in saving a life one must consider every possibility."

Subsequent authorities reinforced the same point, viz., where there are no signs of life whatsoever, there is no reason to delay burial out of consideration of some miraculous revival. The point was made explicit by the Maharsham, as we have seen. Likewise in the late eighteenth century R. Ḥayyim Azulai discourages any delay, and would disregard any instructions left by the deceased to delay burial pending absolute certainty of death. Such delay, he says, cannot be condoned, and is not included in the honor due the dead.[69] Similar sentiments are encountered in a responsum by the Radbaz as quoted by the Ḥatam Sofer.[70] Thus, while the halakhic literature does include a number of instances of mistaken pronouncements,[71] such occurrences are sufficiently rare to be disregarded as a rule. Contemporary authorities, in accepting this position, add the proviso that in cases of sudden death, where shock, drug overdose, or other misleading factors might be present, extra care must be exercised before burial is undertaken.[72]

69. *Responsa Ḥayyim She'al* 2:25, also his *Responsa Yosef Omer* 89.
70. *Responsa Radbaz* 1:87.
71. For a listing, see Y. Levy, *Noam* 12 (5729): 299–300.
72. *Responsa Ẓiẓ Eliezer* 9:46.

SUMMARY AND CONCLUSIONS

In examining the halakhic determination of the time of death, the central talmudic text is found in *Yoma* 65a, which yields the conclusion that death is to be established by the absence of breathing. Rashi's commentary implies that breathing per se is not synonymous with life, but it is the most immediate proof or sign that life remains in the body. Hence where there are other signs that indicate persistent life, even in the absence of breathing, life must be presumed to exist. A slightly different view can be attributed to Maimonides. As explained by Rabbi Aaron Soloveichik, Maimonides views death as a process, beginning with the cessation of breathing, and ending with the failure of the other organs. *Yoma* 65a teaches that the Sabbath is not to be violated once the death process has begun—unless the process can be completely reversed. This interpretation of Maimonides is corroborated by one reading of his *Guide*, which states that death does not necessarily occur until some time after breathing has stopped, i.e., when the heart has ceased to beat.

A pivotal gloss of the Rema seems to yield the same conclusion. He forbids an incision into the abdomen of a woman in labor immediately after she dies, for in the haste to save the baby, the incision might be made before she is really dead. Apparently the fact that she no longer breathes does not establish that death has occurred. The Ḥakham Ẓvi for one, insists that death occurs only when the heart ceases to function—a point in time usually marked by the cessation of breathing. Any subsequent movement is of no significance, in the absence of heartbeat.

A key responsum was that of the Ḥatam Sofer. It identified three criteria as the classic halakhic determinants of death, namely, the absence of breathing, of heartbeat, and of movement. All three must be present, according to the Ḥatam Sofer. Of these, the absence of breathing derives from *Yoma* 65a; the absence of heartbeat reflects certain ambiguities in Maimonides' *Guide*, which accepts that life continues even after breathing has stopped (and the heart still beats), and also the view of those like Rabbeinu Baḥya who consider life to reside ultimately in the heart; and the absence of movement reflects Rashi's comments to *Yoma* 65a as well. Maharsham in turn added to the criteria, by saying that any unusual signs or phenomena related to the body must preclude an assumption that death has occurred. Taken together, these responsa became widely accepted.

It was but left to modern authorities to add that further caution is in order given the state of medical knowledge in modern times. Thus medicine recognizes that states of shock, sedation, or drug overdose may sometimes cause a temporary absence of vital signs that is entirely reversible. In addition, consideration must be given to the possibility of artificial resuscitation or of a mistaken assessment as to the presence of the three vital signs. Authorities holding such positions include Rabbis Feinstein, Waldenberg, Auerbach, Unterman, and Shternbuch.

Additional considerations are raised by Rabbi Feinstein. This includes his view that it is not absence of heartbeat which counts, but rather absence of all heart function, including any activity that can be recorded on an electrocardiogram; also his view that the absence of breathing must be carefully monitored over several minutes in case faint momentary breathing occurs; as well his opinion that life may continue even in the absence of both heart and breathing for some time. In a subsequent responsum, he explains that a comatose patient entirely dependent on a respirator for breathing may be dead already. The problem occurs in attempting to determine whether in fact there is any residual ability to breathe unaided—and Rabbi Feinstein suggests that if for some reason the respirator has to be disconnected anyway (e.g., for servicing the machine), and it is clear that breathing does not occur unaided, death can be pronounced unequivocally. He adds that blood-flow tests should be administered, to determine that in fact there is no oxygenated blood reaching the brain or brain stem.

This responsum of Rabbi Feinstein has been carefully examined and debated. While there are those who see it as being consistent with his earlier insistence that there is life as long as there is heart function, most understand his view to have changed, and to actually accept so-called brain death as a necessary and sufficient determinant of death. Those who understand him in this fashion include Rabbis Tendler, Bleich, and Waldenberg.

Starting in 1970, a number of attempts have been made to formulate a halakhic acceptance of brain death. Rabbi Gedalyah Rabinowitz and Dr. Konigsberg argued at that time that brain death can be viewed as the functional equivalent of decapitation, irrespective of heart function. They argued that the brain coordinates all integrated movement, hence it must be considered the seat of life. And they posit that the absence of breathing is accepted by the Gemara only because such absence must inexorably cause the brain cells to die within minutes. Seen thus, continued heartbeat is irrelevant, because the heart may function after death, as in decapitation, or after the brain ceases to function entirely.

This view has been debated pro and con. A number of writers took issue with its conclusions, including Drs. Levy and Steinberg, and Rabbis Waldenberg, Barukh Rabinowitz, Blidstein, and others. Yet in more recent years, it would appear, some more sympathetic positions have emerged, expressing views quite akin to those of Rabinowitz and Konigsberg. Included in this group are Rabbis Feinstein (in its majority interpretation), Goren, Tendler—and Dr. Steinberg upon reconsideration of his earlier position. They all share the view that the Gemara *Yoma* yields the conclusion that it is the ability to breathe independently that distinguishes the living from the dead, while any residual heartbeat is to be viewed as mere postmortem muscular activity. Rabbis Goren and Israeli go so far as to state that even the Ḥatam Sofer considers breathing to be the single critical consideration, being completely dependent on brain function. But it is Rabbi Feinstein's concurrence that gives this view its real credibility, in the face of those who voice opposition to the notion of brain death. Unfortunately, Rabbi Feinstein did not spell out his revised views fully in a definitive responsum prior to his death. Nonetheless, it did suffice to eventually bring the Israeli Chief Rabbinate in 1986 to rule in favor of the brain-death definition as being analogous to decapitation, or functional separation of the brain stem from the rest of the body.

On the issued of delayed burial, we have seen a number of opinions. Within the first hour, every possible effort to resuscitate should be made, especially where death was unforeseen or accidental. Rabbis Feinstein and Waldenberg do feel, however, that it is improper to resuscitate if by so doing one artificially prolongs pain and suffering that will in any case not bring long-term survival. Failing successful resuscitation, the body should be left immobile for some time, to ensure that no error has been committed. This period is variously fixed at fifteen, twenty, thirty, or even sixty minutes. Past this time period, however, no delay should be contemplated in making burial arrangements.

The reason for this urgency in expediting burial derives from the scriptural prohibition against leaving a body unburied overnight after execution. The Mishnah and the *Sifri* both extend this to cover all cases of death, and they assume that the reasoning involves the honor of the dead. Hence it is only when delay can be justified as bringing greater honor to the dead that such postponement can be contemplated. In the eighteenth century Moses Mendelssohn attempted to justify delayed burial, in the wake of a local government decree based on the possibility of a mistaken pronouncement of death, and he even quoted *Semaḥot* as precedent. In his view, such precautions could be considered an act of honoring the dead. Nonetheless, his view was overruled on halakhic grounds by his contemporary, Rabbi Jacob Emden, who argued that the Halakhah does not recognize or legislate on the basis of miraculous or extremely rare eventualities. Hence, he argued, the classic criteria of death are to be taken as conclusive and sufficient to expedite burial in accordance with the mandate of the Torah.

The position of Rabbi Emden was substantially upheld by subsequent authorities, most notably the Ḥatam Sofer, R. Azulai, and Maharsham. Contemporary authorities concur—with the added caveat that every medical effort at resuscitation be made.

We are now in a position to answer our original question. The case involves what is apparently a brain-dead individual whose heart continues to beat. Is he dead? Clearly, the issue remains unsettled, and several approaches can be considered within the spectrum of legitimate halakhic opinion. Nonetheless, an emerging majority opinion would declare such a patient deceased, if all the relevant tests and criteria are satisfied, and permit the respirator to be disconnected.

3

Organ Transplantation

Introduction

Few areas in modern medicine or science have generated as much debate and discussion as the field of human organ transplantation. The prospect of mass replacement of ailing human organs with healthy human parts procured in morally legitimate fashion has excited the public imagination. Organs that are currently viewed as able to be transplanted include kidneys, livers, corneas, bones, bone marrow, hearts, lungs, skin, and cartilage. Many of these procedures are viewed as life-saving for the recipient patients.

Organ transplantation currently occurs on a widespread basis: as of 1987, in the United States, on an average day, one heart, twenty kidneys, and sixty-five corneas were being implanted. It seems that all that prevents an even greater level of this surgery is the shortage of suitable donor organs. According to one estimate, as many as twenty-two thousand potential donors each year do not give their organs, leaving many who hope for such organs to die before medically matched donors are found.

Yet organ transplantation surgery raises many questions for professionals, ethicists, religious leaders, and laymen alike. These questions came to the fore in the late 1960s with the first heart transplants, but many of them apply to other organs as well. The initial issue involved high-risk procedures that promised little chance for long-term survival. Then the problem of organ procurement arose: were donors really dead at the time their organs were removed; if alive, was the surgeon committing homicide by shortening that life? Where the donor continued to live, what risk factors could be considered acceptable? What of the use of organ banks to store organs indefinitely, not just for implantation, but for purposes of research and teaching?

The questions were made the more pressing with the widespread medical use of so-called brain-death criteria to establish that the donor has in fact died. In a number of states laws were passed to facilitate and encourage the donation of organs immediately following death, either through prior consent (such as driver's-license consent forms) or state laws requiring hospitals to approach next of kin to consider organ donation from the deceased. As of the end of 1987, federal law has required all hospitals to identify all such potential donors, so that their families might be approached to consider such organ donation.

Yet many are troubled by these developments: are all brain-dead patients truly dead and without hope of resuscitation? What of ever more sophisticated means of resuscitation? How are scarce organs allocated—by what criteria are recipients chosen when choices have to be made? Furthermore such transplants can be extremely costly—taking away resources from other more conventional medical treatments and priorities—is this justifiable?

More recently attention has been focused on the use of babies born without most of their brains, but with the brain stem intact, as donors, and the morality of keeping such infants (known as anencephalics, practically all of whom die within days of birth) alive on respirators, so as to remove their organs for transplantation into other infants at the appropriate moment. The question, inter alia, is whether it is permissible to prolong human life for the sole purpose of providing organs to another?

For the Halakhah these questions are magnified by several other considerations. On the one hand there is the clear awareness of the imperative to save lives at almost any cost, human life being of infinite value. But on the other hand there are concerns for the rights of the donor—both in life (not to shorten life by one iota) and in death (so as to avoid the desecration of the cadaver, and to carry out proper burial). Many halakhically sensitive individuals are confronted with a dilemma over the permissibility of signing cards that would permit postmortem use of their organs to save the lives of others; is such permission forbidden, obligatory, or merely permitted? Thus it becomes a question of achieving a delicate balance: how to fulfill one commandment, without at the same time violating another—always a problematic situation. These concerns are heightened by traditional texts and customs that have served over the centuries to define life and death, procedures and practices hallowed since time immemorial.

The issue for Jewish law is how to respond to these issues, which are on the cutting edge of modern science, in a balanced yet forthright fashion. It is to the halakhic response to this challenge that this chapter is devoted.

The Question

A fifty-year-old man suffers from severe degenerative heart disease. His physicians inform him that unless he undergoes heart transplant surgery, he cannot expect to live more than three months at most, during which time he will be bedridden and in pain. If a compatible heart can be found for him, and if transplant surgery is undertaken, he has a good chance of extending his life for three years or more, while enjoying a relatively normal existence. On the other hand, given his weakened condition, he might not survive the surgery at all, and there is the possibility that the transplanted heart might fail or be rejected by his body. Should he agree to become a candidate for a heart transplant?

This case raises the following questions:

1. When may a seriously ill patient risk whatever life remains to him in order to gain long-term life-expectancy?
2. A donor heart will need to come from an accident victim, and be removed at the earliest possible moment to preserve the viability of the organ. What is the earliest time that the heart, or other organs, can be removed from the donor's body?
3. Where there is no question that death has already occurred, are there any prohibitions regarding the removal of the cadaver organs for transplantation, given the concerns of Jewish law that the cadaver be treated with utmost respect?
4. Is it permissible to transplant organs other than the heart that come from living donors who wish to sacrifice an organ, thereby possibly endangering their own lives in order to save another?
5. In the matter of the artificial heart, we can ask whether there can be life without any natural heart, or is life synonymous

with the heart? Is there any difference in this regard between the temporary use of a heart-lung machine during surgery and the use of an artificial heart?

The Sources

A. Deuteronomy 21:23

His body shall not remain all night upon the tree, but thou shalt surely bury him the same day.

B. Exodus 21:12

He that smiteth a man so that he dieth, shall surely be put to death.

C. Mekhilta, Exodus 21:12

From here we learn that one is not put to death, unless the victim was a viable person [*ben kayyama*].

D. Mishnah, Avodah Zarah 29b

The following objects, owned by idolaters, are forbidden for benefit to the Jew: . . . the heart of an animal . . . (*Rashi* to 32a: idolaters would remove the heart of an ox while it was still alive, through a round hole they made in the chest of the animal.)

E. Avodah Zarah 29b

How do we know that a cadaver is one of the things that may not be utilized for some other benefit? It is learnt by analogy to the sacrificial calf, where the word *sham* appears, just as it does at the death of Miriam, teaching that just as the calf is known to be forbidden, so is the human cadaver. And how do we know that the calf is forbidden? The school of Yannai prove it by analogy to Kodashim.

F. Sanhedrin 78a

All agree that one who kills a *treifah* (Rashi: such as one whose windpipe or brain membrane are perforated) is not liable to punishment (*Rashi:* the unanimity implies that as a result of the evident damage to his vital organs, he is considered as a dead person, a *gavra katila*.)

G. Nedarim 22a

Ulla was on his way to Israel when he was joined by two men from Ḥozai. All of a sudden one arose, killing his fellow. He turned to Ulla and said, "Was I right?" Ulla answered, "Yes, and go ahead and cut his throat all the way." When he came before R. Yoḥanan, he said, "Perhaps I encouraged the criminal improperly?" R. Yoḥanan, answered, "You [correctly] saved your life."

H. Sanhedrin 46a–47a

Whoever delays the burial of the dead transgresses a negative commandment, but if he delays it to honor the dead, or to bring a casket and shrouds, there is no transgression. . . . We have learned that for the sake of honor it may be delayed. Is this for the honor of the deceased? No, it is for the honor of the survivors. Do we really delay burial for the honor of the survivors? Yes, for the verse says that you may not leave him unburied on the tree (A), i.e., delay that involves shame, similar to being left on the tree. Thus where there is no such shame, it is not forbidden (Rashi: thus where the honor of the survivors is increased, there is no shame, and delay is permitted).

I. Ḥullin 11b

Said Rav Kahana: we derive the principle of majority (*rov*) from the murderer. For the Torah mandates the death penalty, yet how can we ever be sure that the victim was not a *treifah* (about to die anyway), and the crime is not punishable? Apparently from here we learn that we follow the majority of cases. And if you say that this is not true, in that we always examine the victim, and therefore do not rely on *rov*, how is that possible, for such an examination will certainly violate the cadaver? And if you say that we should indeed violate the cadaver in order to save the life of the accused, we can answer that such an examination is never conclusive, in that it is always possible that the evidence of dire sickness in the victim could have been obliterated by the sword of the killer at the time of the killing. Thus it must be that we rely on *rov*.

J. Bava Meẓia 84b

When R. Elazar b. Simon was about to die he said to his daughter: "I know that the sages are angry with me. (*Rashi:* because I was responsible for the arrest of many thieves, some of them related to the sages.) Consequently they will not take care of my remains in the proper manner. When I die place my body in the attic and have no fear." [Many years later] the daughter reported that the body had been left there no less than eighteen years, and possibly even twenty-two years.

K. Arakhin 7a–7b

Mishnah: We may use the hair from the cadaver of a dead woman. *Gemara*: Why is this permitted, is it not one of the things that are prohibited for use? Said Rav: "It speaks of a case wherein she had left instructions to give her hair to her daughter." And if she were to say, "Give my daughter my arm," would we do that? Said Rav: "We are speaking of a false wig of hair."

L. Maimonides, M.T. Hil. Roẓeiaḥ 2:8

One who kills a *treifah*, if the *treifah* can eat, drink, or walk in the street, is not punished in a human court. Every person is presumed to be fully viable [*shalem*], hence a killer is to be executed unless it is known for certain that the victim was a *treifah*, in that physicians attest that the victim had suffered from an incurable and terminal condition that would have killed him had nothing else intervened.

Discussion

1. HAZARDOUS TRANSPLANT SURGERY: FACING THE ODDS

We have seen in chapter 1 that there is a rabbinic consensus that would permit patients with a limited life-expectancy to undergo hazardous treatment or surgery in the hope of acquiring long term survival, even where that treatment poses a threat of immediate death. "Limited" in this context is generally assumed to refer to a period up to twelve months' duration.

A critical question is the degree of likely success or failure involved, i.e., what is the risk from that procedure? From our examination it would be appear that there is significant disagreement on this matter. The view of the Aḥi'ezer and *Shevut Ya'akov* is that even low odds of full recovery suffice to endorse hazardous surgery where death is imminent without that procedure. Rabbi Moshe Feinstein at first (in 1961) concurred with this view, but by 1972 had revised his position to agree with the *Mishnat Ḥakhamim* to say that a patient may elect to undergo hazardous surgery only if there is a fifty-fifty chance of success. He then adds that where the odds favor a successful outcome of the proposed procedure (i.e., more than a fifty percent chance of success), such surgery should be considered mandatory.

In addressing the risks involved in heart-transplant surgery, these considerations obviously are important. Thus in a responsum of 1968, Rabbi Feinstein bases his clear opposition on the overwhelming failure of the procedure to extend the life-expectancy of the recipients, which in his view falls far short of what is required by the Halakhah for such hazardous undertakings. He also pointed out that in many cases there is a significant possibility that the recipient would live in any case for a number of years without the transplant. For such patients, he says, such a transplant makes no sense whatsoever, given the comparative survival rates. Indeed Rabbi Feinstein expresses surprise that the civil authorities permit such transplants, and in his view those who carry out the surgery should be prosecuted for double homicide, insofar as patient consent is based on misleading counsel and information.[1]

At about the same time, Rabbi Eliezer Waldenberg came to very similar conclusions: he too requires fifty-fifty odds of a successful outcome, as opposed to the then current mortality rates of two out of three. In addition he questioned whether such radically new and experimental procedures are included in the Torah's mandate to the physician to heal.[2]

Rabbi Isser Yehudah Unterman also addressed this issue in an article written in 1969. Taking note of the poor success rate of heart transplants, he issues an unequivocal prohibition against the procedure. He then goes on to consider the minimal survival rates necessary to permit this surgery, and in so doing goes one step beyond Rabbi Feinstein's position. He argues that those authorities who permit hazardous procedures or therapy where there is only a small chance of success do so because, to start with, the patient possesses a legal presumption of life (*ḥezkat ḥayyim*). But where that presumption is inoperative or absent, even they would admit that one cannot rely on an unlikely possibility of recovery. Rabbi Unterman then postulates that it is the very act of removing the diseased heart of the recipient that compromises his *ḥezkat ḥayyim*, in that the heart is synonymous with, and represents, life itself. Consequently one may not rely on minimum odds of success to recover from the surgery. One would need to have a strong likelihood of success (i.e., much better than fifty-fifty odds) before undergoing such a procedure.[3]

Others, however, disagree with Rabbi Unterman's thesis. Thus Rabbi Menaḥem Kasher argues that while it is true (as we saw in chapter 2) that the Ḥakham Ẓvi is of the opinion that the moment the heart is removed life ceases,[4] other authorities differ with this position. Notably Rabbi Joseph Saul Nathanson, in the *Responsa*

---

1. *Responsa Iggerot Moshe, Y.D.* 2:174 (1).
2. *Responsa Ẓiẓ Eliezer* 10:25 (5). The responsum is undated.
3. Rabbi I. Ẏ. Unterman, *Torah she-be'Al Peh* 11 (5729):15–18. This was reprinted and enlarged in the author's collected essays entitled *Shevet mi-Yehudah*, pp. 367 ff. See also *Noam* 13:1–9 and 16:13 ff.
4. See above, Chapter 2.

Sho'el u-Meshiv, points to several talmudic passages that describe how an animal may live for some time after its heart has been removed (D). Accordingly, Rabbi Kasher concludes, a transplant recipient does not lose his *ḥezkat ḥayyim*, his presumption of life, upon removal of his heart—he remains fully alive for some time, at least until the new heart is implanted.[5] He adds that this is certainly true where the functions of the heart are assumed by a heart-lung machine, so that the blood continues to circulate throughout the body. Rabbi Feinstein too, in a responsum of 1970, makes it clear that in his view life can continue for some time after removal of the heart; and the recipient who lives for some months thereafter has the full status of a living human being.[6]

Even so, Rabbi Kasher forbids heart transplants, given the poor success rate as of the writing of the article (in 1970). He does anticipate improvements in this regard (even mentioning the artificial heart as a possibility), but stipulates that even so every case would have to be adjudicated separately and on its own merits and circumstances. Rabbi Moshe Shternbuch also issued a strong rejection of heart transplants, given the track record as of 1969,[7] as did Dr. Ya'akov Levy, an Israeli physician and author.[8]

In a subsequent responsum, written in 1978, Rabbi Feinstein returned to the subject once more, only to reiterate his opposition on the grounds of the poor prognosis facing the recipient. While he recognizes that a few patients might have their lives extended by a few months, such a benefit is severely vitiated by the great pain and suffering that they must experience.[9] He notes that as of his writing the transplant procedure had been largely suspended, with the exception of certain "expert" surgeons by way of research. This he attributes to the fact that "the nations of the world are not sensitive to murder." Thus he remained completely opposed to the resumption of such surgery, as of that date.[10]

---

5. Rabbi M. Kasher, *Noam* 13 (5730): 10–20. Rabbi Kasher notes that this article was written in response to a request by Rabbi Unterman, in the latter's capacity as Ashkenazi Chief Rabbi of Israel.

6. *Responsa Iggerot Moshe, Y.D.* 2:146 (at end).

7. Rabbi Moshe Shternbuch, *Ba'ayot ha-Zeman le'Or ha-Halakhah* (Jerusalem, 1969).

8. Y. Levy, *Noam* 12 (5729): 306 ff.

9. It should be noted that this concern is consistent with his position, seen in chapter 2, that is opposed to the need to resuscitate where great suffering will be the result.

10. *Responsa Iggerot Moshe, H.M.* 2:72.

As a result of these and other rabbinic pronouncements, whether or not they were in agreement with Rabbi Unterman's approach, an early consensus emerged in opposition to the procedure. Indeed the medical community itself came to share these conclusions, faced with the overwhelming negative survival rates of heart-transplant patients (about two hundred of whom died within a short time). As Rabbi Immanuel Jakobovits pointed out in prohibiting the surgery in 1975, the rabbinic rejection of the procedure represented "an impressive example of religiously motivated suspicions and hesitations anticipating, and eventually being vindicated by, the subsequent conclusions of scientific evidence."[11]

In spite of these negative views, however, more recent data have shown encouraging developments that would eliminate this halakhic concern. Since 1978 there has been significant improvement in the long-term survival of heart recipients, when compared to those candidates for transplant surgery who do not undergo the procedure for lack of a donor organ. While there are several reasons for these improvements, the major factor has been the use of the immunosuppressive drug Cyclosporine. As described in the 1984 report of the International Heart Transplantation Registry,[12] the four-year survival rate of patients undergoing a heart transplant since 1978, when treated with Cyclosporine, is seventy-one percent. Without benefit of this drug, the rate drops to thirty-five percent. The one-year survival rate with Cyclosporine is close to ninety percent. These figures become all the more significant when it is recognized that among those candidates accepted into heart-transplant programs, but for whom an appropriate donor heart could not be found, more than ninety percent died within three months of being admitted to the program for transplantation.[13] Given such success rates, there is room to argue that at least for those patients who can benefit from Cyclosporine, heart transplants should no longer be classified as experimental, but as therapeutic in nature.[14]

---

11. Rabbi Immanuel Jakobovits, *Jewish Medical Ethics* (New York, 1975), pp. 286–290.

12. Michael P. Kaye et al., *Journal of Heart Transplantation* 4, no. 3 (May 1985): 290–292.

13. See also Rabbi R. Fink, *Journal of Halakhah and Contemporary Society* 5 (Spring 1983): 63–64.

14. Such too is the conclusion of Rabbi Tendler, as recorded in *Mount Sinai Journal of Medicine* 51, no. 1 (January/February 1984): 55.

Such a conclusion would seem to follow from our earlier discussion wherein authorities such as Rabbis Feinstein and Waldenberg permit hazardous procedures as long as there is a fifty percent chance of success. With the rising rate of long-term survival, most objections based on medical prognoses would be answered. It will be recalled that one of the views discussed in the chapter on hazardous therapy was the view of R. Jacob Emden, who insisted that such therapy pass the test of being proven, i.e., beyond the experimental stage. This would appear to be the case with these latest statistics, at least for certain patients and in certain institutions. As well there has been a more careful screening procedure, in that candidates must have end-stage cardiac disease (i.e., without the transplant their prognosis is less than twelve months' life). This eliminates the concern that patients might live indefinitely anyway without the hazards of surgery. In any case the entire question of *ḥezkat ḥayyim* was raised only by way of requiring more favorable odds of success, a requirement which would appear to be satisfied by these ongoing improvements in mortality rates.

We should also address the related, although somewhat different, question raised by kidney transplants. Patients with chronic kidney failure have access to either dialysis or a kidney transplant, using either a live donor or a cadaver organ. The question may be formulated thus: where a patient can continue to receive dialysis treatment indefinitely, thereby prolonging his life, under what circumstances may he choose to receive a kidney transplant, thereby freeing himself of the constraints associated with dialysis, but at the same time exposing himself to the higher risks associated with such surgery?

Again some recent statistics are in order, based on Canadian results. In 1984 thirty percent of all dialysis patients were on waiting lists for transplantation. Only eight percent did not want such surgery, the rest were simply medically unsuitable. Of those on the waiting list about seventy-five percent were actually transplanted. Of the total transplants performed, eighty-four percent were successful—and the rest returned to dialysis. As to survival rates, those receiving kidneys from live donors boasted an eighty-seven percent three-year survival rate, whereas cadaver organs enjoyed a fifty-nine percent three-year survival. For patients under sixty-five years of age, the rates were eighty-nine percent and eighty-five percent respectively.[15]

Rabbi Moshe Meiselman contends that the decision to have a kidney transplant should depend entirely on respective survival rates, not considerations of convenience or pain. He quotes the Magen Avraham that a Jew is required to undergo a measure of pain and discomfort if that will prevent the loss of his fellow's life,[16] and he argues that this should be even more true of saving one's own life. Thus he feels that the inconveniences associated with dialysis should not figure in the decision to undergo the surgery, which should be based entirely on the likelihood of survival.[17] Rabbi Meiselman, it would appear, does not consider the fact that even in the eventuality of failure of the transplanted kidney, conventional dialysis can be resumed as before, thus eliminating the threat of failure of the transplanted organ.

Of course one could argue that the actual transplantation surgery itself is dangerous, as with all surgery that carries a statistical possibility of death. The question is similar to the one raised in the context of elective cosmetic surgery, i.e., may one choose to undergo surgery that is not medically required? The consensus on that issue has clearly been to permit such surgery where the goal is to eliminate psychological stress, whether it be in finding employment or a marriage partner. As Tosafot to *Shabbat* 50b puts it, a state of mind which prevents a person from commingling with people constitutes pain as the Halakhah would understand the term.[18] In the case of dialysis, few would disagree with the premise that ongoing dialysis is fraught with discomfort, pain, and a significantly restricted lifestyle that hampers normal social interaction. Accordingly, the issue of statistical danger of surgery might well be disregarded.

What if kidney transplantation offers a better chance of survival, as is often the case? Here Rabbi Meiselman agrees that surgery becomes permissible, by reason of safeguarding and extending life, i.e., one may choose a risky procedure if it bears the best hope of long-term survival.

---

15. *Canadian Renal Failure Register*, December 1985, pp. 97–119.
16. *Magen Avraham* to *Y.D. O.H.* 156.
17. Rabbi M. Meiselman, *Halakhah u-Refuah*, 2:114–121.
18. A useful summary of the literature on this topic is found in Rabbi J. David Bleich, *Judaism and Healing* (New York, 1981), pp. 126–128.

Of course here, too, the earlier described minimum odds would be required. In addition, as we shall see, there is the question of risk to the kidney donor.[19] Interestingly, in 1984 there was actually a decrease in the number of kidney transplants using the organ of a living related donor (from fifteen to eleven percent). This may represent concern about the future prospects of the donor with respect to overall health and the risks of life with only one kidney.[20]

It is clear, then, that kidney transplantation has gone beyond the realm of the experimental. It is an accepted medical procedure, and organ recipients enjoy a high success rate, with dialysis available as a backup option. Thus it would appear that in evaluating the permissibility of kidney transplantation, the success rates and likelihood of failure should not currently pose a halakhic problem.

2. REMOVING ORGANS FROM THE BRAIN-DEAD BODY

In chapter 2, we discussed the halakhic definition and determination of the time of death. That question is central to the issue of heart transplantation, in that donor hearts are necessarily taken from patients who are no longer living. At the same time, a successful transplantation requires that the donor heart be removed immediately following death, while it is viable, fresh, and capable of resuming all its cardiac functions. Thus in practice most donor hearts are taken from brain-dead patients, whose hearts continue to beat until they are removed. Consequently heart transplants are predicated for the most part on the acceptance of brain death as sufficient proof that death has occurred. It is of utmost importance, therefore, that the criteria of death be established and agreed upon, especially vis-à-vis brain death.

As we saw in the earlier chapter, the classic halakhic criteria of death as formulated by the Ḥatam Sofer (at least as he was understood by most commentators) require the total absence of independent breathing, heartbeat, and movement. The presence of any one of these, therefore, indicates that death has not yet

---

19. This is especially true where the kidney malfunction can be traced to some hereditary factor which may turn up at a latter stage in the donor, who is directly related to the recipient.

20. See *Canadian Renal Failure Register*, p. 99.

occurred. Later authorities require in addition that even where these vital signs are absent, death may not be declared until some time has elapsed, indicating that the lack of vital signs is irreversible. But what if a patient depends on artificial life-support systems that "maintain" his vital signs? Here we encounter a difference of opinion.

On the one hand is the view that as long as the heart continues to beat unaided, life persists, even though breathing can only be maintained with the help of a respirator. This argues that life is identified with the heart—and brain death must be accompanied by heart failure before a patient may be certified as dead. According to this view, if the heart or organs are removed from such a patient, it would be tantamount to murder, and be clearly forbidden.

Yet others disagree, and feel that brain death, properly defined, is the functional equivalent of death by decapitation in the Halakhah. This, they argue, is true whether or not the heart continues to beat, for it is not the heart that is the seat of life, but the brain (including the brain stem), in its coordinating and integrative capacity. This view, identified primarily with the revised opinion of Rabbi Moshe Feinstein, would permit the removal of the heart from such a "patient," in that the patient is, correctly speaking, deceased already.[21] As we saw in that chapter, by the end of 1986 this position was endorsed by the Israeli Chief Rabbinate, which permitted removal of the heart from brain-dead patients, under carefully controlled guidelines.

Yet it is still possible that even the restrictive view might contemplate permission on other grounds. Specifically, is it possible that even if the so-called brain-dead patient is still alive, the Halakhah would consider him either a *treifah* (because of his condition he has less than twelve months to live) or a *goses biyedei adam* (about to die as a result of human malfeasance)? According to the Talmud (F), there is no statutory punishment

---

21. In a symposium dedicated to this issue, and published in the Israeli journal *Assia*, 5739, pp. 183–201, several views are put forth, including one by Rabbi Barukh Rabinowitz. In his article he permits removal of life support to facilitate organ transplantation, yet makes this dependent on a certainty that, once disconnected, both heart and lungs of the donor will cease to function. Putting aside the question as to how such certainty can be ascertained, his position is basically similar to that of Rabbi Feinstein.

for killing a *treifah* (which is also true, according to the majority view, of the *goses biyedei adam*).[22] Maimonides accepts this principle and codifies it into law (L). Does it follow, then, that such a patient might be sacrificed if that will allow another to live indefinitely?

This very question was debated in the nineteenth century by Rabbi Ezekiel Landau (the *Noda bi-Yehudah*) and his contemporary Rabbi Isaiah Pick. The former states categorically that it is forbidden to sacrifice the life of a *treifah* to save the life of a *shalem* (one who enjoys a normal life expectancy).[23] He invokes the rhetorical question of the Talmud, "Why do you think your blood is redder than his?" Yet Rabbi Pick disagrees. So too does R. Joseph Babad (the *Minḥat Ḥinukh*), when he permits a group of Jews facing a murderous enemy to sacrifice one of them who is a *treifah*, if that will indeed save the rest of the group, because "such a person is not considered a *nefesh* [a viable human being]."[24]

Rabbi Yehudah Gershuni, discussing these various views,[25] notes that the position of the *Noda bi-Yehudah* is quite consistent with the *Mekhilta* (C) to the passage in Exodus (B), which does not apply capital punishment to the killer of a *treifah*, yet does imply that the act itself is forbidden as homicide. And even Maimonides (L), in removing the death penalty from the killer of a *treifah*, implies that the act is illicit, and punishable at the hands of God. As a matter of fact, R. Meir Simḥah of Dvinsk notes that Maimonides' formulation leads to the conclusion that while a court does not punish this homicide, the Israelite King can carry out the death penalty for this crime, in his capacity as administrator of extrajudicial law.[26]

On the other hand, those agreeing with Rabbi Pick, to permit the sacrifice of the *treifah*, consider homicide to refer only to where the victim is a *ben kayyama*, i.e., has long-term viability. As the Talmud puts it, *gavra ketila katal*, "he is killing a dead man," in the interests of saving a live one. This reasoning is taken

---

22. See *Encyclopedia Talmudit* 5:396, 1:160.
23. *Responsa Noda bi-Yehudah, Mahadura Tinyana H.M.* 59.
24. *Minḥat Ḥinukh*, positive commandment 296.
25. Rabbi Y. Gershuni, *Kol Ẓofayikh*, pp. 375 ff. This is an expanded version of his article in *Or ha-Mizraḥ* 18, no. 1 (Tishri 5729): 133–137.
26. On this subject, see *Jewish Ethics and Halakhah*, vol. 1, pp. 155 ff.

one step further by R. Israel Lipschutz, to permit the sacrifice of a person whose death is certain and imminent, even where there is only a doubtful chance that it will save a second life.[27] He brings support for this contention from the Gemara in *Nedarim* 22a (G), where it is recounted that Ulla found himself alone with two violent men. One arose and struck the other, fatally. As the victim lay dying, the attacker turned to Ulla and, with a threatening demeanor, inquired whether he approved of the act. Fearing for his life, Ulla agreed with the man, urging him to finish the job and decapitate the victim completely. The only justification that R. Lipschutz can find for Ulla's response is to say that while Ulla could have remonstrated with the murderer, such overt disagreement might have raised the killer's ire and cost Ulla his own life. Thus he decided to encourage the killer to hasten the victim's death, in a desperate attempt to save his own life, even though his own survival remained in jeopardy anyway. From this he concludes that "even though we must safeguard momentary life, that is only where there is no counterbalancing life. Where there is viable life on the other side, certainly that life is to be preferred to the momentary life at hand, even where the latter is certain and the former is doubtful."

Given these two views, which is the correct one? Rabbi Eliezer Waldenberg considers the question in the context of heart transplants and emphatically rejects the lenient view.[28] (Parenthetically he considers an accidental victim facing death to be, not a *treifah*, but a *goses be-yedei adam*, similar to one who was attacked by his fellow.) He further quotes Maimonides' view that the courts themselves can carry out the death penalty on an emergency basis, even in those cases where the death penalty cannot be implemented by conventional means.[29] He also invokes Maimonides' view that prohibits the killing of one to save another, an act which Rabbi Waldenberg finds analogous to removal of a beating heart for transplantation. It should be noted, though, that Maimonides does not explicitly include killing a *treifah* in this prohibition.

But what of the permissive view of the *Minḥat Ḥinukh?* As a

27. *Tiferet Yisrael, Boaz,* to *Yoma* 8:3.
28. *Responsa Ẓiẓ Eliezer* 10:25 (5).
29. Maimonides, *M.T. Hil. Roẓeiaḥ* 2:5.

matter of fact, Rabbi Waldenberg quotes an even earlier authority, the late-thirteenth-to-early-fourteenth-century Meiri, who states clearly that when confronted with a threat to their lives, a group of Jews may properly sacrifice one of them who is a *treifah* rather than all be killed.[30] To these views, Rabbi Waldenberg answers as follows:

1. The *Noda bi-Yehudah* is supported in his view by several other important authorities, including the *Tiferet Ẓvi* and the Maharam Lublin, who came to their conclusions even though the view of the Meiri was known to them through secondary sources. Accordingly, one can presume that they discounted the view of the Meiri.

2. Even though the Meiri merely permits the group to hand over the *treifah* to the enemy, this does mean that he would also allow them to kill the *treifah* with their own hands, as does the surgeon who removes a beating heart.

3. In referring to the case of Jews confronted with a murderous enemy, the request is for an unspecified member of the group, all of whose members are equally at risk. Accordingly each Jew can argue that the *treifah* should be the one selected, given his limited life-expectancy anyway. But in the heart transplant, the *treifah* is not threatened with immediate death to start with, he is simply being selected to save another. And it makes no difference that the *treifah* is in agreement, for such a decision would be considered invalid on the grounds that it is made under duress or despair. And even if this were not true, his life is not his to give away.[31]

Yet Rabbi Gershuni disagrees, and inclines to permit the removal of the heart of a *treifah*, or *goses*, in order to save the life of another. He furthermore understands Maimonides to be saying (L) that whereas the *treifah* status of an animal is completely determined by the signs of disease as defined by tradition, this is not the case with human *treifot*, whose status and prognosis are to be ascertained by the attending physician.

In yet another responsum, Rabbi Yiẓḥak Ya'akov Weiss strenu-

30. Meiri to *Sanhedrin* 72a, quoted too in *Shiurei Knesset ha-Gedolah, Y.D.* 157, and by Rabbi Jacob Emden, *Even Boḥen* 1:79. On this passage in Meiri, see below, p. 000.

31. See *Jewish Ethics and Halakhah*, vol. 1, chap. 3, for a discussion of suicide and voluntary euthanasia.

ously opposes the removal of the heart for transplantation.[32] In the first place he points out that it is forbidden to shorten the life of the *goses* by any active means. Furthermore, he argues, most authorities agree that we even suspend the laws of the Sabbath in order to save the momentary life of a *goses*. And as the *Shevut Ya'akov* states, the only time that we may properly handle and move a *goses* is where the intention is to attempt a treatment that offers some hope of his recovery or stabilization.[33] Failing that intent, we dare not do anything that might speed up his death (although we can remove anything which impedes the natural course of events leading to death).[34] In addition one cannot argue from the view of the Jerusalem Talmud that a person is obligated to endanger himself to save the life of his fellow.[35] For that obligation is suggested only where the danger to oneself is uncertain, and one might well survive the peril. It certainly does not apply where the contemplated course of action involves the certain death of the intercessor. Thus Rabbi Weiss concludes that it is forbidden to shorten the life of a *goses* in order to lengthen the life of another person, especially where the results of the transplant are in doubt anyway.

In another article, Rabbi Ḥayyim Dubber Gulevsky takes up many of these issues.[36] First he establishes that it is forbidden for an individual to give up his own life to save that of another. What is permissible, even according to the *Noda bi-Yehudah*, is self-sacrifice to save many lives, as found in several places in the Talmud. Rabbi Gulevsky quotes the Radbaz[37] to the effect that there is no obligation to donate one's organs to save another. But while the Radbaz indicates that one who puts himself in danger by sacrificing such an organ is a *ḥasid shoteh*, an overzealous fool, there is no prohibition per se against doing precisely that, for after all "he does save an Israelite soul." Going one step beyond this, Rabbi Gulevsky then refers to the *Yad Eliyahu*, who states that an individual may choose to endanger himself to save the life

32. Rabbi Yiẓḥak Ya'akov Weiss, *ha-Ma'or* 20, no. 7 (Ellul 5728): 3–7.
33. *Responsa Shevut Ya'akov* 3:75.
34. See *Jewish Ethics and Halakhah*, vol. 1, chap. 3, for a discussion of this distinction as it emerges from the halakhic sources.
35. See above in chap. 1.
36. *Ha-Ma'or* 21:1, pp. 3–16; 21:2, pp. 22–28; 21:3, pp. 11–12.
37. *Responsa Radbaz* 1052.

of one wiser than he. Thus he concludes that such self-exposure to danger is not forbidden, even though a third party may not shorten one life to save another.

As to the *treifah* and *goses*, Rabbi Gulevsky is of the view that an accident victim is in the category of a *goses biyedei adam*, his condition being the result of a specific act or event; thus one who hastens his death is not subject to judicial punishment. Nonetheless the act itself is prohibited, as demonstrated by the *Noda bi-Yehudah*. Rabbi Gulevsky adds that this is especially true in light of the fact that some time must pass after death has occurred before death can be certified, by which time the organs will have deteriorated beyond the point of viability.

Thus it is that those halakhists who consider the brain-dead patient to be alive, for the most part (with the exception of Rabbi Gershuni) oppose removal of his heart even if he is categorized as a *goses* or *treifah*. It is only those who accept brain death who would favor the removal of vital organs, once it has been established that true brain death has occurred, giving rise to a situation of functional decapitation.

3. THE USE OF CADAVER ORGANS

The human body possesses a special aura even after life has departed, hence it must be treated with dignity and respect. More specifically there are several prohibitions that must be observed in dealing with the final remains, prohibitions that are relevant to the use of the cadaver organs for transplantation. There are three major issues: dishonor of the body (*nivul ha-met*), utilizing the body (*hana'ah min ha-met*), and timely burial (*halanat ha-met*).

Nivul ha-Met

The Torah in Deuteronomy (A) demands that the body of an executed criminal not be left unburied overnight, but is rather to be accorded a speedy and dignified burial. The *Sifri* extrapolates from this that any maltreatment bringing dishonor to the body is forbidden. And the Gemara in *Sanhedrin* (H) takes this as the basis of a general principle that extreme care must be exercised to ensure that the body not be exposed to indignity (*bizayon*).

This consideration would apply to any defacement or mutilation of the cadaver. Does this then forbid incisions such as those necessary to remove the cadaver organs for transplantation? The question is essentially whether there are any legitimate circumstances in which the integrity of the cadaver may be violated. What if there is no intentional *bizayon* or indignity, but rather the fulfillment of the wishes of the deceased?

The Gemara *Ḥullin* 11b (I) provides the basis of a solution to this question. In establishing the biblical sanction of *rov*, by which we rely on statistical majorities, it refers to the death penalty mandated for homicide. The question is this: how can the death penalty ever be carried out, given the possibility that the victim was a *treifah*, which as we have seen voids the death penalty of his killer? It must be, says the Gemara, that majority rule applies, and we can assume that he was not a member of the tiny minority of *treifot*. But is it not possible that the cadaver is thoroughly examined, and we do not rely on such presumptions alone? The answer of the Gemara is that such an examination is not done, for it would violate the cadaver. But why not do so anyway, after all a man's life is at stake (i.e., that of the accused)? The answer: such an examination would not be conclusive, for the killer's sword might have obliterated all the evidence of mortal illness, hence there is no justification for postmortem violation of the cadaver.

It is quite clear from this passage that the prohibition of *nivul ha-met*, mistreatment of the cadaver, is biblical in origin (although others debate this question). Furthermore, in theory at least, the prohibition would be set aside if in so doing the life of another human being could be effectively saved. These considerations lie at the basis of the major halakhic discussion of the propriety of autopsies, given the integral role of dissection of the dead in the cause of the advancement of medical knowledge, and the ineluctable fact that all autopsies involve the mutilation of the body in one degree or another. With the establishment of the State of Israel, and its medical requirements, the issue became a cause célèbre, generating an extensive corpus of halakhic literature. From that debate certain principles do emerge, impacting directly on the issue of cadaver organ transplantation.

The key halakhic exchange occurred in the nineteenth century, occasioned by a responsum written by the same R. Ezekiel Landau, the *Noda bi-Yehudah*. It was his view that a cadaver may be violated when the intent is to bring direct benefit to a living patient who is "before us" (*be'faneinu*).[38] In his view such an act cannot be considered a gratuitous or unjustifiable assault on the human body; to the contrary it may be taken as an honorable gesture redounding to the credit of the deceased. But the key caveat to emerge from this responsum is that such a procedure may not be done in the context of a general intent to advance the cause of science of medicine. Such a nonspecific framework is too vague, its concrete and direct effects are too unreliable, to justify the very specific and immediate violation of the corpse at hand. Thus it is only where the autopsy will provide immediate knowledge to benefit another known sufferer from the same disease that we can permit that particular autopsy to be performed. Other contemporary authorities concurred with this ruling of the *Noda bi-Yehudah*, most notably the Maharam Schick.[39]

Opposed to this relatively lenient ruling stood R. Jacob Ettlinger, author of the *Responsa Binyan Ẓion*.[40] He argued that it is unfair to compromise the prior rights of the deceased even if it is in order to save the life of an endangered human being. To buttress his view, he quotes Rashi's comments to *Bava Kamma* 60a, that it is forbidden to save oneself at the cost of the assets of one's fellow. He likewise points to several talmudic passages that forbid self-preservation involving the exploitation or compromise of the rights of others, whether it involves their bodies, their possessions, or their reputations.

But what if the deceased had indicated prior to death his willingness to have his body violated for a particular purpose? Can *nivul ha-met* be set aside by prior agreement, or where it is clear that the deceased would have wanted or favored such a step? R. Malkiel Tannenbaum of Lomza answered the question in 1901, by saying yes.[41] He argued that to honor the wishes of the dead is quite consistent with the honor due them. Thus even where there is no express agreement, if it can be reliably established that such would be his wishes, or that such a step would be to his honor (*likhvodo*), his body may be disinterred and an autopsy

38. *Responsa Noda bi-Yehudah, Mahadura Tinyana, Y.D.* 210.
39. *Responsa Ḥatam Sofer, Y.D.* 336.
40. *Responsa Binyan Ẓion* 170–171.
41. *Responsa Divrei Malkiel* 5:60.

performed. This would be the case where the intent would be to identify his killer for the sake of justice, or to prevent the death of others.

A similar view was articulated in the nineteenth century by Rabbi Joseph Saul Nathanson,[42] to permit the suspension of the prohibition against *nivul ha-met* for the sake of identifying the remains to facilitate the remarriage of an *agunah*, i.e., a woman whose husband had disappeared. In so doing, Rabbi Nathanson lays down the general principle that what is prohibited is unnecessary violation of the dead, but where there is legitimate need (*ẓorekh gadol*), the corpse may be violated. In other words, it is not just to save life that *nivul ha-met* is set aside; other situations qualify as well.

In applying this discussion to the question of transplants, contemporary authorities make a number of careful distinctions. Rabbi Isser Yehudah Unterman, in the context of corneal transplants, points out that underlying the ruling of the *Noda bi-Yehudah* is the concern for *pikuaḥ nefesh*, the saving of life, so that even if violating the cadaver is incompatible with benefiting another, still the prohibition would be set aside in the interests of saving another's life, as are other commandments of equal or greater severity.[43] Nonetheless the potential beneficiary must still be present, as required by the *Noda bi-Yehudah*.

But what does "present" mean, in an age where there is instantaneous communication over large distances, where organs can be transported thousands of miles in a matter of hours, while they are yet fresh and viable? Rabbi Unterman answers unequivocally that as long as the intended recipient of the organ, or of the pertinent information, can receive it timeously, the patient must be considered "present," even if he be across the country, "for the entire country must be considered *be'faneinu*, or as if right here." But where the harvest of information or organs is intended to be stored or banked for some future use, the prohibition of *nivul ha-met* is triggered.

It is still necessary, however, to determine what is or is not properly considered of a lifesaving nature. While the issue is

42. *Responsa Yosef Da'at, Y.D.* 363, as well as his *Responsa Shoel u-Meshiv* 1:231.

43. *Shevet mi-Yehudah*, p. 368.

relatively simple in the context of vital organs, there is some debate regarding other organs, most notably corneal transplants. While all would agree that a person who is completely blind is in heightened danger of a fatal accident, and therefore a transplant for such a person would be permitted by most authorities, some are opposed to *nivul ha-met* where the intended recipient does have one functioning eye. Thus Rabbis Yekutiel Greenwald and Yeḥiel Weinberg are opposed in this case, while Rabbis Unterman and Yiẓḥak Liebes permit it.[44] In addition Rabbi Greenwald insists that where the entire eye is removed from the cadaver, once the cornea has been implanted, the rest of the eye tissue must be properly buried. One authority, Rabbi S. Hubner, is opposed to corneal transplants altogether, on the grounds that even a totally blind person cannot be considered in any special danger of his life.[45]

Rabbi Ovadiah Yosef likewise finds grounds to permit the removal of the eye for a corneal transplant, but he adds several caveats. Firstly this should, if at all possible, not be done to a Jewish cadaver when there is a Gentile cadaver available; secondly, permission should be secured from the potential donor while he is yet alive; thirdly, once the cornea itself has been utilized, the rest of the eye should be returned for burial. In any case, even in the absence of these conditions, Ovadiah Yosef permits the use of cadaver organs "after the fact" (*be'di'eved*), where the potential recipient wishes to avail himself of organs improperly harvested.[46]

The area of non-Jewish cadavers presents a separate area of discussion, i.e., does the prohibition of *nivul ha-met* apply equally to Jewish and Gentile cadavers? Here too there is a significant difference of opinion. On the one hand there are those who believe that the prohibition is aimed at Jews alone. This is the view of Rashi, Tosafot Yomtov (R. Yomtov Lipman Heller), and the Ḥatam Sofer, as well as the *Responsa Or ha-Meir*.[47] On the other hand, Naḥmanides and, in our own time, Rabbi Joseph Dov Soloveitchik consider the prohibition to apply equally to non-

44. See respectively *Kolbo al Aveilut* 1:45, *Responsa Seridei Esh* 2:20, and *Noam* 14:28 ff.

45. *ha-Darom* (Nissan 5721): 54–64.

46. *Responsa Yabia Omer* 3, *Y.D.* 23.

47. See Rashi to Deut. 21:33, and *Responsa Or ha-Meir* 34.

Jews.[48] As to the rationale of the former view, the words of Rabbi Abraham Isaac ha-Kohen Kook are relevant: the prohibition of *nivul ha-met* is uniquely applicable to the Jew, an extension of the commandments that require the Jew in his lifetime to sanctify himself with special foods and other behavioral patterns. Just as the Gentile does not observe those commandments intended to preserve the sanctity of the Jewish body and the singular spirituality of the Jewish people during life, so too there should be a clear appreciation of the unique halakhic concerns affecting the Jewish body after death.[49]

Hana'ah min ha-Met

The Gemara in *Avodah Zarah* 29b (E) substantiates the prohibition against the benefit or use of a cadaver by analogy to the ritual of the *eglah arufah*, or slaughtered calf, as encountered in Deuteronomy 21. Maimonides too codifies this law that it is forbidden to use a cadaver for some other purpose or extraneous benefit.[50] Furthermore, according to most authorities, including Rashi, Rabbeinu Tam, Naḥmanides, the Shakh, and the Ḥatam Sofer, the prohibition is based on the Torah itself.[51] How then can we permit the use of cadaver organs to benefit another party?

One approach is based on the view of R. Jacob Emden. He is of the opinion that the prohibition is not biblical in origin but merely rabbinic, and thus, like all rabbinically prohibited substances, it may be permitted for medical treatment.[52] Another approach is found in the writings of R. Solomon Kluger, who writes that the reason for the prohibition in the first place is to ensure a timely burial that will prevent the dishonor of the cadaver, but once the bulk of the remains have been buried, the law allows that individual organs may be utilized without going against the original prohibition. As pointed out by Ovadiah Yosef

48. See Naḥmanides' comments to Deut. 21:23; *Torah she-be'Al Peh* 6:64. For a review of this question, see Rabbi J. David Bleich, *Contemporary Halakhic Problems* 2:56–60.

49. *Responsa Da'at Kohen* 199.

50. Maimonides, *M.T. Hil. Avel* 14:1.

51. Respectively, in Rashi to *Sanhedrin* 47b; Rabbeinu Tam as recorded in *Sanhedrin* 48a; Naḥmanides as mentioned in the *Kesef Mishnah, M.T. Hil. Ma'akhalot Asurot* 4:4; *Sh.A. Y.D.* 79:3; and *Responsa Ḥatam Sofer*, Y.D. 336.

52. *Responsa She'elat Yaveẓ* 1:41. See also Rema to *Sh.A. Y.D.* 155.

and others, this line of reasoning could well apply to the posthumous implantation of individual organs, as long as the rest of the body is properly buried.[53]

Rabbi Unterman offers an original solution to the problem of using cadaver organs by suggesting that upon implementation the organ is no longer to be considered dead tissue. Being literally revitalized in the body of the recipient, the prohibition of *hana'ah min ha-met* is no longer applicable to it. He brings support for his view from the fact that whereas the Talmud in *Niddah* inquires whether those resurrected from death are a continuing source of impurity, it does not inquire whether such people, having been dead, may be of benefit to others. Rabbi Unterman concludes that once revivified, the body and its organs are no longer prohibited for use.[54]

There is yet another avenue of leniency. It is the view of the Radbaz that even if the prohibition is biblical in origin, what is forbidden is only conventional uses of the cadaver, but not non-conventional ones, such as medical treatment.[55] Others, such as Rabbi Akiva Eiger, disagreed.[56] In considering these views, Rabbi Moshe Feinstein concluded in a responsum of 1958 that even for medicinal purposes, cadavers are forbidden; but he does permit the beneficial use of non-Jewish bodies.[57] Such a position is based on the Jerusalem Talmud, the Shakh, and R. Elijah of Vilna—all of whom are of the opinion that a Gentile cadaver is not subject to this prohibition.

Other contemporary authorities also prohibit the use of a Jewish cadaver. Such is the view of R. Yiẓḥak Ya'akov Weiss, who argues that it is unreasonable to assume that the deceased has any obligations toward the living, for the dead are free of any and all commandments.[58] Rabbi Waldenberg also prohibits the removal of organs from a Jewish cadaver for purposes of implantation. He agrees with R. Shalom Gagin (the Yismaḥ Lev,) that under no circumstances may an organ be removed from the dead,

53. *Responsa Yabia Omer* 3 (*Y.D.*): 178; *Responsa Tuv Ta'am ve'Daat* 285. See Rabbi Gershuni, *Kol Ẓofayikh*, pp. 384 ff.
54. *Shevet mi-Yehudah*, pp. 54–57.
55. *Responsa Radbaz* 3:548. See also *Responsa Shivat Ẓion* 62.
56. See his comments to *Sh.A. Y.D.* 349.
57. *Responsa Iggerot Moshe, Y.D.* 1:229.
58. *Ha-Ma'or* 20:7; *Responsa Minḥat Yiẓḥak* 5:7–8.

in light of the credo of the future resurrection of the dead in both body and soul. Rabbi Waldenberg does, however, allow the use of a Gentile cadaver.[59] He also permits, after the fact, the implantation of organs improperly taken from a Jewish cadaver, i.e., where the organs had been removed and stored—and are now available to a particular recipient in some danger of his life. In other words, while the organ may have been improperly removed, once done, it may be utilized.[60]

Yet there are others who take a more lenient stance. Ovadiah Yosef does side with the Radbaz and a long list of subsequent authorities, including R. Solomon Kluger and the Ḥida, who are of the opinion that nonconventional benefit from a cadaver is not prohibited. Thus, for medical purposes, and certainly in the context of organ transplantation, Ovadiah Yosef permits the use of cadaver organs, even those of a Jew.[61]

Halanat ha-Met

In an earlier chapter we saw that the Torah requires that the deceased be accorded a speedy burial.[62] Thus there is a question that arises when an organ is removed and permanently implanted in another—is the burial of that organ improperly delayed?

The Mishnah itself (H) indicates that the obligation to carry out immediate burial is set aside in order to accord honor to the dead, i.e., where more time is required to complete proper funeral arrangements.[63] The Gemara (H) explains that the original concern is for *bizayon*, or shameful treatment, or as Rashi puts it, that any delay might demonstrate a lack of concern for the dignity of the body.[64] This being the case, it follows that where the delay is intended to add dignity or honor to the deceased, even a delay of several days can be allowed.[65] Indeed there is a story, recounted in *Bava Meẓia* (J), that R. Eleazar b. Simon instructed his family not to his bury his body for many years, out of fear that the burial

59. *Responsa Ẓiẓ Eliezer* 13:91.
60. Ibid. 14:84. For this and several other sources, see A. Abraham, *Nishmat Avraham, Y.D.* pp. 261 ff.
61. *Responsa Yabia Omer* 3 (*Y.D.*) 21.
62. See chap. 2, sec.3.
63. *Sanhedrin* 46a.
64. Rashi ad loc.
65. *Piskei Tosafot, Sanhedrin* 105.

would not be accorded due respect by his colleagues, and as a result it was left unburied for at least eighteen years.[66] While such a case was surely unusual, it did nonetheless establish a precedent for legitimate delayed burial. Yet it is not clear that even this precedent can apply to transplanted organs, for the intent in that and other talmudic cases was always to preserve and enhance the honor of the deceased himself, whereas in transplants there is no tangible benefit to the donor; it is rather for the benefit of the recipient.

Yet there is room for a different approach to the problem of organ burial. Is it possible that once the major part of the body has been buried, the requirement of burial has been satisfied? In other words, is there an obligation to bury individual organs, even after the rest of the body has been interred? The Jerusalem Talmud implies that burial necessarily refers to the entire body (the expression is *kulo ve'lo mikẓato*),[67] and Naḥmanides appears to accept this principle.[68] In addition, the Tosafot Yomtov rules that as long as a single organ remains unburied, the obligation of burial has not been fulfilled.[69] Yet others disagree. Thus the *Mishneh le'Melekh* points out that the Jerusalem Talmud itself no longer considers a cadaver to be a *meit miẓvah*, or body in need of burial, once the head and major portion of the remains have been buried.[70]

Among contemporary halakhists, there is a significant difference of opinion. Rabbi Yekutiel Greenwald, in agreeing with the Tosafot Yomtov, is of the opinion that individual organs do indeed require burial. He points out that the Jerusalem Talmud permits a priest to defile himself in the process of burial of such organs, even after the rest of the body has been properly buried. Indeed, as he points out, the *Shulḥan Arukh* accepts this as law. And he argues that even the saving of the life of the recipient is not sufficient cause to suspend the requirements of burial, in that unlike the case of the living, there is no obligation on the deceased to compromise its dignity to save the life of another.[71]

66. See *Bava Meẓia* 84b, and the Maharsha ad loc. On this passage see Rabbi Ben Ẓion Firer, *Noam* 4 (1961): 202.

67. J. T. *Nazir* 7:1.

68. Naḥmanides, *Torat ha-Adam* 43a.

69. Tosafot Yomtov to the Mishnah, *Shabbat* 10:5.

70. *Mishneh le'Melekh, M.T. Hil. Avel* 14 (end).

71. *Kolbo al Aveilut*, pp. 46–47, with reference to *Sh.A. Y.D.* 374, and Shakh, ad loc. See also in the same volume, p. 183.

Similarly, Rabbi Waldenberg stands opposed to deferred organ burial, arguing that it will interfere with the eventual resurrection of the dead, which requires that the body be buried intact—or at least to be so intended by the deceased, before death.[72]

Yet others disagree, on the grounds that the early sources are referring to cases where there is no subsequent burial at all of the organs in question. Thus, Rabbi Meir Steinberg points out that when the Gemara in *Arakhin* (K) forbids a woman to bequeath her arm to her daughter, it assumes that the arm will never be buried. This, he argues, is not the case with organ transplantation, insofar as upon the eventual death of the recipient, the organ will surely be accorded full burial rights.[73] And along similar lines, Rabbi Unterman, invoking the principle of revivified organs (see above), sees no need to insist on burial of an organ that has come back to life, and is no longer in need of burial, at least until the death of the recipient.

In an extended examination of this question, Rabbi Yiẓḥak Liebes reviews the discussion in the Jerusalem Talmud, and concludes that while the latter is of the opinion that the entire body must be buried, all of the major codifiers disagree, once the major part of the cadaver is properly interred. The reason is the familiar principle of majority (*rov*) (I), which in this instance considers the major part of the body to account for the entirety (*rubo ke'kulo*).[74]

There is another consideration in favor of delayed organ burial. As we have seen, delay is permitted for the honor of the deceased. Thus if it be true that the donation of his organs after death accrues to the credit of the deceased, and brings general approbation to his memory, then it could fairly be argued that organ donation is sufficient reason to allow indefinite deferral of the burial of that organ until the eventual death of the recipient. This would certainly be the case where prior to death, the deceased indicated his desire to donate the organ, on the basis of the principle that "it is to a man's credit to have his wishes fulfilled"

72. *Responsa Ẓiẓ Eliezer* 13:91.

73. Rabbi M. Steinberg, *Noam*, 3:94, 4:202. See Rabbi R. Fink, "Halakhic Aspects of Organ Transplantation," *Journal of Halakhah and Contemporary Society* 5 (Spring 1983): 48–49.

74. Rabbi Yiẓḥak Liebes, "be'Inyan Hashtalat Evarim," *Noam* 14 (1971): 51–59.

(*reẓono shel adam zehu kevodo*).[75] Even Rabbi Ettlinger, in forbidding autopsies where a beneficiary is present, does allow an autopsy where the deceased had given express permission prior to death.[76]

Such is the variety of views engendered by the juxtaposition of two simultaneous obligations—the one requiring proper treatment of human remains, and the other that calls for the saving of one's fellow's life. Faced with their conflicting demands, the various halakhists resolve the issue in a variety of ways, but always faithful to the dictates of rabbinic sources and reasoning.

4. TRANSPLANTING ORGANS FROM A LIVING DONOR

While the issue of living donors does not arise in heart transplants, for obvious reasons,[77] other procedures, such as kidney or bone marrow transplants, do pose the risk of acceptable risk to the donor. Thus we may well ask if it be permissible to sacrifice one kidney to a sibling with kidney failure, leaving the donor with only one remaining kidney.

In chapter 1 we examined the issues of self-endangerment in general. We saw that while according to most authorities a person may not expose himself to certain death in order to save another, the situation is different where death is unlikely to follow from such risk. There are two major schools of thought, one being the Jerusalem Talmud (which requires self-endangerment to save another), and the other the Babylonian Talmud (which does not, at least according to the majority of codifiers). It was the Babylonian view which became normative.[78]

Granted, however, that one is not obliged to endanger oneself to help another, does that mean that one is forbidden from such self-exposure even if one wishes to take the chance? Clearly the minority view that accepts the Jerusalem Talmud (including the Ḥavvot Yair and Rabbi Unterman) would see no prohibition here. But what of the majority? And more specifically, what if it is not simply some possible danger from which one might emerge com-

75. *Sefer Ḥasidim* 152; J.T. *Peah* 1:1.

76. *Responsa Binyan Ẓion* 170; Steinberg, p. 93.

77. One reported exception occurs where a donor himself receives a transplanted heart/lung combination, as a result of deterioration of his own lungs.

78. See above, chap. 1, sec. 2.

pletely unscathed, but the certain and permanent loss of an organ of one's body?

The key text on this issue is a responsum of the Radbaz. The question, as put to him, was whether a Jew could agree to the demand of a tyrant to remove his ear, by way of saving the life of an imprisoned fellow Jew. The questioner reasoned thus: surely if the Sabbath, a cardinal principle of Jewish law, may be desecrated in order to save life, an organ may be sacrificed for the same purpose. The Radbaz answered as follows: if we do set aside the Sabbath to save life, that is only where the danger originated in heaven, and was not of human making. But it is unheard of to expect a man to have to sacrifice an organ, when to do so might conceivably endanger his life. For this reason, he argues, the sages refused to take an eye for an eye—lest it somehow lead to death. More generally, he states,

> The laws of the Torah should be understood as fostering a harmony that is in full agreement with rational thought. Hence it is inconceivable that a person should agree to be blinded in one eye, or have a hand or foot amputated, so that others not kill his fellow. Therefore I see no basis for such a law, other than when undertaken as a voluntary act of piety, and blessed is the man who can reach such a level. But if there is the possibility of danger to his life [*safek sakanat nefashot*] then he who does this is a pious fool [*ḥasid shoteh*], for his life [when exposed to even doubtful danger] takes precedence over that of his fellow [even though it be certain danger].[79]

This responsum gave rise to a number of varying interpretations in the context of organ donors. On the one hand it has been understood to prevent any action that could pose risk to the life of the donor. Thus, in an undated responsum, Rabbi Waldenberg refers to the Radbaz as the primary source for his view that opposes any risk whatsoever on the part of a donor. He furthermore takes the position that even the Jerusalem Talmud and the *Hagahot Maimoniyyot* would agree. For they allow self-endangerment only because one can rely on a measure of Providence to emerge unscathed from the danger—which is not the case where

79. *Responsa Radbaz* 627.

the organ will certainly be removed, and permanently so. Thus he forbids the removal of an organ unless there is clear medical evidence that there is no danger to the donor whatsoever.[80] Likewise the *Minḥat Yiẓḥak* quotes the Radbaz in support of his contention that because the loss of an organ represents significant, albeit statistical, danger to the donor, whether at the time of the surgery or subsequently when he might have need of that organ, it is forbidden to donate such an organ.[81] Rabbi Pinḥas Barukh Toledano, reviewing the sources, comes to the same conclusion.[82]

But others rely on the Radbaz to come to a more permissive position. Thus Ovadiah Yosef understands Radbaz to be speaking only of real danger, i.e., a fifty percent possibility of death.[83] He quotes the Radbaz elsewhere as saying that even Maimonides allows a small risk in saving a drowning fellow, and that therefore it is only a fifty-fifty risk (*safek shakul*) that must be avoided by a donor. Where the risk is of far lesser order, one is required to act, or else to risk being in violation of the prohibition against standing idly by at the impending death of one's fellow. Accordingly, says Ovadiah Yosef, because kidney donors have but a one percent or two percent risk of death, the procedure is certainly permissible. In a similar vein Rabbi Shaul Yisraeli comments that the Radbaz refers only to the loss of organs that impede the full functioning of the donor and would render him a *ba'al moom*, physically defective. But where the body can function fully without that organ, and the medical risk factor is very small, as in the case of a kidney donor, there is no convincing reason to forbid the procedure.[84]

So too Rabbi Moshe Meiselman extrapolates from the Radbaz that as long as the kidney recipient stands a better chance of survival than he does with dialysis, anyone who wishes to donate a kidney for that recipient may certainly do so. He furthermore avers that this is true even where the likelihood of success is only

80. *Responsa Ziẓ Eliezer* 9:45.
81. *Responsa Minḥat Yiẓḥak* 6:103.
82. *Barkai* 3 (Fall 1985): 23–36.
83. *Responsa Yeḥaveh Da'at* 3:84; *Halakhah u-Refuah* 3:61.
84. *Barkai* 3 (Fall 1985): 35–36, in his editorial comments.

slightly more than fifty percent.[85] One case where a donor should not sacrifice a kidney, as pointed out by Rabbi Moshe Hershler, is where the donor may be susceptible to the same hereditary kidney disease as the recipient, especially where donor and recipient are related to each other. In this case the donor's own remaining kidney is at risk, obviously a direct threat to life.[86] Rabbi Hershler adds that while we permit kidney donation, this is not the case where the intent is merely to avoid the inconvenience of dialysis as an alternative to transplantation. For while we are prepared to condone some risk in order to save an endangered life, where dialysis provides an equally effective safeguard of life for the intended recipient, even the Radbaz would forbid the removal of the donor kidney. This leads to the conclusion that such a patient should rather receive a cadaver organ if he wishes to avoid the difficulties involved in protracted dialysis. Of course this assumes that the issues raised earlier in the context of cadaver organs are properly addressed.

Rabbi Waldenberg, it would appear, has since changed his position. In a later volume of his responsa,[87] while repeating his concerns and reservations, he recognizes that the Radbaz in fact differentiates between danger to life and danger posed to a specific organ. Thus, in spite of his reservations, Rabbi Waldenberg accepts the principle of organ donation as long as the overwhelming odds are favorable to the donor. In so doing, he quotes Rabbi Jacob Emden, who permits the removal of an organ in order to save the life of a fellow human being.[88] This is as long as medical opinion is confident that both donor and recipient will in all likelihood survive.

In addition there are some authorities who do not merely permit organ donation, but actually require it, if in so doing one will save a life. This seems to be the opinion of Rabbi Yeḥiel Mikhel Epstein, author of the *Arukh ha-Shulḥan*, who says that it is improper to miss an opportunity to save another life.[89]

---

85. *Halakhah u-Refuah* 2:118. While Rabbi Meiselman speaks of identical twins whose success rate is relatively high, current success rates would allow for matching of donors and recipients beyond such limiting circumstances or immediate family connections.

86. Ibid. 2:125.

87. *Responsa Ẓiẓ Eliezer* 10:25, pp. 5–12.

88. *Migdal Oz be'Even Boḥen* 1:83.

89. *Arukh ha-Shulḥan H.M.* 426:4. This is consistent with the writings of R. Menaḥem Recanati, in the fourteenth century.

Finally, we can mention a lengthy responsum by Rabbi Moshe Feinstein, who also understands the Radbaz as permitting a person to expose himself to merely possible danger (*safek nefesh shelo*) in order to avert certain danger to one's fellow.[90] Again Rabbi Feinstein stresses that while such selflessness is praiseworthy, it is no way to be considered obligatory. And even though it is normally forbidden to expose oneself to danger in the process of avoiding a Torah prohibition, nonetheless here a life is to be saved—thus a possible risk may be permitted. A similar view is attributed to Rabbi Shelomoh Zalman Auerbach,[91] and is also articulated by Rabbi Liebes.[92]

5. *THE ARTIFICIAL HEART: LIFE WITHOUT A HEART*

In an earlier chapter, in discussing the determination of death, we encountered the question of the possibility of life without a heart.[93] Likewise, earlier in this chapter, in section 1, we examined in brief the question of the presumption of life in the absence of a fully functioning heart. This issue is central to the matter of the artificial heart and its effect on the continuity of life. Thus it would be helpful to take another, more detailed look at the issues raised there.

There were two diametrically opposed positions: the Ḥakham Ẓvi was of the opinion that without a natural, functioning heart, life ceases immediately (even though some nerve and muscle activity might continue temporarily). R. Jonathan Eibeschutz, on the other hand, accepted the remote possibility that other organs might assume the function of the heart, thus allowing for life without a heart present.

The Ḥakham Ẓvi makes it quite clear, in the course of his responsum, that his view is that the tradition viewed the soul as residing in the heart, and that the other organs depend completely on a fully functioning heart. In this, he says, there is no difference between humans and animals.[94] And even according to

90. *Responsa Iggerot Moshe, Y.D.* 2:174 (4).
91. *Nishmat Avraham, Y.D.*, p. 66.
92. *Noam* 14 (1971): 28–35. See also R. Yehudah Gershuni, *Kol Ẓofayikh*, pp. 391–397.
93. See above, chap. 2, sec. 1.
94. *Responsa Ḥakham Ẓvi* 77.

R. Eibeschutz, life may continue without a heart only because there is some other natural organ that takes its place and provides its function. If so, one may legitimately ask whether by removing the diseased heart from a patient, and replacing it with an artificial pump, is one not removing the basis of his life, effectively rendering him a nonviable human being?

Sure enough, on the basis of the Ḥakham Ẓvi, certain contemporary halakhists forbid heart transplants and artificial heart implants. Thus Rabbi Unterman writes that even Rabbi Eibeschutz assumed life to persist without a heart only because he believed some other natural organ took its place. Where there is no such natural transfer, but merely the surgical removal of the heart, the basis for life too is negated. Thus Rabbi Unterman introduced the notion of *ḥezkat ḥayyim*, the presumption of life, which in his opinion is irreparably destroyed by the very act of the removal of the recipient's own heart.[95] Accordingly, he concludes, the surgery must be forbidden, as it constitutes homicide. Rabbi A. L. Grossnass agrees with this conclusion, and adds that were such a person to be killed at a later time, his murderer would technically not be guilty of homicide. Such considerations would obviously extend to the implantation of a permanent artificial heart. Rabbi Waldenberg apparently also agrees with Rabbi Unterman that upon removal of the heart, the patient is no longer to be considered living—until such time as he is literally brought back to life with a transplanted natural heart.[96]

Yet it is precisely this point which is a matter of debate. Rabbi Joseph Saul Nathanson quotes the Gemara in *Avodah Zarah* (D) which refers to the pagan rite that removed the heart from a living ox, apparently intending the unfortunate beast to live for a short while thereafter.[97] And the author of the *Da'at Torah* endorses this conclusion by quoting the analogous passage in the Jerusalem Talmud that compares the removal of the heart to the severance of the windpipe without severing the gullet of an animal—an act which certainly does not cause instantaneous death.[98] In line with this, the *Knesset ha-Gedolah* ruled, in

95. *Shevet mi-Yehudah*, pp. 371 ff.
96. *Responsa Ẓiẓ Eliezer* 10:25 (5).
97. *Responsa Sho'el u-Meshiv* 108.
98. *Da'at Torah, Y.D.* 40, with reference to J.T. *Avodah Zarah* 2:3.

opposition to the Ḥakham Ẓvi, that a chicken found to be without a heart is to be considered nonkosher and defective.[99]

On the basis of these sources, Rabbi Menaḥem Kasher comes to the conclusion that death is not the automatic consequence of the removal of a functioning heart, for life can continue for some time thereafter. And if physicians can extend that time period until a replacement heart can become functional, death can be said to have been averted altogether.[100] He reinforces this view by referring to several other passages: *Ḥullin* 32b assumes that a cow's life can continue for some time even after the heart has been effectively stopped (in this case by the severance of the windpipe); the Rashba considers an animal to remain alive as long as there is residual movement (*pirkhus*) even after severance of both windpipe and gullet;[101] and Jonathan b. David ha-Kohen of Lunel explicitly extends this assumption to humans, saying that a man who gives a writ of divorce subsequent to the severance of his windpipe and gullet, is considered to have acted while alive.[102] In other words, says Rabbi Kasher, such a person can be said, in the talmudic phrase, "to have passed from life, but not to have reached death." This state of suspended animation prevails until the situation is resolved with finality either way. And if an artificial heart is implanted, it too prevents the onset of death. Where the life-expectancy is extended indefinitely, the person with the artificial heart is to be considered fully alive.[103]

Very similar conclusions are reached by Rabbi Ḥayyim Dubber Gulevsky. He argues that the Ḥakham Ẓvi was referring only to the overt absence of a natural heart without any obvious substitute. Where substitute means provide the functions of the heart, even the Ḥakham Ẓvi would admit that life has not ceased. This, says Rabbi Gulevsky, is surely the case in all instances of open-heart surgery where the heart is temporarily immobilized and its functions taken over by artificial pumps. Why should the physical

---

99. *Knesset ha-Gedolah, Y.D.* 40.

100. Rabbi Menaḥem Kasher, *Noam* 13 (1970): 10–20.

101. Rashba, *Torat ha-Bayit he-Arokh, Hil. Treifot* 2:3.

102. *Avodat ha-Leviyyim* to *Ḥullin* 29b, in Kasher, pp. 14–15.

103. It should be noted that as of 1987, such permanent implantation of the artificial heart is no longer performed; instead the artificial heart is used exclusively as a bridge until a suitable donor heart can be found and transplanted. This in turn raises other ethical questions, most particularly that of triage, i.e., who gets the donor hearts that are in such demand?

removal of the diseased heart, while its functions are assumed by the same machines, be any different? Thus it is his view that life would continue without interruption even in the case of the permanent artificial heart.[104]

Rabbi Moshe Hershler makes the point that the Halakhah does not recognize any nonmiraculous revival of the dead. Where a patient is resuscitated by medical means, after a complete absence of vital signs, it must be said that death did not occur in the interim—whereas life persisted in some residual undetected form, until the vital signs were restored. The result of this thesis is that the removal of a diseased heart that is followed by implantation of a donor heart, is to be viewed as uninterrupted life.[105] Furthermore, he asserts, the heart does not possess any inherent spiritual status as separate from the brain, in that it is an organ that can be replaced without violating the spiritual integrity of the person. Thus the principle of the artificial heart does not in his view present any unique halakhic problems.

One other contemporary halakhist who takes issue with Rabbi Unterman is Rabbi Ḥayyim David Regensburg. He argues that if the presumption of life is vitiated upon removal of the diseased heart (as Rabbi Unterman argues), the same would have to be true of all open-heart surgery that involves the temporary immobilization of the heart. This, he says, is demonstrably not the case, in that patients subject to such surgery continue all other functions in normal, uninterrupted fashion. Furthermore he questions the very issue of "presumption of life" in this context, saying that in halakhic literature this principle is invoked only where there is genuine ignorance as to the whereabouts or condition of a person known previously to have been living. But in this instance, the person is present, and the facts of his condition are known. Thus there can be no question whatsoever that he is to be presumed, and pronounced, a living human being.[106]

Finally we can refer to the responsum of Rabbi Moshe Feinstein, written in 1970 in response to Rabbi Gulevsky. Although he says that the function of the heart goes beyond merely pumping blood, and that it maintains life even after it has stopped beating,

104. Rabbi Ḥayyim Dubber Gulevsky, *ha-Maor* 29; no. 1 (1969): 27–28.
105. Rabbi M. Hershler, *Halakhah u-Refuah* 4:87–89.
106. Rabbi H. D. Regensburg, *Halakhah u-Refuah* 2:3–8.

nonetheless it is his considered view that life does continue even after the heart has been physically removed. As he explains, life is a function of both heart and brain, but if their role can be effectively taken over by other means, life will persist. And he specifically affirms the continuity of life through the process of a heart transplant, even though he stood opposed, as of that time, to the implementation of the heart transplant on other grounds, i.e., the poor record of success.[107] While Rabbi Feinstein does not refer to the artificial heart, it is a short step from this reasoning to an endorsement of the principle of the artificial heart as a means to extending life, all other concerns being satisfied.

Thus it would appear that for the majority of authorities, life can be said to continue uninterrupted in the absence of a heart—as long as some alternative means of blood circulation is adopted. If the use of an artificial heart does that, it can be utilized without compromising the spiritual integrity of the recipient. In addition the artificial heart would eliminate certain other doubts relative to the natural heart transplant, i.e., determination of death, the use of cadaver organs, and the shortage of donors, as seen earlier.

SUMMARY AND CONCLUSIONS

It is evident that there is no shortage of questions, answers, and opinions generated by the availability of organ transplants, especially heart transplants. We may summarize our major findings as follows:

The first question relates to the likelihood of successful surgery. While some authorities allow hazardous procedures or treatment with even a small likelihood of success (notably the Aḥi'ezer and the *Shevut Ya'akov*), most modern authorities require that at the very least there be even odds of success (i.e., a fifty percent chance of surviving twelve months with the new organ). This group includes Rabbis Feinstein, Waldenberg, Unterman, and Kasher. Given the dismal success rates in the first years of heart-transplant surgery, this meant an effective consensus opposed to the procedure.

Since 1978, however, the statistics have improved the average life expectancy of such recipients well above the fifty percent

107. *Responsa Iggerot Moshe, Y.D.* 2:147 (end).

mark, even approaching ninety percent in many cases. These are patients who would without the surgery be expected to live no longer than a few months. Given such results, the halakhic concerns on the issue of effectiveness are largely disposed of. Indeed, according to Rabbi Feinstein at least, the surgery might be considered requisite, being an effective lifesaving step.

This is equally true of renal (kidney) transplants, in that the results are, if anything, even better than for cardiac transplants, with the added bonus that in the unlikely eventuality of transplant failure, dialysis can be resumed indefinitely. While Rabbi Meiselman feels that kidney transplants should not be attempted where dialysis offers better chances of long-term survival, there would appear to be no major problem in performing such a transplant where the success rates are high and the discomforts of dialysis are keenly felt.

The second question, in heart transplants especially, is raised by the problem of organ procurement from the deceased. This requires a precise definition of the moment of death. Two views, or trends, are discernible in the halakhic literature. The first cannot countenance or allow any assumption that death has occurred as long as the heart continues to beat unaided. This is the position of Rabbis Waldenberg, Weiss, and Bleich, amongst others. This view, then, would forbid a determination of death based exclusively on brain-death criteria, and thereby effectively eliminate heart donation.

The other view takes brain death as the functional equivalent of decapitation, which in Jewish law is the equivalent of death, irrespective of heart function. Once it is clinically determined that the brain and brain stem are irreversibly out of commission, and all autonomous breathing is absent, then death can be certified, and the organs can be removed, under certain circumstances. This is the view of Rabbis Feinstein, Goren, and Tendler—and most recently of the Israeli Chief Rabbinate.

We have also examined the question whether the restrictive view might consider other grounds to permit removal of organs for transplantation from brain-dead patients. Specifically, the issue is whether a *treifah*, with extremely limited life-expectancy, can be sacrificed with permission, to enable another person to enjoy long-term survival. To the *Noda bi-Yehudah*, the answer is in the negative, but R. Isaiah Pick and the *Minḥat Ḥinukh* answer positively. Subsequent authorities split over the issue, so that while Rabbis Waldenberg and Weiss stood opposed, Rabbis Gershuni, Gulevsky, and Rabinowitz were more favorably disposed to a permissive ruling.

The third question relates to the issue of the appropriate treatment afforded the cadaver, when its organs are needed for transplantation. We have seen that there are three prohibitions. The first was *nivul ha-met*, or dishonoring the body, by physical disfigurement. While every effort at respectful treatment must be made so as to avoid dishonor, the *Noda bi-Yehudah* does permit such disfigurement where the beneficiary of that action is both known and present. This is based on a talmudic dispensation to set aside the prohibition in order to save life. While the *Responsa Binyan Ẓion* opposed this lenient ruling (except where express permission had been granted prior to death), most subsequent authorities accepted it, including the Ḥatam Sofer, Maharam Schick, and R. Saul Jonathan Nathanson. It was left to Rabbi Unterman to make the point that under current conditions, given instantaneous worldwide communication and rapid transport facilities, the range of "immediate" beneficiaries is greatly extended. Nonetheless, even the lenient view would prefer where possible to utilize a Gentile cadaver, and to obtain prior consent from the donor.

The second prohibition involves the utilization of the cadaver for others. R. Solomon Kluger permitted such benefit once the bulk of the body had been buried; R. Emden allowed medical utilization; and Rabbi Unterman found room for leniency on the assumption that the transferred organs are no longer dead, strictly speaking. The Radbaz and, following him, Ovadiah Yosef permit nonconventional use of organs, although others disagree. In this area too, Rabbis Waldenberg and Weiss are opposed to the utilization of such organs, and disagree with these various mitigating considerations.

Delayed burial of the transplanted organs poses another problem. Here too, however, other factors enter: delay can be contemplated in order to bring honor to the deceased; some (*Mishneh le-Melekh*, Rabbis Steinberg, Unterman, and Liebes) permit such deferment, as long as the bulk of the body is buried right away; but others (Naḥmanides, Tosafot Yomtov, Rabbis Greenwald and Waldenberg) disagree and insist on burial of the entire remains.

There is a fourth question: the risk to the living donor. Here there is a significant movement toward some kind of consensus. Whereas the Jerusalem Talmud requires possible self-endangerment to save another from certain death, the more authoritative Babylonian Talmud disagreed. A pivotal text is a responsum by the Radbaz, variously interpreted. Some, such as Rabbis Weiss, Toledano, and initially Waldenberg, understand the responsum to forbid any exposure to risk whatsoever, especially when the certain result will be the permanent loss of a vital organ. But others, notably Rabbis Ovadiah Yosef, Meiselman, Hershler, Yisraeli, and eventually Waldenberg, understand his view to be that while the Babylonian Talmud does not require any exposure to risk, it does allow for personal predilection, whereby one can take a chance to save another, as long as the chances of successful outcome are at least fifty percent. Indeed according to this view, such selflessness is praiseworthy. Rabbi Feinstein also agrees with this latter group, while disagreeing with those who, like the Jerusalem Talmud, would require self-exposure.

The final question that this chapter has dealt with relates to the artificial heart. Does the Halakhah accept the possibility of viable life without the heart? On the one hand the Ḥakham Ẓvi says no, arguing that at most he can be considered a *treifah*. His view is reflected in the writings of Rabbis Unterman, Grossnass, and Waldenberg. The other view, however, is that where there is a reliable substitute for the heart, life may indeed continue. This would encompass the opinions of Rabbis Feinstein, Kasher, Gulevsky, Hershler, and Regensburg. They argue that the artificial heart is no different than the heart-lung machine in use during conventional open-heart surgery while the heart is incapacitated.

On November 2, 1986, the Israeli Chief Rabbinate issued its ruling to permit physicians at selected Israeli hospitals to perform heart transplants under careful rabbinic scrutiny and supervision. As explained at the time, the ruling was based on a number of considerations.[108] In the first place, there was the recognition of the high odds favoring successful implantation and survival of the recipient. Secondly, it was understood that donors are indeed

---

108. The full text of the ruling, together with various addenda, letters, and explanatory articles by Ashkenazi Chief Rabbi Mordecai Eliyahu, and Rabbi S. Israeli, is found in *Barkai* 4 (Spring 5747): 7–41.

demonstrably brain-dead, completely devoid of any independent breathing function, and irreversibly comatose, hence classifiable as deceased. Thirdly, the rabbis satisfied themselves that every precaution against error or premature judgment was to be taken, by way of various clinical tests and procedures. Fourthly, they required written consent from the donor or the family, and finally the rabbis were assured of periodic review of the procedures involved at every stage. Besides these explicit grounds, it is evident that these rabbis were able to satisfy themselves on the various additional questions and potential problems raised in this chapter, by relying on the permissive views that we encountered in each instance.

This ruling was a remarkable illustration of halakhic process and dynamics, involving change and responsiveness to evolving realities in modern life. Whereas but twenty years previously the rabbinic consensus had been to condemn the heart-transplant procedure for a variety of reasons, during the intervening years a significant proportion of rabbinic authorities arrived at radically new conclusions, based both on medical changes and improvements, as well as a careful reconsideration of traditional halakhic texts. Of course other halakhists remained opposed to the procedure, preferring to stay with their original approaches and perceptions. One such recent view is that of Rabbi Immanuel Jakobovits, Chief Rabbi of the British Commonwealth, who argues that the brain-death criteria are themselves far from scientifically proven, being subject to ongoing debate in the medical world. He also has difficulty in dispensing with the traditional role of heart function and blood circulation as part and parcel of the halakhic definition of death.[109]

This variety of opinions, too, has served to highlight the pluralistic nature of post-Sanhedrin halakhic conclusions, which has always, within reasonable bounds, allowed for a measure of dissent, variety, and internal debate.

In examining the many and complex halakhic issues involved in organ transplantation, it becomes clear that there can be no simple answers to the questions we posed at the beginning of our

---

109. See his article in *Jewish Chronicle*, May 29, 1987, p. 29. Likewise see his unequivocal statements, leaving no room for dissent, in "Ethical Problems Regarding the Termination of Life," *Jewish Values in Bioethics*, ed. Rabbi L. Meir (New York, 1986), p. 92.

investigation, especially not where heart transplants are involved. The entire area is an admirable specimen illustrating how halakhic positions emerge and evolve in a living process subject to many factors: scientific progress, changing social realities, and then textual interpretation and reinterpretation in the light of preexisting attitudes toward sacrosanct principles of faith, tradition, change, and reverence for life, in the face of death.

In conclusion then, should our fifty-year-old patient have the surgery? It depends on whom you ask. But a number of rabbinic authorities would tend to permit, and indeed encourage, a heart transplant, if in so doing there is a good likelihood of a successful outcome. It would also appear that many authorities would permit donation of one's vital organs, where intended to save the life of the recipient, with the proviso that the organ removal at the time of death follows carefully prescribed directions, i.e., brain death as halakhically defined and rabbinically supervised. Yet on this question, too, others would dissent.

As for the rest, we can be sure that the issue will continue to be debated and argued for a long time to come, as further medical developments occur, and new rabbinic insights into the talmudic and responsa literature evolve. Here, as elsewhere, we should be mindful of the rabbinic prescription that says, in the words of the Talmud, *zil gemor*, "go and study for yourself."

4

Violence in Self-Defense and the Defense of Others

Introduction

All civilized societies presume the rule of law, the purpose of which is to regulate social behavior so as to prevent any individual or group from acting in ways that are injurious to others who live in that society. Thus, by a so-called social contract, those who live in a particular society are presumed to have given up certain freedoms and prerogatives in return for receiving the protection and privileges provided by those who govern that society.

It follows from this that most systems of government are opposed to the idea that individuals or groups should be free to renege on this "contract." It is difficult, to say the least, to permit individuals to function as a law unto themselves, carrying out their own justice, living by their own standards of right and wrong, without reference to the conventions of the larger society in which they live. Yet there are circumstances in which the laws of the land or society are inadequate for the protection of its law-abiding individuals. Thus there arises the question as to when it is permissible to have recourse to actions deemed necessary to preserve life or limb—when the government or society does not, or cannot, provide for such needs.

The issue occurs most commonly in cases of violent attack. How may a person dispose of that peril to himself or others? The context may be an urban setting in which a man or woman is robbed while threatened with physical injury; it might occur in more politicized situations, in which members of a group feel physically threatened by the overt or covert actions of another group. Instances of such situations have abounded in recent years, wherein individuals or groups have taken up arms in defense of the innocent, causing injury or death to those they deem a threat. In the United States there is a widespread and popular image of the vigilante who takes the law in his own hands to bring "justice" in the face of an "inefficient" system of justice; individuals who have attempted to maim or kill their alleged "muggers" are often seen as public heroes; and the right to bear arms for self-defense is promulgated by a powerful national lobby which maintains that the right of self-defense is a basic guarantee of the American system of law. In the State of Israel the issue has taken on the additional weight of religious and nationalist sentiment and doctrine, most particularly in the angry debate over the so-called Jewish Underground, many of whose members were observant Jews, responsible for certain violent (and homicidal) actions directed against Palestinians perceived as being Arab terrorist sympathizers. On another level, the issue of preemptive war raises similar questions: i.e., may a sovereign state, or society, unleash preemptive war or battle when they perceive (as did the Israelis in 1967) that they are about to be attacked?

Responses to such cases are varied. On the one hand, there are those who consistently oppose the use of violence to stem violence. They argue that no civilized society can permit individuals, no matter how innocent or provoked, to take up arms in violation of the social contract. Violence, it is said, merely begets more violence. Some, as did Gandhi, advocate forms of pacificism or social reform to remove the "underlying causes" of violence, claiming that in the long run, this is the only hope for a just society. Others, along similar lines, argue that the state alone can be empowered to use force of arms, thus the coercive power of the state must be strengthened, even though individual lives may be forfeit in the short run. Common to these views is the fear of the anarchy that might result were any individuals to be permitted to act with violence to bring about their own vision of justice: where would we draw the line on this slippery slope?

On the other hand, there are those who see individual rights as primary. What is good for society is what is good for its individuals, especially those who are weak and without immediate recourse to justice. Thus society, it is argued, must allow an individual to protect himself or his fellows under all reasonable circumstances. In this view, laws are often impractical and faulty, and a person should not be required to sacrifice his life or limb for some long-term gain to society. To the contrary, if people are allowed to defend themselves or other innocent victims, society will benefit, in that criminals will perceive the need to act in lawful fashion. But if such preventive action is not permitted, and criminals are permitted to "get away with murder," all of society will suffer, in that such aggressors will feel free to pursue ever-wider circles of violence.

In between these opposing viewpoints stand a number of others, qualifying the terms and conditions under which recourse to arms can be endorsed. For them it becomes a question of circumstances, intent, background of the assailant, perceptions and subjective judgments, and the degree of violence that might be permitted as a response, as well as the issue of direct vs. indirect threat.

In this debate, the Halakhah treads a careful path, as always attempting a delicate balance of opposing principles: a deep respect for government, yet also a sensitivity to the primacy of the individual; the affirmation of the surpassing value of each human being, yet the need to safeguard societal structures and institutions. In discussing this issue, we will deliberately avoid politics and ideology, leaving it to the reader to draw his own conclusions in such matters.

The Question

A man is arraigned in a court of law and charged with an act of homicide. He had been sitting in a park when approached by two young males demanding his wallet. When he refused them, they proceeded to make aggressive gestures, insisting that he give them money, without, however, explicitly threatening his life. While bystanders looked away, he tried to escape, to no avail. Finally, feeling himself in danger of his life, he drew a licensed gun, firing one shot into the chest of one of the young males. While the other fled, the one so shot died a short while later of his wounds. When questioned by the police, the defendant indicated that he felt his life had been in imminent danger and had acted in self-defense, adding that the bystanders had not come to his help, nor had his attempts to dissuade his assailants yielded positive results.

This case raises a number of questions that require clarification of several halakhic principles:

1. Where a person is being, or is about to be, physically attacked, does the Halakhah mandate violent intervention by either the potential victim or by others?
2. Where the nature of the aggression is not absolutely clear, and there is some doubt as to the intent of the assailant, who determines the proper response, and how? May subjective judgments be made by the potential victim or others?
3. Is any preventive response, even homicide, permitted, or does the Halakhah require a proportionate or reasonable response, e.g., some attempt to disable or wound the attacker?
4. Where the threat is the result of indirect or involuntary action by an attacker, may the one so threatened (or others) injure or kill the assailant?

The Sources

A. Exodus 22:1–2

If a thief be found breaking in, and be smitten so that he dieth, there shall be no bloodguiltiness for him. If the sun be risen upon him, there shall be bloodguiltiness for him—he shall make restitution.

B. Numbers 25:16–18

And the Lord spoke unto Moses saying: "Attack the Midianites and smite them. For they attack you by their wiles by which they have beguiled you in the matter of Peor."

C. Deuteronomy 22:25–26

If a man find a damsel that is betrothed in a field, and the man take hold of her and lie with her, then the man only that lay with her shall die. But unto the damsel thou shalt do nothing . . . for as when a man riseth against his neighbor, and slayeth him, even so is this matter. For he found her in the field, the betrothed damsel cried, and there was none to save her.

D. II Samuel 2:12–3:39

And Abner the son of Ner . . . went out from Maḥanaim to Gibeon. And Joab the son of Ẓeruiah . . . went out, and they met together. . . . And Abner said to Joab: "Let the young men, I pray thee, arise and play before us." . . . And the battle was very sore that day; and Abner was beaten, and the men of Israel, before the servants of David. And the three sons of Ẓeruiah were there, Joab and Abishai and Asahel; and Asahel was as light of foot as one of the roes that are in the field. And Asahel pursued after Abner . . . And Abner said to him: "Turn thee aside to thy right hand or to thy left" . . . but Asahel would not turn aside from following him . . . wherefore Abner . . . smote him in the fifth rib . . . and he fell down there, and died in the same place. . . . But Joab and Abishai pursued after Abner. . . . then Abner called to Joab and said:

"Shall the sword devour forever? Knowest thou not that it shall be bitterness in the end . . ." So Joab . . . pursued after Israel no more, neither fought they anymore. . . . And when Abner was returned to Hebron Joab took him aside into the midst of the gate to speak with him quietly, and smote him there in the fifth rib that he died, for the blood of Asahel his brother. And afterward when David heard it, he said: "I and my kingdom are guiltless before the Lord for the blood of Abner the son of Ner; let it fall upon the head of Joab, and upon all his father's house . . . these men the sons of Ẓeruiah are too hard for me; the Lord reward the evildoer according to his wickedness."

E. Sanhedrin 72a

Said Rava: why is the killer of a thief found breaking in not subject to prosecution? The answer is that there is a presumption that no man will tolerate the loss of his possessions without resistance. Knowing this, the thief reckons that the homeowner will stand his ground and resist the intruder. Faced with this resistance, he intends to kill the homeowner. Accordingly, the Torah has said, "if a man comes to kill you, kill him first." (*Rashi*: the words "there shall be no bloodguiltiness for him" teach that insofar as he comes to kill you, you should kill him first.)

F. Sanhedrin 72a

The Sages have taught: " '. . . there shall be no bloodguiltiness for him. If the sun be risen upon him . . .'—surely the sun does not rise up only upon him? Rather the intent is that if it is as clear to you as the sun that his intentions toward you are not peaceful, then you may kill him, but if not, do not kill him." However, another tannaitic statement says: " 'If the sun be risen upon him, there shall be bloodguiltiness for him.' Surely the sun does not rise up only on him? Rather the intent is that if it is as clear to you as the sun that his intentions toward you are peaceful, then you may not kill him, but if not, kill him." Do these two anonymous statements not contradict each other? The answer is that the first is describing the case of an intruder who is the father of the homeowner, while the second deals with a case where the intruder is the son of the homeowner. (*Rashi*: this latter case includes by extension all other men, for they are to be killed when there is any doubt, for they can be presumed to have entered intending to kill upon meeting any resistance. The only exception is where it is as clear to you as the sun that the intruder is mercifully disposed, as in the case of a father who intrudes upon his son.) Said Rav: I will kill any man whom I discover intruding on my home, except for Rav Ḥanina bar Shila, because I know for certain that he has mercy on me as a father on a son.

G. Sanhedrin 72b.

The sages have taught: The verse refers to "breaking in" [*maḥteret*]; what about the case where the thief is encountered on the roof, in the courtyard, or an outdoor enclosure? When the verse says "if the thief be found," it intends them to be included. If so why does it say "breaking in"? The answer is that term teaches that once he breaks in he needs no warning before being killed. (*Rashi*: by a forced entry, he demonstrates careful forethought with a readiness to kill, whereas if the thief is encountered outdoors, or coming through an open door, he must be warned first, for in such a case we can say that it was an opportunistic crime, without homicidal intent, in that he intended to run away if discovered.) Said Rav Huna: If a pursuer is a minor he may be killed. It would appear that Rav Huna believes that a pursuer does not require forewarning [before being killed], thus it makes no difference whether he be an adult or a minor. But Rav Ḥisda disagrees, saying: where the head of a fetus has emerged from the birth canal [and the mother's life is in danger], we may not kill the fetus, for we do not take one life in order to save another, according to Rav Huna this makes no sense, for the fetus should be killed, because it pursues the mother to kill her? The answer of Rav Huna is that the fetus itself is not pursuing her, rather it is from heaven. It would appear that support for Rav Huna is found in the statement that where one person is in pursuit to kill another, he is warned as follows, "You are pursuing a fellow Jew, and for this you can be killed . . . " (*Rashi*: the pursuer may be killed, even though he does not explicitly accept the warning.)

H. Sanhedrin 73a

Mishnah: The following are saved (*Rashi*: from committing the transgression) even if they have to be killed: a person who is pursuing another either to kill him or to commit homosexual rape, or to rape a betrothed woman.

Gemara: Whence do we derive permission to kill a man in homicidal pursuit of another? From the verse "you shall not stand idly by the blood of your fellow" [Lev. 19:16]. . . . And how do we know that we may even kill him? It is derived by extension from the law of the betrothed woman: for surely if the Torah permits us to kill a man whose intent is merely to defile a betrothed woman, certainly we may do that where the intent of the pursuer is murder. But it is not proper to derive such a punishment by inferred reasoning! The school of Rebbe answers that there is in this case a legitimate analogy, in that the text of the betrothed woman itself refers to homicide, saying, "for as when a man riseth against his neighbor, and slayeth him, even so is this matter." Why does the Torah invoke the murderer? . . . we can learn therefrom that just as the rapist can be killed, so too the one intending homicide. But how do we know that the rapist himself can be killed? The school of Reb Ishmael teaches that the words "and there was none to save her" imply that if there was someone able to save her, he is obligated to do so with any means at his disposal. (Tosafot: There is an obligation to save another.)

I. Sanhedrin 74a

R. Jonathan b. Saul said: When a person (*Rashi*: either the intended victim or an onlooker) can stop a homicidal pursuer by disabling part of his body, but does not do so (*Rashi*: instead he kills the pursuer outright), he is subject to the death penalty. What is the source for this? The Torah says: "And if men strive together and hurt a woman with child, so that her fruit depart, and yet no harm follow, he shall surely be fined . . . but if any harm follow, then thou shalt give life for life" [Exod. 21:22–23]. R. Eliezer learns from this last phrase that the men had homicidal intent, otherwise why "life for life"? But even though the intent was homicidal, the Torah says that there is a monetary fine [where the fetus is lost]. This, [reasons R. Jonathan b. Saul], can only make sense if we assume that the attacker does not forfeit his right to life, for if he does indeed forfeit his right to life, then he would be automatically exempt from any monetary fine resulting from his action, so a monetary fine would be impossible. The fact that he is not exempt here, but rather "shall surely be fined," teaches that he does not automatically forfeit his life. [Thus a person may not stop him by killing him, if he can stop him by merely disabling part of his body.]

J. Sanhedrin 49a

Joab was summoned to the court. The King said to him: "Why did you kill Abner?" Joab answered: "I was the blood-avenger of Asahel." Said he, "Asahel was pursuing Abner with the intent to kill him [so Abner acted in self-defense]." Said Joab: "Abner should simply have disabled Asahel in part of his body." Said the King: "He was not able to do that." Said Joab: "If Abner was able to pierce precisely the fifth rib from the bottom, could he not have disabled another part of his body?" Said he: "Let the case of the death of Abner be dismissed." (Rashi: you are acquitted of the death of Abner.)

K. Maimonides, M.T. Hil. Roẓeiaḥ 1:6, 7, 9, 13, 15

All Israel is commanded to save a person being pursued for his life, even if it means killing the pursuer, and the pursuer is a minor.

Thus, if warning is issued, and he continues to pursue, the pursuer can be killed even without his acknowledging the warning. But if the pursuer can be stopped by disabling part of his body, by striking him with an arrow, a stone, or a sword, to cut off his hand, break his leg, or blind him, then that should be done. . . .

And this is a negative commandment, i.e., not to take mercy on the life of a pursuer. Thus the sages taught that it is permissible to take apart the fetus of a woman whose life is threatened in labor. This can be done by medication or by surgery, for the fetus is considered a pursuer threatening her life. But once his head has emerged, he may not be harmed, for we do not take one life to save another, and this occurs in the course of nature [*tiv'o shel olam*].

Whoever can save the victim by disabling part of the pursuer's body, but does not take care and instead kills the pursuer, then that person is a murderer, and is guilty of a capital crime, however a court does not execute him . . .

If a person sees another pursuing his fellow to kill him or to rape, and can save the victim but chooses not to—such a person has negated a positive commandment, which is "and thou shalt cut off her hand" [Deut. 25:12], and he has transgressed two negative commandments, which are "thine eye shall have no pity" [ibid.] and "thou shalt not stand idly by the blood of thy fellow" [Lev. 19:16].

L. Maimonides, M.T. Hil. Melakhim 9:4

If a Noahide kills another person, even an unborn fetus, he is subject to the death penalty . . . And likewise if he kills a homicidal pursuer, when he can disable him in one part of his body, he is subject to the death penalty. But this is not the case with an Israelite. (Ravad: The case of Abner poses a problem for him.)

M. Maimonides, M.T. Hil. Ḥovel U-Mazzik 8:15

If a ship is about to founder because it is overloaded, and one of those on board casts part of the cargo overboard, he is not liable for the value of the lost cargo. For it is like a pursuer intent upon killing them, so by his action he performed a great service and saved their lives.

Ravad: In this matter there is neither rhyme nor reason [in Maimonides' words]. For this case has nothing at all to do with the law of the pursuer. And it is not the same as the case of the ass that was cast off from the ferry in *Bava Kamma* 117b. Instead in such a case, where one man casts it overboard, the cost should be shared by them all.

N. Meiri, Sanhedrin 72a

Where does the Torah state that (D) "if a man comes to kill you, kill him first"? It is explained in the Midrash Tanḥuma as coming from the verse (B) "attack the Midianites . . . for they attack you," i.e., they habitually attack you, hence you may attack them in view of the fact that they are disposed toward attacking you.

O. Sefer Ha-Ḥinukh 600

We are commanded to save the victim of a homicidal pursuer, even at the cost of his life, i.e., we are commanded to kill the pursuer, if we cannot save the victim without killing the pursuer. Regarding this it says, "thou shalt cut off her hand, thine eye shall have no mercy" [Deut. 25:12]. On this the *Sifri* comments that "and she taketh him by the secrets" teaches that where the aggression poses a mortal danger, the limb of the attacker is to be cut off, but if that is not possible, then "thine eye shall have no mercy" teaches that his life is forfeit . . . and this is true of every such person.

P. Shulḥan Arukh, Ḥoshen Mishpat 425:1

A homicidal pursuer who continues to pursue after he has been warned, even though he be a minor, all Israel is commanded to stop him by injuring his limb. And if that cannot be done without killing the pursuer, then the killer can be killed, even though he has not yet killed.

Rema: A thief who is found breaking in has the status of a pursuer. But if it is known that he only came for financial reward, so that if the homeowner should offer resistance he will not kill the homeowner, it is forbidden to kill the thief. And the *Tur* says that if an individual endangers many by engaging in counterfeiting where the government is punitive, he is in the category of a pursuer, and can be denounced to the government.

Discussion

1. MEETING VIOLENCE WITH VIOLENCE

In an earlier chapter we saw that, generally speaking, the Halakhah does not favor the exchange of one life for another, i.e. it is forbidden to sacrifice one life in order to save another.[1] More particularly, where deliberate homicide is involved, and an individual must choose between killing an innocent man or being himself killed, there is a clear and unambiguous talmudic ruling that forbids the taking of such innocent life, even at the cost of one's own equally guiltless one.[2] Thus the taking of innocent life is one of the three so-called cardinal commandments (the other two are idolatry and prohibited sexual liaisons of the most severe kind, *arayot*) for which *yehareg ve'al ya-avor,* i.e., one should submit to be killed rather than transgress.

Furthermore, where an individual is known to be guilty of a capital offense, even then his life is not forfeit. Thus Maimonides enumerates as one of the 613 commandments the law that witnesses to a capital crime may not themselves execute the criminal prior to his proper appearance in a court adjudicating the case.[3] Clearly the Halakhah does not countenance either the saving of

1. See chap. 3, where, in the discussion of heart transplants, it is forbidden to sacrifice or shorten even momentarily the life of a donor, moribund and facing imminent death, in order to save the life of a potential recipient. See also *Jewish Ethics and Halakhah for Our Time,* vol. 1, chap. 2, where, at the other end of the lifespan, if the fetus has partially emerged from the birth canal and a crisis arises to threaten the life of the mother, we may not sacrifice the newborn to save the mother, for "we do not sacrifice one life to save another." This general principle is articulated in the Mishah *Ohalot* 7:6 and codified by Maimonides in *M. T. Hil. Yesodei ha-Torah* 5:6–7.

2. The classic formulation reads: "What makes you think that your blood is redder than his—maybe his is redder than yours!" See *Pesaḥim* 25b, *Yoma* 82b, *Sanhedrin* 74a.

3. Maimonides, *Sefer ha-Miẓvot,* prohibition 292.

one life at the expense of another or the punishment by execution of a murderer without full due process under judicial sanction.[4]

Yet were one to conclude from this that it is always forbidden to kill a person outside of full judicial proceedings, such an inference would be in error. To the contrary, in the very next commandment, Maimonides explicitly enumerates the law of the pursuer (*rodef*), a law that does not merely condone, but actually insists upon the nonjudicial attack to be carried out against a person, e.g., a homicidal man stalking another, where the assailant poses a mortal threat to his intended victim. Such extreme action is called for if necessary to save the life of another, in apparently total circumvention of all due process.

Such is the dialectical tension characteristic of the halakhic prescription for the saving of life: on the one hand, no life is more valuable than another, no exchanges or substitutions can be contemplated; but on the other hand, there is a clear acceptance of the principle of violent, and if necessary murderous, attack against any person who represents a threat to the life of his fellow, and is about to implement his purposes.

Now it is necessary to examine the parameters of this rather startling law of the *rodef*, or pursuer. For it is the key to understanding the halakhic attitude toward the use of force in self-defense, or for that matter the defense of others.

The Mishnah in *Sanhedrin* 73a (H) enunciates the law of the pursuer, saying that the pursuer himself is to be "saved" from his transgression, even at the cost of his life. Included under this rubric are pursuers who intend murder, homosexual rape, or the rape of a betrothed woman. The Gemara, discussing the issue (H), finds sanction for the principle in the biblical admonition, found in Leviticus, against doing nothing to save one's fellow who's life is in jeopardy, i.e., "you shall not stand idly by the blood of your fellow" (Lev. 19:16) But this only teaches that "something" must be done—how do we know that "something" extends to an

4. As a matter of fact, Naḥmanides goes so far as to forbid wounding of a man, even if by wounding him the life of another would be saved. For he includes wounding under the rubric of *avizraihu de'reẓiḥah*, i.e., a derivative of murder, equally forbidden under all circumstances. See *Torat ha-Adam* in *Kitvei ha-Ramban*, p. 14. Rabbeinu Yonah of Gerondi went so far as to prohibit the public shaming of a man (*halbanat panim*) where intended to save another's life. See his *Sha'arei Teshuvah* 3:137–139. This view did not become normative.

act of killing? To this question the Gemara invokes another biblical passage, this time in Deuteronomy (C). The passage deals with the case of a betrothed woman who is raped—a capital crime. In fact the verse itself explicitly equates such an act to the crime of murder, she being the entirely guiltless victim of aggression. The Gemara, in the name of R. Ishmael, infers from the phrase "and there was none to save her" that had a bystander been present, he would have been obligated to save her—by any means whatsoever, even the killing of the rapist. Once this principle is established, says the Gemara, it can properly be extended to murder *per se*, the Torah itself having invoked homicide in this very context. Actually the Gemara could just as well have quoted the early rabbinic Midrash known as the *Sifra* in its comments to the verse in Leviticus, for the *Sifra* derives from that verse an actual obligation to save such intended victims by killing the attacker if necessary, but perhaps the Gemara chooses to avoid this source, because the verse does not really specify this principle of *rodef* in sufficient degree. As opposed to the *Sifra*, the *Sifri* to Deuteronomy does invoke the passage of the betrothed woman, as does the Gemara here.[5]

This is not the only source of the principle of *rodef*. Deuteronomy 25:11–12 describes the case of a woman who, to protect her husband, attempts to mortally wound his antagonist—and the Torah permits an onlooker to disable her, saying "thou shalt cut off her hand, thine eye shall have no mercy" (O). The *Sifri* concludes from this formulation that if need be, the woman may be killed to prevent her from killing her intended victim. And Maimonides, in the *Sefer ha-Miẓvot*, and the *Mishneh Torah* (K), as well as the author of the *Sefer ha-Ḥinukh* (N), both quote this source as providing sanction to interdict murderous intent.[6]

But perhaps the most significant paradigm for the law of the pursuer, especially vis-à-vis action by the intended victim him-

5. See *Sifra* to *Kedoshim* 2:4–5, and the *Sifri* to *Kee Teẓe* 243. For these sources, see Rabbi E. Ben Zimrah, "Shefikhut Damim mi-Tokh Ẓorekh," *Shenaton ha-Mishpat ha-Ivri* 3–4 (1976–77): 123.

6. See Maimonides' *Sefer ha-Miẓvot*, prohibition 293, where he effectively combines this source with that of the betrothed woman discussed earlier. Yet in his *Mishneh Torah* (K), Maimonides pointedly omits any reference to the talmudic derivation of *rodef* from the rape of the betrothed woman in Deuteronomy. On this, see below. The *Sefer ha-Ḥinukh* concludes that one who does not intercede is guilty of the infraction of one positive and two negative commandments.

self, is the law of the thief found breaking in (*ha-ba be'maḥteret*). Exodus 22:1–2 (A) posits the law that if a thief is encountered while breaking and entering, and the resident kills the thief on the premises, he is not held liable for such a homicide, except if "the sun be risen upon him." The Gemara in *Sanhedrin* 72a (E) quotes Rava to explain why there is no liability for what is ostensibly a grossly disproportionate response to a mere act of theft: there is a generally valid presumption that no man on his own domain will give up his possessions without a struggle of some sort. Thieves who intrude onto private property know this, and thus if they persist anyway, it must be that they are prepared to overcome such resistance by any means necessary, not excluding the possibility of killing any person encountered. Thus one who discovers a thief in the act is in mortal danger of his life. If he kills the intruder, the act must therefore be classified as one of self-defense. Rava concludes with the words, "for the Torah says 'if a man comes [ready] to kill you, kill him first.' "

Now this passage is not without problems. In the first place it is not clear where the Torah "says" what it is reported as saying, for the words as quoted are not found in the Torah itself. Secondly, the verses in the passage in question are themselves unclear: What does "breaking in" include? And why is there a difference if the sun is up or not?

Rashi, it would seem, feels that Rava here is simply stating that this passage itself is the source of the principle, i.e., by holding the person guiltless for killing an intruder, the Torah is here teaching the principle of the legitimacy of self-defense.[7] The Meiri, however, is of a different view, for he quotes the *Midrash Tanḥuma,* which sees the source in the biblical exhortation to the Israelites to attack the Midianites (B), in the light of the ongoing Midianite practice of attacking them.[8] The same source is quoted by the Midrash in *Numbers Rabbah* 21.

But the question of the source or prototype aside, it is necessary to determine the parameters of the law of the thief found breaking in. What does "breaking in" include, what are the

7. See Rashi's comments to *Berakhot* 58a, and 62b, where he refers to this passage in the Torah as the source of the principle. Likewise see his comments to *Bava Kamma* 117b.

8. See Meiri's comments in his *Beit ha-Beḥirah* to *Sanhedrin* 72a, quoting the *Tanḥuma* to *Parshat Pinḥas*, chap. 3.

essential, defining characteristics of such an intruder that would carry over to aggression in general? In this matter there is a basic disagreement between Rashi and Maimonides. Rashi, in his comments to *Sanhedrin* 72b (G), is of the view that the manner of entry is the critical factor, in that if it is evident that the thief made a forced entry, breaking through a physical barrier, it can be concluded that the crime was planned, to the extent that violence would be used where necessary. Where there is such forced entry, no warning need be given the intruder prior to disabling or killing him. But where the entry occurred in a manner that would indicate an opportunistic crime, e.g., where the thief chanced upon an open door or window, and enters to steal without foresight or prior intent, we can assume that the intruder might well flee if accosted. In that case, he cannot be killed without prior warning, for he is not strictly speaking, "breaking in," according to Rashi. This latter case includes any situation where the thief is found in the open air (on the roof, backyard, etc.). Maimonides, on the other hand, defines the intruder as any thief who enters private property to steal where he knows it is likely he will find someone within.[9] It is this probability of encountering resistance that is the key—and it makes no difference whether it be indoors or out; he can be killed without warning, on the presumption that he knew, or should have known, that he would encounter resistance. According to Maimonides, therefore, the term *maḥteret* (which he would translate as "indoors") simply reflects the location where thieves are most commonly encountered.

Rabbi Moshe Feinstein examined several aspects of the law of the intruder, based on this passage in Maimonides.[10] He notes that Maimonides classifies this law in the Laws of Theft (*Hil. Geneivah*), and not in the Laws of Assault (*Hil. Gezeilah*). He concludes that Maimonides, paradoxically, applies the law of the intruder only where the thief enters as a *ganav*, i.e., where he does not intend to take things by physical force, but rather by avoiding detection. Apparently, such a thief, if actually confronted, is liable to react with deadly force because of his genuine

9. Maimonides, *M. T. Hil. Geneivah* 9:8, 12. See especially the comments of the Maggid Mishnah ad loc.

10. *Responsa Iggerot Moshe*, 2:54 (1), dated 1980.

fear. But where entry is made as a *gazlan*, i.e., where the thief is certain of his physical prowess and his ability to intimidate any opposition, then apparently Maimonides feels that there is a greater likelihood that the thief will flee if he encounters real and unexpected resistance. Thus in the latter case (the *gazlan*) warning needs be given, but not in the former (the *ganav*). The problem, however, is that elsewhere, Maimonides' position reflects the majority view in a Tosefta in *Bava Meẓia* that a thief (*ganav*) who enters intending to avoid detection and confrontation, is not to be considered homicidal, even if he is armed, and thus a guard who discovers him should stand his ground.[11]

Rabbi Feinstein resolves the two passages by noting that the latter speaks not of the owner of the premises, but rather of the guard. In such a case the thief feels that a guard will not endanger his life as would the proprietor, and consequently the thief will not resort to force against him, thus in turn the guard should stand his ground. But where two such thieves come together, giving reason to believe that they are indeed ready to attack a guard who might discover them, then he need not stay and confront them. By contrast, where two thieves come openly and brazenly (*gazlanim*), there is room to conclude that anyone who discovers them should stand his ground, in that their intent is to take by intimidation, not actual force—and if unexpectedly confronted, they will probably flee the scene. Accordingly Rabbi Feinstein suggests that a guard openly accosted by two thugs should theoretically offer resistance, either verbal or physical, thereby thwarting their attempt to intimidate him. For there is reason to believe that behind their bravado they are not as strong as they appear. Yet he concludes that this is not what the Gemara is saying, but rather that one should consider the real possibility that they will kill him for having the gall to stand up to their threats. Indeed Rabbi Feinstein points out that most authorities agree with the minority view of the Tosefta, i.e., an armed thief (*ganav*) is to be considered homicidal so that the guard may withdraw, and in addition if there are two thugs (*gazlanim*), then even if they are not armed, it is not necessary to offer resistance or stand one's ground.

On the basis of this, one can conclude that on one's own

---

11. See Maimonides, *M. T. Hil. Geneivah* 1:3; Tosefta *Bava Meẓia* 8:6.

property, if accosted in aggressive fashion by a single armed thief, or two or more who are not armed, a person should properly consider his life in danger, and act accordingly. If he cannot defend himself he should accede to their demands, but if he is capable of defending himself he may do so, even if it involves taking their lives. And this is true even where there is no explicit death threat made by the attackers. For the law of the *maḥteret* renders the intruder at the mercy of the person within. And according to the *Mekhilta*, this is true whether the intrusion be by day or night, whether the intent of the intruder be peaceful or injurious.[12]

What if a person is attacked, but it is quite clear that homicide is not a factor, in that the intent is merely to injure the innocent party? The Rosh, on the basis of the statement in the Jerusalem Talmud that "where one man injures another, and the attacker is himself injured, there is no liability," permits self-defense that causes injury to the attacker.[13] He also allows a third party to intervene, whether it be a relative coming to the defense of a family member, or even an unrelated observer who wishes to prevent the attack on an innocent man. Such action, while not required (as in the case of a life-threatening attack) is permitted, in order to safeguard the innocent victim and prevent the commission of a transgression (as Maimonides puts it, it is forbidden to raise one's hand against one's fellow, whether or not one strikes him).[14] Yet he also makes it quite clear that such a response must be proportionate; i.e., if it is not necessary to kill the assailant, then the least injurious response is called for. This is based on the Torah's uncompromising response (O) to the actions of the woman whose husband is under attack, if she acts overzealously in his defense. Similar sentiments are expressed by the thirteenth-century *Hagahot Maimoniyyot* (R. Meir ha-Kohen) and the Maharam Rothenburg.[15] So, too, R. Joshua Falk (the Sema) does not limit such preventive action to the victim or a

12. *Mekhilta de'R. Ishmael, Mishpatim* 13. The *Mekhilta de'Rashbi* is somewhat more restrictive, holding the person within responsible if circumstances would have allowed a less violent response.

13. *Piskei ha-Rosh* to *Bava Kamma* 3:13 and the comments of the *Nimmukei Yosef* ad loc. See also the *Tur H. M. Sh.A, H. M.* 421.

14. Maimonides, *M. T. Hil. Ḥovel u-Mazzik* 5:2, based on *Sanhedrin* 52a.

15. See *Responsa Or Zarua* 25, in the name of the Rosh, and *Teshuvot Maimoniyyot, Nezikin* 15. See *Encyclopedia Talmudit* 12:744.

relative but extends it to cover any fellow Jew privy to the impending act of aggression.[16]

R. Joseph of Trani, expanding on the Rosh, explains that where one man raises his hand to strike another, the intended victim may certainly strike him in anticipation—but only at that moment, not in the course of any subsequent heated argument, unless of course the attacker renews his threatening posture.[17]

From a responsum of the Radbaz, R. David b. Abu Zimrah, seen in an earlier chapter, it would appear that he would even allow the potential victim to take the life of his attacker where the attacker threatens only a limb. The responsum dealt with the question of sacrificing an ear in order to save another person, and Radbaz had answered in the negative; i.e., it is not necessary for one person to lose a limb in order to save the life of another, in that the loss of a limb could well turn out to be a threat to his own life.[18] In other words, any possible threat to one's own life takes precedence over the definite danger to the life of another person. Rabbi Israel Shepansky extrapolates from this principle that where another person is about to endanger one's limb in a manner that might subsequently turn out to be a potential threat to one's life, one need not tolerate the loss of that limb, but may instead kill the attacker.[19] He then goes one step further, to say that this principle of *rodef*, or pursuer, includes situations where the attacker intends "merely" to inflict some permanent injury on the body of his victim. He derives this from the fact that the Gemara in *Sanhedrin* (H) chooses to derive the law of the pursuer from the biblical case of the rapist. For it may be asked why such biblical sanction is necessary—can one not, by pure logic, conclude that threat to one life can be removed by killing the assailant, if necessary? It must be, says Rabbi Shepansky, that from the law of the rapist we learn the additional principle that even where the attack threatens only the physical "wholeness" of the victim by permanently disfigurement or *pegimah* (in rape, the victim is not killed but permanently scarred in body or mind), even there the assailant should properly be killed. This, of course,

16. See *Sema* to *Sh. A. H. M.* 421:25, 28.

17. *Responsa Maharit, Y. D.* 29, in the case of a messenger of the court who encounters a violent response.

18. See above pp. 116 ff.

19. See Rabbi Israel Shepansky, *Or ha-Mizraḥ*, 1970 (20), pp. 24–25.

is not the case where the injury to the innocent party is of a temporary nature, one from which the victim would in time fully recover.

Two other halakhists also took sides in this issue. Where one man attacks another, but without posing a threat to his life, and the one so attacked responds by killing his assailant, R. Solomon Luria considers him subject to the death penalty for not being more careful.[20] But as opposed to this, R. Jacob Emden tends to exonerate the intended victim, arguing that given the provocation, and the anger at being attacked, it is not proper to condemn him to death for his retaliatory action.[21]

There is one other assault that can be thwarted at the cost of the aggressor's life, and that is the situation of betrayal to alien authority (*mesirah*). Of the many crimes that a Jew might commit, the denunciation of a fellow Jew to a capricious authority was always considered of particularly heinous character. For such duplicity might lead not only to the unjust death of that one Jew, but also to the death of many of his coreligionists. For this reason, this crime was subject to the death penalty at the hands of rabbinic courts during the Middle Ages, and even later.[22] Now where it becomes known to the intended victim, or another person, that someone is about to commit an act of *mesirah*, or threatens to do so, there is a clear talmudic mandate to treat that person as a *rodef* in the fullest sense. A number of such instances are recorded in the Gemara, where several amoraim killed *mosrim* and thereby prevented their acts of betrayal.[23] And while in these instances the killing was carried out only by outstanding scholars, Maimonides' formulation of the law clearly allows the masses of the Jewish people to act in similar fashion.[24]

Before concluding this section, we can attempt to conceptualize the notion of *rodef*, at least as seen through the eyes of Maimonides. For Maimonides invokes the *rodef* principle even beyond human acts, to situations where inanimate objects qualify under the rubric of pursuer. Thus, in *Hilkhet Ḥovel u-Mazzik* (M), he postulates, based on the Gemara *Bava Kamma* 117b, that where

---

20. *Yam Shel Shelomoh* 3:26.
21. *Responsa Yaveẓ* 2:9.
22. See *Jewish Ethics and Halakhah*, vol. 1, chap. 6.
23. *Berakhot* 58a, *Bava Kamma* 117a.
24. Maimonides, *M. T. Hil. Ḥovel. u-Mazzik* 8:10–11.

a ship is in danger of sinking because it is overloaded, the offending cargo may be cast overboard because it is "like a pursuer," and the person who acts thus is not liable for restitution to the owner of the sacrificed goods. His classic interlocutor, the Ravad (M), differs sharply and asserts that the financial loss is to be shared by the owners of all the cargo. While subsequent commentators attempt to explain these respective views,[25] and take sides accordingly, it is clear that for Maimonides the principle of *rodef* extends to any threatening situation where the immediate cause of the threat is readily identifiable and can be removed.

However, it is necessary to make a careful distinction between two facets of the law of *rodef* according to Maimonides. The distinction, as first formulated by R. Ḥayyim ha-Levi Soloveichik,[26] is between the law of the pursuer (*din rodef*) and the obligation of the pursuer (*ḥiyyuv rodef*). The former occurs in all cases of pursuit not involving a conscious act by the source of the threat. In such cases, the threat is to be removed forthwith, and without establishing prior intent to kill or harm. Such cases include the unborn fetus or the cargo that threatens to capsize the ship and endanger human life. But where the source of the threat to life comes from a human possessed of a soul, then it is first necessary to establish prior intent to harm, before the principle of *rodef* can be acted on. Such a case includes a baby already born and a human aggressor at any subsequent point. Thus Maimonides accounts for the fact that once it is born, the baby, being fully human, cannot be killed to save the mother, for the baby does not actually intend the mother's death.

And so it is evident that the law of the pursuer was extended to embrace a significant spectrum of threatening behaviors, not all of them actual physical assault. Common to them all, however, was the principle that unless the aggressor is thwarted, there will follow the destruction of the life or limb of his victim or victims. In so doing, the assailant effectively abrogated his presumption of innocence, and relinquished his own right to life or limb, as

25. See Z. Kaplan, "Sefinah she-Ḥishvah le'Hishaver," *Sinai* 67 (5730): 38–42, who offers an insightful analysis of Maimonides' position.

26. *Ḥiddushei R Ḥayyim ha-Levi*, as quoted in R. Isser Zalman Melzer, *Even ha-Ezel* to *M. T. Hil. Ḥovel u-Mazzik* 8:15. See Shepansky, p. 23, and Kaplan, p. 42.

the case might be. The Halakhah, in not merely permitting, but actually requiring, a preemptive response, was demonstrating its awareness of the need to respond to violent aggression as and when needed, not merely after the fact. And if, in so doing, the principle of not substituting one life for another was to be vitiated or weakened, that was apparently an acceptable price to pay in the long-term interest of maintaining a law-abiding society.

2. SUBJECTIVE AND OBJECTIVE DETERMINATIONS OF AGGRESSION

Where there is doubt whether an act of pursuit is being committed, or there is a question as to the nature of the harm that is liable to occur (*safek rodef*), i.e., the intent of the attacker is unclear, there is a real question as to whether action may be taken against that attacker. May the decision properly be taken based on a subjective judgment, or must certain objective requirements be satisfied first?

As pointed out by Rabbi Eliyahu Ben Zimrah, the evaluation of the real intent of the attacker depends in the first place on his prior behavior and record.[27] Only thus can we account for the rather contradictory reports found in various talmudic passages on the subject of proper response to aggressive or threatening behavior. Thus R. Naḥman is quoted as saying that "men threaten much but do little,"[28] but on the other hand a number of instances are recorded where such threats were taken seriously.[29]

The Gemara in *Sanhedrin* (G) again constitutes an important source for the resolution of this question. Specifically, there is the question of *hatra'ah*, or forewarning, as it applies to the *rodef*. Normally such warning must be given a transgressor before punishment may be meted out by a court, in order to assure that the infraction was committed with full knowledge of the improper nature of the act, as well as its consequences. In the case of the *rodef*, is this warning necessary before the assailant is disabled or killed? If so, it would appear that the reason is that it is

27. Rabbi Eliyahu Z. Ben Zimrah, "Shefikhut Damim mi-Tokh Ẓorekh," *Shenaton ha-Mishpat ha-Ivri* 3–4 (5736–37): 117–153, esp. p. 127.
28. *Shevuot* 46a.
29. *Gittin* 14b, *Nedarim* 22a.

necessary to establish the real intent of the assailant beyond any reasonable doubt.

In fact, warning the assailant is required before he can be disabled, as codified by Maimonides (K). Clearly the intent of the *rodef* must be established. Must warning always be given? In (G), Rav Huna and Rav Ḥisda debate the question of a minor who pursues another with the apparent intent to do harm. Rav Huna feels that such a minor may indeed be killed, if necessary, for warning is not required for a minor. Rav Ḥisda disagrees, arguing that warning is always necessary, but in the case of a minor it cannot be given, and thus he may not be killed or disabled as a *rodef*. In discussing their differences, the Gemara—at least as understood by Rashi—brings proof for the view of Rav Huna from a Beraita that permits the killing of a pursuer even though he did not explicitly acknowledge the warning given him. Yet another Beraita is quoted in support of Rav Ḥisda, yet Rav Huna counters that as with the thief who breaks in, warning is not required. There is some question as to the precise position of Rav Huna. Rabbi Shepansky is of the view that while it is not necessary for the minor to acknowledge the warning, nonetheless even Rav Huna agrees that such warning must be given. Ben Zimrah, on the other hand, considers Rav Huna to dispense with the need for warning in this case. In any event, most subsequent authorities accepted the view that a pursuer must be forewarned, even though he be a minor, and whether or not he acknowledges the warning thus given. Such is the view of Maimonides (K), and the *Shulḥan Arukh* (P).

Yet there is a prominent minority view that sometimes dispenses with the need for warning. Thus the Sema, in commenting on this law in the *Shulḥan Arukh*, indicates that where it is not feasible, warning may be dispensed with, and "the proof is from the case of the minor who cannot discern warning, but nonetheless can be killed if in pursuit." Likewise the *Minḥat Ḥinukh*, in commenting on (O), quotes the Sema and allows the killing of a pursuer where warning is not given, for it is *safek nefashot*, i.e. a life is at stake.

Others too make certain pertinent distinctions. R. Isaac bar Sheshet (the Rivash), quoting R. Aaron ha-Levi, exempts the potential victim himself from the need to issue a warning to his assailant, for "he is in fear of his life, concerned to save himself, therefore he is not required to issue warning—instead, when he sees the attacker coming to kill him, he may act first to become the attacker himself."[30] Indeed as far as R. Aaron is concerned, this dispensation is universally accepted. Among other medieval authorities, it was the Meiri who formulated the mandate to the intended victim to act in cases of doubt. Thus he says that where the life of a woman in labor is threatened by a fetus that has partially emerged from the birth canal, she herself may dismember the fetus that is a *rodef*—even though others present are forbidden to do so because as far as they are concerned it is unclear who is threatening whom, she the baby, or the baby her. Nonetheless, insofar as she is the putative victim, she need have no such dilemma, and she may act with all necessary force to remove the threat.[31] As pointed out by Ben Zimrah, this view is based on the Jerusalem Talmud.[32]

As to an onlooker who intervenes, the Rivash indicates that while he must issue a warning, that is only if there is sufficient time prior to the attack. In other words, under normal circumstances a pursuer should be warned so as to clarify his real intent, prior to a third party taking action against him—unless such warning would cause such a delay that the life of the intended victim might be lost. But the intended victim himself need not issue such warning to ascertain the nature of the threat to his life; he may act without delay. Such a formulation would seem to allow for a significant measure of subjective judgment by the putative victim under most circumstances, and by a third party in certain limited situations, e.g., where time is of the essence. And as we have seen above, the Radbaz permits the taking of the life of an aggressor even where the threat is not to one's life per se, but merely to a limb of one's body; even there, it would appear, warning is not always required.

Earlier in this chapter, we saw the special status of an intruding thief (*ha-ba be'maḥteret*), whose life is forfeit if confronted on the premises. In Exodus (A), this dispensation is dependent on the sun not having "risen upon him," in that if the sun has

30. *Responsa Rivash* 238, in agreement with the view of Rav Huna in *Sanhedrin* that warning is not always necessary. See the note preceding.

31. Meiri to *Sanhedrin* 72b, in the name of "the sages of the generations."

32. See Ben Zimrah, p. 124, n. 34, with regard to J. T. *Sanhedrin* 8:9 and 26:3.

risen, then indeed he may not be summarily killed by his discoverer. Now the Gemara in *Sanhedrin* (F) examines these verses carefully, quoting certain contradictory tannaitic statements, and concludes that where there is any doubt about the intentions of an intruder, he may be killed. It is only where it is "as clear as day" that his intentions are peaceable (as in the case of a father intruding on the property of his son) that the intruder may not be killed. Rashi, commenting on this passage, extends the mandate to take preemptive action against all intruding strangers. Yet in a parallel passage in *Pesaḥim* 2b, the opposite conclusion seems to prevail, i.e., the intruder may be killed only where his homicidal tendencies are known, but where any doubt exists, he may not be attacked. And as explained by Rashi there, this is true of all men, not merely where the intruder is the father. Rabbi Shepansky, in discussing these passages, suggests that as a rule there is no doubt that an intruder is homicidal (as in Rava's principle, seen earlier). In such a case, no warning is necessary. But where there is genuine doubt as to the intent of the intruder, indeed warning must be given prior to taking any action.

Here again, it would appear that a distinction is to be made between the intended victim and a third party. While a third party should, by warning, clarify the intent of the assailant wherever any doubt exists, an intended victim is not under any such obligation, and may kill an intruder upon contact. And such a conclusion is supported by a careful reading of Rava's principle in *Sanhedrin*: as Rabbi Naftali Ẓvi Yehudah Berlin (the Neẓiv) notes, it should really not be necessary to introduce the principle "if a man comes to kill you, kill him first"; after all, an intruder is a *rodef*, and that by itself should suffice to take action against him. If, therefore, it is introduced, it must be to add an extra dimension to the notion of self-defense that does not exist in the conventional *rodef* dispensation, and that dimension is to kill him "first," i.e., without the delay or hesitation involved in forewarning the intruder.[33]

In summary, it would appear that an individual about to be attacked, whether in the privacy of personal property or in the public domain, is entitled to react in a preemptive manner, and moreover to do so as a result of his own subjective perception or

33. See Neẓiv, *Bimromei Sadeh, Yoma* 85, as quoted in Shepansky, p. 21.

judgment of the gravity of the situation. While it would certainly be preferred for some independent or objective determination to take place, the Halakhah recognizes that the intended victim cannot be held responsible or blameworthy for acting with immediate force. In the final analysis, it is his judgment which must be accepted. But this is not the case for a third-party witness to the intended attack, for such an outsider must perforce establish the intent of the assailant by some objective means, notably by warning the assailant and then seeing him persist in his path; only then may, nay must, he properly intercede even at the cost of the assailant's life.

Of course there is the further question posed by the potential self-endangerment of such a third party who "gets involved." As we have seen in an earlier chapter, it is a real question whether any individual is required or even permitted to endanger himself for the sake of another whose life is in danger. To say, as Maimonides does, that there is a positive commandment to stop an assailant does not mean that it is obligatory irrespective of the danger to oneself. For the majority view, including that of Maimonides, is that one is not required to endanger oneself for the sake of saving another's life. Thus again it is for the third party to make a subjective judgment as to the relative dangers posed to the life of the intended victim and to his own life if he chooses to confront the assailant.

3. CHOOSING A REASONABLE RESPONSE: INJURY OR DEATH?

Once it is determined that an act of aggression is about to be committed, the question then arises as to an appropriately violent preventive act. When may the aggressor be killed, and when merely disabled? A useful distinction may be drawn between a situation where it is a third party who intercedes aggressively and the situation where the intended victim is the one to respond with violence.

Third-Party Intervention

The early rabbinic Midrashim made it clear that where possible the response to aggression should use minimal violence. Thus the *Mekhilta De'R. Ishmael* derives from the Deuteronomic case of rape (C) that a violent response is appropriate only where there are no peaceable alternatives.[34] The reason: gratuitous violence is not only unnecessary, it is also subject to punishment. Likewise, the *Sifri* to Deuteronomy 25:12 (O) requires a graduated response, i.e., first only those limbs necessary to commit the act of aggression are to be removed, and only where this proves ineffectual may the aggressor be killed. This in turn served as the basis for the tannaitic statement, found in the Tosefta, that described the appropriate incremental response to a murderous attack: "first he cuts off one of his limbs, but if this does not stop him, he should kill him preemptively."[35]

This demand for an incremental response that seeks where possible to avoid the death of the aggressor was subsequently codified as law by Maimonides (K), the *Minḥat Ḥinukh* (O), and the *Shulḥan Arukh* (P). At the same time, however, there was some debate among the medieval halakhists as to whether such care was necessary in dealing with the threat of an intruder on the one hand, or the threat of denunciation of a fellow Jew to hostile authority on the other. Maimonides, for one, did not require it, whereas the Ashkenazi authorities (such as the Mordecai and Maharam Rothenburg) generally did.[36]

What if, in spite of this ruling, an assailant is summarily killed without any attempt at an incremental response? Can the person who acted thus be punished for his overzealous response? This question is addressed for the first time in *Sanhedrin*, in the name of R. Jonathan b. Saul (I). In his opinion, such gratuitous killing is indeed categorized as culpable homicide subject to the death penalty. His view is based on the passage in Exodus 21 that seems to assume that an aggressor does not automatically forfeit his life, but rather is subject to lesser penalties (whether financial or otherwise). Maimonides, in codifying this law (K), accepts the principle of culpability, but adds that in practice the sentence is not under normal circumstances carried out by a court of law.[37]

---

34. *Mekhilta De'R. Ishmael, Mishpatim, Nezikin* 13.

35. Tosefta *Sanhedrin* 11:10.

36. See *M. T. Hil. Geneivah* 9:7–8, *Hil. Ḥovel u-Mazzik* 8:10–11. On this point see Ben Zimrah, p. 133, n. 85.

37. Ben Zimrah is of the opinion (ibid., p. 133) that Maimonides in this passage does not differentiate between homicide committed by the intended

Such a distinction between guilt and punishment is a Maimonidean trademark: it is found as well in his insistence that while it is forbidden for a Jew to submit to idolatry, even under the pain of death, nonetheless if he does submit, he is exempted from punishment, in that he acted under duress.[38]

When It Is the Victim Who Responds

While there is no significant dissent or debate involving the appropriate and graduated response required of a third party presented with an imminent attack, there is such a controversy when it comes to self-defense by the intended victim.

The discussion revolves around two biblical incidents. The first occurs in Genesis 32, where Jacob anticipates an epochal confrontation with his estranged brother Esau, and experiences deep fear. *Genesis Rabbah* is puzzled at this fear; after all, Jacob was a man of great faith. It answers, as quoted by Rashi to Genesis 32:8, that Jacob's fear was that he might in self-defense kill Esau's cohorts in battle, an act of bloodshed which he wanted to avoid. R. Elijah Mizraḥi, in his classic commentary to Rashi, notes the fact that Jacob was not fearful of killing Esau, at least not on moral grounds. Why not? Mizraḥi answers that as for the cohorts, Jacob honestly did not know their true intent, and were he to kill them rather than injure them, he would be culpable—but as for Esau himself, his murderous intent was clear to Jacob, and on moral grounds Jacob would be within his rights to kill Esau in self-defense, without resort to inflicting a disabling injury.[39] Thus, Mizraḥi concludes, the intended victim himself may properly kill his attacker, even without any prior attempt to disable him.

The second biblical narrative occurs in the Book of Samuel (D), in the days of King David. In the internecine intrigues of the day,

victim and that by a third party. Yet a careful reading of the passage in question, especially halakhah 15, gives the clear impression that Maimonides in these laws has in mind only actions committed by a third party who comes to the aid of an intended victim. This would be a precise reflection of his understanding of R. Jonathan b. Saul, as opposed to Rashi's interpretation. On this see below.

38. See Maimonides, *M. T. Hil. Yesodei ha-Torah* 5:4: ". . . even so, if he transgresses against his will he is not given corporal punishment, and certainly not put to death by a court, even if he killed against his will [*be'ones*]".

39. Mizraḥi to Gen. 32:8, s.v. *va-yeẓer lo.*

David's lieutenant Joab got into a confrontation with Abner ben Ner, and on one occasion, Abner found himself pursued by Joab's brother Asahel. Abner attempted to dissuade his assailant, but to no avail, whereupon he turned on Asahel and stabbed him to death. Some time later, in spite of a promise to foreswear violence against each other, a vengeful Joab lured Abner to a secluded spot and killed him in cold blood—much to the consternation of King David.

In elaborating upon this narrative, the Gemara in *Sanhedrin* (J) recreates the scene in the courtroom wherein Joab is taken to task by the King, who accuses him of murdering an innocent man (Abner) who had acted in self-defense. Joab's answer is that, given his expertise with the sword, Abner could have simply injured his assailant (Asahel), without actually killing him, i.e., he could have used an incremental response. This defense by Joab was accepted, and the case against him dismissed. It would appear both from the narrative and this talmudic adumbration that even the intended victim (in this case Abner) should properly attempt to disable his attacker before resorting to the ultimate response, i.e., homicide. If this is indeed the conclusion yielded by this passage, it would stand diametrically opposed to the view of Mizraḥi, who, as we have seen, allows summary homicide under such circumstances. If so, it is necessary to clarify the relationship of these two biblical passages and the conclusions that follow from them.

Rabbi Ovadiah Yosef sets out to clarify this matter at some length.[40] In his view it is quite possible to reconcile the position of Mizraḥi with the acquittal of Joab, in that he might have been acquitted for other reasons, e.g., Joab acted on the spur of the moment, or out of ignorance of the correct law (i.e., that Abner was entitled to kill his pursuer). The fact that he was acquitted, therefore, does not in and of itself indicate that Abner acted improperly. And the fact that Abner did not attempt to justify his killing of Asahel might merely have been because he chose not to answer Joab's charge. In any case, Mizraḥi would argue that Abner was not required to adopt a graduated response, for being in danger of his life he was under extreme stress, and thus was permitted to kill Asahel.

---

40. *Responsa Yabia Omer*, vol. 4, *H.M.* 5:4.

A number of other sources tend to agree with the position of Mizraḥi. Thus the *Tur* codifies the law that a pursuer who causes damage to material goods is exempt from liability, because his life is automatically forfeit at the hands of his intended victim.[41] And others who take a similar position include the *Mishneh la-Melekh* and the Levush.[42] Among the moderns, Rabbi Samuel Alkalai goes one step further: it is entirely up to the perception of the individual who intercedes to stop the attack, whether it be the victim himself or a third party, right then and there, it being unnecessary in his view to establish what might have been the response of some hypothetical reasonable man.[43] Yet many authorities do not accept the position of Mizraḥi. What is the reason?

Rashi, in comments to the passage of R. Jonathan b. Saul in *Sanhedrin* (I), explicitly extends the principle of an incremental response to the actions of the victim himself (an extension that he repeats in *Sanhedrin* 57a). And the Tosafot, in commenting on the narrative of Jacob and Esau, indicate that Jacob's fear was that he would improperly kill his attackers, Esau included, without first disabling them as the Torah requires.[44] In other words, Tosafot too is of the opinion that the intended victim has to exercise caution in responding to his assailant. Other medieval authorities who side with Rashi include R. Meir Abulafia (the *Yad Ramah*) and Meiri.[45]

What is the basis for Rashi's position? In the first place, it is Rashi's interpretation of R. Jonathan b. Saul. But what makes him read it this way, and not as excluding the victim? There is the fact that Joab was acquitted for having killed Abner, even though the latter acted in self-defense in killing Asahel. Yet Ovadiah Yosef, as above, finds room to defend the position of Mizraḥi, further quoting the view of the *Iyyun Ya'akov* that the case is quite analogous to an intruder who may be summarily killed by the person whom he confronts within.

What is the position of Maimonides? From his formulation of these laws in the first chapter of *Hilkhot Roẓeiaḥ* (K), it would

41. *Tur H. M.* 380, 425.
42. See *Mishneh la-Melekh* to *M. T. Hil. Ḥovel u-Mazzik* 8:10.
43. Responsa Mishpetei Shmuel 93.
44. *Moshav Zekenim on the Torah* to *Vayishlaḥ*, Gen. 32:8.
45. See the *Yad Ramah* to *Sanhedrin* 49b and 57a; Meiri to *Sanhedrin* 73a.

appear that, unlike Rashi, he considers the view of R. Jonathan b. Saul to be speaking only of a third-party intervention. Thus he describes the need to limit the response to such provocation in terms of the third-person singular. And while we have seen too that Maimonides certainly favors the use of minimal force wherever possible, preferring some disabling action rather than outright homicide in the prevention of an attack, nonetheless in *Hilkhot Melakhim* (L) it would appear that he sides with Mizraḥi, when he states that an Israelite may kill an assailant and not be subject to the death penalty, even though he could have simply disabled him instead of killing him. Interestingly, Maimonides' classic contender, Ravad, takes issue with this ruling, and as prooftext quotes the case of Abner and Joab, in which Abner was ostensibly held accountable and put to death by Joab for killing Asahel without the proper effort to disable him. It would appear that Ravad identifies with the view of Rashi. Similarly in *Hilkhot Roẓeiaḥ* (K), Maimonides states that an Israelite is not executed by the court for killing an assailant when he could have injured him instead. Why does Maimonides disregard the case of Abner? One Maimonidean commentator, the *Mishneh la-Melekh*, comes to his defense, explaining that the case of Abner has nothing to do with normal cases of self-defense, in that Joab was acquitted on other grounds, i.e., he was a blood-avenger (*go'el ha-dam*) whom the Torah permits to exact retribution for the killing of his brother.[46] Thus Abner was not really subject to judicial execution, in that he acted in self-defense. Any other person who might have killed him would have been guilty of murder. Thus it is that Abner was not liable, and this would be true of all similar situations.[47] Yet Ovadiah Yosef contends that this is not quite true, in that Joab could not have been acquitted merely on the grounds that he was a blood-avenger, for Abner had not killed in error (*be'shogeg*), and thus the entire concept of blood-avenger is extraneous to this case.

Subsequently R. Jacob Reischer too examined the question, and substantially corroborated the position of Rashi, as opposed to Mizraḥi and Maimonides. A similar conclusion is arrived at by

46. For the laws of the blood-avenger, see Numbers 35 and the extensive treatment in *Encyclopedia Talmudit* 5:220–233.

47. *Mishneh la-Melekh, M. T. Hil. Ḥovel u-Mazzik* 8:10.

R. Ḥayyim Benveniste (author of the *Knesset ha-Gedolah*),[48] and R. Israel Ginzberg (author of the *Mishpatim le'Yisrael*).[49] Given this preponderance of halakhic authority, Ovadiah Yosef considers the possibility that even Mizraḥi himself does not give a blanket dispensation to all intended victims to take the life of their assailants, but instead refers only to wartime conditions. In war, death is widespread and largely uncontrolled, as was the case in the biblical narrative of the battle confrontation of Jacob and Esau. Accordingly, Mizraḥi intended merely extreme combat situations, to the exclusion of more conventional circumstances. Indeed Ovadiah Yosef finds reason to believe that such was the intent behind David's reprobation of Joab, in that it was a time of war, and Abner was entitled to act as he did, in self-defense. Malbim, in his comments to the story of Abner and Joab, appears to make the same distinction. The *Knesset ha-Gedolah* also distinguishes between peace and wartime, saying that under conditions of war, even a third party does not have to try to wound the assailant but may kill him outright, in that there are many assailants who might attack even as the present one is wounded.[50]

Rabbi Eliezer Waldenberg attempts to understand why Maimonides in (K) insists that while he is guilty of the death penalty, a man may not be executed by a court for not taking less drastic action, in apparent contradiction to R. Jonathan b. Saul.[51] R. Joseph Karo, in commenting on this passage in Maimonides, had answered that in fact this was the intent of R. Jonathan b. Saul, to say that his culpability was in theory only, i.e., death at the hands of heaven, but not judicial execution, given the defendant's circumstances at the time. Rabbi Waldenberg, however, has a different answer, namely that Maimonides understands the story of Abner to yield the conclusion that where a man acts (improperly) to kill an assailant, he can be killed with impunity by a blood-avenger of the dead man, even though a court may not kill him. A similar position is taken by the Ḥazon Ish, when he states that even though Abner killed his assailant intentionally, and was

48. See *Responsa Yabia Omer* p. 388, par. 6, who locates this view in Benveniste's *Dina de'Ḥayyei*. Ben Zimrah, on the other hand, is of the opinion that the *Knesset ha-Gedolah* agrees with Mizraḥi, but in this instance Rabbi Yosef appears the more correct.

49. Ginzberg, *Mishpatim le'Yisrael*, p. 337, no. 72.

50. *Knesset ha-Gedolah, H. M.* 388:62.

51. *Responsa Ẓiẓ Eliezer* 4:24.

therefore not really committing accidental homicide, nonetheless Joab can fairly be considered a blood-avenger, who may kill and not be held culpable, and for this reason was acquitted by the court.[52] This approach differs markedly with that of Ovadiah Yosef, in arguing that Joab was acquitted as a blood-avenger, even though Abner's original act was not punishable by a court. Hence Maimonides rules that a court may not execute for such gratuitous violence. In any case, in the view of Rabbi Waldenberg, Mizraḥi and his fellow thinkers are contradicted by the story of Abner, who was considered in error for having killed his attacker, Asahel.

Thus, according to Rabbi Waldenberg, Maimonides, far from being impugned by the story of Abner, actually finds his source in that narrative. This is indeed the same answer as given by the *Mishneh le-Melekh* in commenting on (L). But if this is the case, why does the Ravad quote the case of Abner as being in contradiction to Maimonides? Rabbi Waldenberg's novel answer is that the Ravad in this instance is not dissenting at all! By saying that the case of Abner "poses a problem for him," Ravad is merely explaining why Maimonides takes his position, i.e., Maimonides is bothered by the case of Abner and why Joab did not bring Abner before the court to face trial—thus he answers that Abner could not have been convicted or executed for his wanton homicide, and only Joab could act in a nonjudicial capacity, to carry out "justice."

Yet other halakhists for the most part do perceive Ravad as taking issue with Maimonides here. Thus R. Meir Simḥah of Dvinsk explains their differences as follows: There is a distinction between a pursuer who is acting in legitimate fashion (as was Asahel), and one who is not. The former requires of his intended victim that he act with care and attempt to merely disable him, whereas the latter permits summary execution by the intended victim.[53] Maimonides in this law is speaking of the latter instance (i.e., wanton violence), whereas the case of Abner is of the former kind, i.e., Asahel was within his rights (it was a military exercise initiated by Abner himself at which the confrontation occurred), so Abner should have taken care not to kill him, and thus was

52. *Ḥazon Ish, H. M.* 17:1.
53. *Or Sameaḥ, M. T. Hil. Roẓeiaḥ* 1:13.

subject to the death penalty. Ravad, on the other hand, rejects this distinction, and thus finds the case of Abner to be in contradiction to Maimonides. Having said this, R. Meir Simḥah can then explain that Mizraḥi is speaking only of cases where the pursuer is without any legal justification (notably Esau), not where some justification exists.

Ovadiah Yosef has some difficulties with this view of R. Meir Simḥah. Specifically it appears to be contradicted by a talmudic comment regarding the scriptural narrative of Pinḥas and Zimri (Numbers 25:1–9). Zimri, it will be recalled, was in the process of an act of flagrant violation of the law of sexual idolatry. Pinḥas pursues and kills him on the spot. The Gemara *Sanhedrin* 82a posits that had Pinḥas inquired first, he would have been told not to intercede as he did, and that furthermore, "had Zimri ceased his act and turned on Pinḥas and killed him, Zimri would have been innocent of murder, in that Pinḥas was a *rodef*, i.e., a murderous assailant." This, says Ovadiah Yosef, contradicts R. Meir Simḥah, in that Pinḥas was certainly entitled to act as he did, subsequently receiving the divine endorsement for acting correctly. If so, Zimri would have no right to kill his assailant Pinḥas without first deflecting the attack by other means, either by ceasing his provocation or by wounding Pinḥas. Thus it must be, he says, that it makes no difference whether the assailant is justified or not; in neither case is the intended victim held guilty. In addition, says Ovadiah Yosef, it is difficult to maintain that Abner had acted correctly in the first place in initiating such perilous military exercises—indeed the Jerusalem Talmud (*Sotah* 1:8) takes him to task for needlessly endangering the lives of the young men involved, and as a result considers his death at the hands of Joab as divine punishment for such irresponsibility.

Yet on the first point of Ovadiah Yosef, R. Meir Simḥah himself disposes of the objection from the story of Pinḥas, explaining that while the Gemara does say that Zimri would have been acquitted had he killed Pinḥas, nonetheless it remains true that he would have been found guilty had he killed a third party who jumped to the rescue of Pinḥas, without first attempting to wound him, in that such a third party would be under an obligation to save an endangered person. Thus, he concludes, where an intended victim turns on his attacker and is about to kill him, the attacker, who is now in danger of his life, may indeed kill his pursuer, and be held blameless, in that he acted in self-defense at that point.

This last point is a matter of debate between Rashi and the Meiri. Rashi, commenting on the Gemara *Sanhedrin* 82b, explains that if the building collapses on a thief breaking in, there is no obligation to save his life, in that "the moment he breaks in he has forfeited his life." In other words, for the duration of the hostile activity, and until it is completed, he retains the status of a *rodef,* and he may be attacked with impunity—or left to die.[54] Meiri, however, differs, saying that if it is certain that the thief remains alive, there is every obligation to save him, in that at that moment he no longer poses a threat to others' lives, thus his life is no longer forfeit. According to the Meiri, therefore, we judge each stage of the episode separately, and if at one point the pursuer becomes the pursued, then he is accorded the status of an intended victim who may defend himself at all costs. This, apparently, is not the case according to Rashi. Amongst later authorities, R. Moshe Margaliyot takes the side of Rashi.[55] And R. Meir Simḥah would be fully compatible with Meiri, i.e., whosoever is threatened at any given time may act to save himself, irrespective of what may have transpired prior to that point.[56]

In reviewing these sources, it is readily apparent that on the question of the intended victim wounding, as opposed to killing, his assailant, there is a significant divide among the halakhic decisors. As to what the majority view might be, whether in support of Rashi's restrictive position or the more permissive stance of Mizraḥi, it is difficult to tell. Ovadiah Yosef feels that Rashi represents a majority, whereas Ben Zimrah ascribes the majority to the support of Mizraḥi. In any case, there is significant dissent on either side.[57]

A similar picture emerges with situations where it is quite clear that there is no intended threat to the life of a victim, i.e., but the

54. See similarly *Ḥiddushei R. Ḥayyim ha-Levi, M. T. Hil. Roẓeiaḥ* 1:13, and *Encyclopedia Talmudit* 12:698, listing this and the opposing views of the *Responsa Minḥat Bikkurim* and *Ḥasdei David,* which are in more in line with Meiri.

55. *Mar'eh Panim* to J. T. *Sanhedrin* 8:9. See Ben Zimrah, pp. 134–135.

56. On this issue see Rabbi Asher Levitan, *ha-Pardes* 27, no. 3 (1952): 1–3, with reference to a possible Maimonidean position as well.

57. See too Rabbi Y. D. Moseson, *ha-Pardes* 16, no. 11 (1942): 16–18; and Rabbi Eliyahu Ḥazon, *ha-Pardes* 37, no. 2 (1963): 14–16.

assailant is about to hurt his victim. What kind of response is permitted in such instances?

The Rosh, in a passage which we saw earlier,[58] refers to the Torah's prescription for the woman who injures her husband's assailant (O), and concludes that her indiscretion occurred in that she did not first attempt a less drastic response to her husband's situation. She, like her husband himself, is required to make every effort to respond to violence in an effective manner, yet with as little violence as possible.[59] This requirement is echoed by the Meiri, including possibly a requirement that one attempt to withdraw from the scene if at all possible.[60]

Yet here, too, others disagree so as to permit, or at least not to punish, disproportionate violence in response to harmful attack. Thus R. Jacob Weil (the Mahariv) permits an entirely subjective judgment on the part of the victim, given his state of intense arousal at being attacked.[61] And R. Solomon Luria similarly holds blameless anyone who uses gratuitous violence in response to an unwarranted attack on his person, given the heat of the moment and the fear of renewed attack unless completely effective action is taken.[62] This dispensation was subsequently extended by R. David ha-Levi, known as the *Taz*, to include the relatives of a person under attack, on the principle that "a relative is like oneself."[63] These authorities, it would appear, like the Rosh, do permit disproportionate violence in deflecting an attack designed to injure.

4. *WHERE THE THREAT IS UNINTENTIONAL, OR INDIRECT*

Thus far we have seen that the principle of *rodef* permits a violent preventive response, whether by the intended victim or a bystander, where there is a deliberate threat to the life or limb of a person. We can now take up the related question as to the appropriate response in cases where the threat is not consciously

58. See above p. 146.
59. *Piskei ha-Rosh, Bava Kamma* 3:13; *Sh.A. H. M.* 421:13.
60. Meiri to *Bava Kamma* 28a. See Ben Zimrah, p. 138.
61. *Responsa Mahariv* 26.
62. *Yam Shel Shelomoh, Bava Kamma* 3:26.
63. *Taz* to *Sh.A. H. M.* 421:13.

intended by the one who poses the threat—or alternatively, where the threat is indirect.

Maimonides in (K) codified the law that a fetus may be destroyed to save the life of the mother, as long as its head has not emerged. The reason he offers is that "the fetus is considered a pursuer [*rodef*] threatening her life." But once the head has emerged, the baby may not be sacrificed. We saw earlier that this dichotomy is to be accounted for with the distinction between *din rodef* and *ḥiyyuv rodef*, so that once birth has occurred, the status of *rodef* must be preceded by intent to kill or maim. From this formulation of Maimonides it would appear that where humans are involved he requires intent to harm as an integral part of the law of pursuit. In other words, if the "assailant" is impelled by circumstances beyond his control (i.e., *ones*), his life or limb is not forfeit.

What is the basis for this? For it would appear that Maimonides is contradicted by the Gemara in *Sanhedrin* (G) that in the name of Rav Huna considers a minor in pursuit to be a *rodef*; i.e., it is permitted to kill such a minor, even though he technically has no culpable intent (*deiah*). In other words, homicidal intent is not necessary to qualify as a *rodef*.

The question, it would appear, is whether the principle of *rodef* is essentially one of punishment or rather one of rescue. If the reason it is permitted to kill an assailant is because justice requires his punishment, then criminal intent is clearly needed before punishment can figure. But if it is purely rescue of a threatened person, then no such intent is needed. In this regard, Rabbi Ezekiel Landau, the *Noda bi-Yehudah*, points out that this talmudic passage seems to be divided. While Rav Huna considers a minor to be a *rodef*, Rav Ḥisda disagrees, arguing that because the minor cannot properly acknowledge the warning that must be given to him, he cannot be killed.[64] His reasoning, says the *Noda bi-Yehudah*, is that the action is indeed one of punishment. Of these two views, the majority of halakhic authorities side with the definition of rescue as the operative concept in *rodef*.[65] But

64. *Responsa Noda bi-Yehudah, Mahadura Tinyana H. M.* 60. See Shepansky, p. 28.

65. As the author of the *Simḥat ha-Ḥag* points out, the very idea that if possible a *rodef* should be injured rather than killed indicates that it is not a question of punishment, but rather of saving the intended victim, that is uppermost. See *Simḥat ha-Ḥag* 17, and Ben Zimrah, p. 131.

for Maimonides, it would follow, there is the element of punishment too.[66] This understanding of Maimonides can be said to follow from his view of the source of the principle of *rodef*; i.e. as we saw earlier, in his view it is the punishment meted out to the woman who attacks her husband's adversary, and not the rape of the betrothed woman, where the essential concern is rescue of the victim.[67]

Once this principle is established, it follows that even where the assailant acts merely to set up a chain of events intended to lead to the death of his victim, he is to be considered a *rodef*. The technical term here is *gramma*, or indirect action leading to a desired effect. Whereas one who causes a death by such indirect means cannot be executed by a court of law,[68] nonetheless it would appear that the law of *rodef* permits violent interception, if necessary by killing, if that is necessary to save the endangered life in question.[69] Such is the view of the Rivash, the *Hagahot Maimoniyyot*, and more recently, R. Meir Simḥah, the Aḥi'ezer, and Rabbi Unterman.[70]

Both these considerations come together in another set of circumstances that have engendered some interesting differences of opinion. What if a group of people finds itself at the mercy of a murderous band (or, for that matter, government), and they are threatened with death unless they hand over one of their group demanded by their enemy. Can that person be considered a threat to their lives, and if so, does the law of the pursuer apply to him, so that they can sacrifice him? In this case, he neither intends to kill them nor is he the one to kill them himself, yet is he a *rodef* in fact?

The Tosefta *Terumot* 7:23 deals with precisely such a situation, and requires that they all be killed rather than hand over a single soul, unless the demand was for a specific named individual,

66. A similar formulation of Maimonides' position is found in the extensive analysis of Rabbi Yosef Rekhes, "Birur be'din Rodef," *Noam* 13 (1970): 259–268, esp. p. 264.

67. For an analysis of this line of thinking, see Rabbi Meir Blumenfeld, *Moriah*, 2, no. 11 (1971): 21–25.

68. See Maimonides, *M. T. Hil. Roẓeiaḥ* 2:1–5.

69. See Unterman, *Shevet mi-Yehudah*, pp. 355–359, who quotes the *Or Sameaḥ* and several other authorities.

70. *Responsa Rivash* 338; *Hagahot Maimoniyyot, Hil. Roẓeiaḥ* 1, *Or Sameaḥ* ah loc.; *Responsa Aḥi'ezer, E. H.* 19; *Shevet mi-Yehudah*, p. 95.

such as Sheba ben Bikhri, then they may hand him over. In a similar passage in the Jerusalem Talmud, Resh Lakish and R. Yoḥanan differ over this question: regarding the individual who is requested by the adversary, is it necessary that he be guilty of a capital crime, or is that irrelevant, in order to save the lives of the rest of the group? Resh Lakish requires that he in fact be guilty, whereas R. Yoḥanan says that he may be handed over "even if he is not guilty of a capital crime."[71] Of these two views, Maimonides accepts that of Resh Lakish, whereas others, such as the Meiri and Rabbeinu Nissim, accept the view of R. Yoḥanan.[72] Maimonides, in taking this position as opposed to his usual adoption of the view of R. Yoḥanan, appears to be consistent with the notion of *ḥiyyuv rodef*, i.e., there must be an element of punishment present, not simply rescue of threatened lives. Rema, in his comments to the *Shulḥan Arukh*, favors the latter view.[73]

This question became a subject of some debate in this century too. In a rather far-reaching analysis, R. Avraham Yeshayahu Karelitz, popularly known as the Ḥazon Ish, interpreted the view of Resh Lakish to permit handing over an individual, even if according to the laws of the Torah the individual had not committed a capital crime at all.[74] In other words, even the strict view permits his sacrifice as a *rodef* just as long as the enemy has justification by its own laws for his execution. What is the reason? The Ḥazon Ish explains that "it is incumbent upon us to limit as much as possible the loss of Jewish lives." He draws an analogy to the following situation: a man sees a missile about to hit a group of people; if he is able to deflect it he should do so, even if he knows that in so doing he will kill a single individual in the new path he has caused. The reason: we do sacrifice one if that is necessary to save many, and even if the one so sacrificed was not in danger in the first place. In any case, the Ḥazon Ish concludes,

---

71. J. T. *Terumot* 8:10. For a lengthy discussion of this passage and its implicatins, see A. Enker, "Reẓaḥ mi-Tokh Hekhreḥ," *Shenaton ha-Mishpat ha-Ivri* 2 (5735): 161 ff. See also *Jewish Ethics and Halakhah*, vol. 1, chap. 5, pp. 140 ff.

72. Maimonides, *M. T. Hil. Yesodei ha-Torah* 5:5; Meiri to *Sanhedrin*, p. 271; Ran to Alfasi, *Yoma* 82a.

73. *Rema* to *Sh.A. Y. D.* 157:2.

74. *Ḥazon Ish* to *Sanhedrin* 5. See also his comments to *M. T. Yesodei ha-Torah* 5:5.

against Maimonides, that the view of R. Yoḥanan is to be accepted.

Rabbi Unterman takes sharp issue with this view.[75] In the first place he argues that the reason the group may not hand over an individual who had not been named by the besiegers is that if they do so, they themselves become *rodfim*, i.e., they now pose a threat to his life, in that they single him out for death, albeit indirectly in that they do not kill him with their own hands. It is only once he is named by the opposing camp that they can no longer be considered *rodfim*. Furthermore, he says, it is incorrect to consider the named individual a *rodef* just because he was singled out by the enemy for their own reasons; it is necessary in addition that he indeed be guilty of a capital crime according to the Torah. For it is inconceivable to him that Maimonides would, in accepting the view of Resh Lakish, permit the sacrifice of a person whose guilt is not established, other than by some capricious wish of an inhuman enemy.[76] In a postscript, Rabbi Unterman records an incident in nineteenth-century Poland wherein a group of some twenty young Jewish men, on their way to assist a neighboring community suffering a pogrom, were handed over to the authorities by their fellow Jews on the point of death, and immediately executed. For many years thereafter, the inhabitants of the village where they had been handed over were universally ostracized for their act of betrayal.

These two opposing perspectives on this issue are encountered and reflected in several heartrending responsa delivered to Jews during the Nazi Holocaust.

One responsum, adopting a position similar to that of the Ḥazon Ish, was authored by R. Shimon Efrati. The case involved a group of Jews hiding in an underground bunker from the Gestapo. During a search that required absolute silence, a baby in the group started to cry. One of the men covered the baby's face, and as a result the baby suffocated to death. The question

75. *Shevet mi-Yehudah*, pp. 98 ff.

76. In editing the second edition of Rabbi Unterman's work, Rabbi Avraham Bick comes to the defense of the Ḥazon Ish, explaining that the latter's meaning is not to allow such handing over where there is no reasonable justification whatsoever for their demands, but rather that their demand is in accordance with their accepted law or practice, albeit not in accord with the laws of the Torah. Under this circumstance, he argues, that life can be sacrificed in order to save the lives of the others. See *Shevet mi-Yehudah*, p. 100.

arose: did he act in accordance with the Halakhah?[77] Rabbi Efrati examined the question and found two grounds on which to rule that the act had been within permissible parameters. In the first place he points out that the Tosefta in *Terumot* records the view of R. Judah that where the person who poses the threat to the group is part of the endangered group anyway, and therefore will die in any case if he is not given over, then he should be given over whether or not he is guilty of a capital offense. In the case of the baby, says Rabbi Efrati, were the group to be discovered, the baby would die with the rest of the group, thus he can be "given over" to death to save the others. In this, the baby could be said to be like Sheba ben Bikhri, in that both would die in any case. The second principle leading to Rabbi Efrati's conclusion is that of *rodef*. For he considers the baby in this instance to be a *rodef*, albeit one without intent to harm. He argues that even according to the view that where there is no intent to harm the *rodef* may not be killed, nonetheless where the *rodef* himself will die in any case, he may be killed, if that will save the others. Like the Ḥazon Ish, therefore, his position was that the one posing the threat to the life of the group may be sacrificed, even if there is no prior guilt associated with that person.

On the other hand, we encounter a responsum by Rabbi Efraim Oshry, rabbi of the Kovno ghetto.[78] The Germans at one point ordered the Jewish leadership of the community to issue a limited number of life-saving identity cards to members of the ghetto. The leadership carried out the order, and thereby relegated the rest of the ghetto to almost certain death. In the process a number of workers resorted to irregular means to acquire these cards, thereby ensuring that other Jews would be killed. Were these people acting in accordance with the Halakhah? Was it permitted to effectively "hand over" some Jews to save others, or to sacrifice another to save oneself? Rabbi Oshry, in answering these questions in the negative, effectively followed a line of reasoning similar to that taken by Rabbi Unterman. Firstly, he considers Maimonides' acceptance of Resh Lakish's view to be normative and correct, i.e., we may not hand over another person to certain

---

77. *Responsa mi-Gei ha-Harigah*, p. 23. Also see, in detail, Irving Rosenbaum, *The Holocaust and the Halakhah*, pp. 31 ff., and Enker, "Rezaḥ mi-Tokh Hekhreḥ," p. 172.

78. *Kuntres me-Emek ha-Bakha*, no. 1.

death unless that person is guilty of a capital crime, like Sheba ben Bikhri. This is certainly the case where the enemy has not itself named the ones to be handed over to their death, but leaves that determination to the Jews themselves. Hence the Kovno leadership had no right to make such a determination at all.[79] Secondly, he disagrees with the actions of those who saved themselves and thereby condemned others to death. While the Shakh permits an individual Jew to take whatever steps he can to avoid being put to death, even though he knows that another Jew will face death as a result,[80] that is only where the death of the other Jew is not inevitable. This was not the case in the Kovno ghetto. In this sense, those who improperly took the cards for themselves were the direct cause of the deaths of others. This, he argues, is true even according to the Yad Avraham who permitted a person to save himself, but not if it would lead automatically to the endangerment of another.[81]

On another occasion, Rabbi Zvi Hirsch Meisels was confronted with a situation in Auschwitz in which the father of a boy condemned to death was able to save his son by substituting another boy in his stead. The father's question was simple: could he sacrifice one to save another?[82] In responding, Rabbi Meisels could find no clearcut precedent that would permit such substitution, given the fact that the one so substituted was certain to die, as is clear from the position of the Yad Avraham. Further complicating the situation was the fact that it was not a case of a person saving himself at the expense of another, but as a father saving his son, he was acting as a third party. As a result, the father did not attempt to save the boy.

SUMMARY AND CONCLUSIONS

In retrospect, it becomes clear that the law of self-defense in the Halakhah is a multifaceted one. While in general Jewish law

79. Rabbi Oshry himself quotes the view of Rabbi Avraham Shapiro, Chief Rabbi of Kovno at the time, that did in fact advocate cooperation with the Germans, and to "take upon themselves the responsibility of doing whatever needs to be done to save a part of the community." See Rosenbaum, p. 31.

80. Shakh to *Sh.A. H. M.* 163:11.

81. *Yad Avraham* to *Sh.A. Y. D.* 157.

82. *Responsa Mekaddeshei Hashem* 1:3. On this responsum, see Ben Zimrah, pp. 146–147; Rosenbaum, pp. 3–5 and 157–158.

insists on due process and judicial review, it does also permit, under the rubric of the law of *rodef*, nonjudicial violence in the prevention of physical attack on an innocent person. Maimonides enumerates this among the positive obligations incumbent on a Jew. What are the sources for the law of *rodef*? We have seen that they are several: not to stand idly by the blood of our fellow (Lev. 19:16); the Deuteronomic law of the obligation to save by any means a betrothed woman threatened with rape; the sanction to disable a woman who poses a mortal threat to a man fighting with her husband (Deut. 25:11); and most particularly the law in Exodus 22 that permits the killing of a thief found breaking in.

This last principle involves a number of disputes: what is its source (Rashi: it is its own source, vs. Meiri: from the attack on the Midianites); what is included in this law (Rashi: only instances of forced entry, vs. Maimonides: only cases where people would be expected to be encountered within); is an armed thief who enters private property assumed to be homicidal (two views in the Tosefta, as quoted by Rabbi Feinstein). Rabbi Feinstein does consider him homicidal, allowing the intended victim to act accordingly. The same, he says, is true of two or more thieves, even if they be not armed.

Where the intended victim is clearly not in danger of his life, but merely subject to grievous injury, several views are recorded. The Rosh permits, without requiring, a violent response, by either the intended victim or his relative, as long as the least injurious response necessary to stop the attack is used. And the Sema extends such a mandate to any bystander. R. Joseph of Trani likewise permits an immediate preemptive attack to provocation, and the Rivash, it would appear, goes so far as to permit a homicidal response by the intended victim so as to stop a threat to any of his limbs or organs from which he would not be able to fully recover in time. Yet most authorities avoid permitting such an extreme response, leaving the question rather as to whether a homicidal response is indeed a capital crime (as R. Solomon Luria argues) or is forgivable given the provocation (the view of R. Jacob Emden).

We also saw that Maimonides extends the principle of *rodef* to all sources that present a threat to life, animate or inanimate alike. Thus he classifies a ship's cargo as a pursuer if it poses a peril to the ship. As clarified by R. Ḥayyim Soloveichik, such a threat does not need to be intended or conscious to be disposed of in any way possible. It is only when a human, already born, poses a threat that prior intent to harm is necessary before a violent response is mandated.

How do we determine whether a grievous attack is about to occur? Must certain objective criteria be satisfied before preemptive violence is permitted? While it is important to consider the past record of an assailant (if it is available), the major clarification of this issue revolves around the issue of warning (or *hatra'ah*). Based on a dispute between Rav Huna and Rav Ḥisda in *Sanhedrin*, most authorities accept the view that even a pursuer must be forewarned, to establish his intent to harm—and it makes no difference whether the pursuer is a minor or acknowledges the warning given him. A significant minority (notably the Sema, Rivash, and Minḥat Ḥinukh) dissents, and takes the position that under extreme circumstances, where the life of a victim is at stake, warning may be dispensed with.

Certainly, it would appear, the intended victim himself may dispense with warning, and act with all necessary haste (and violence) to dispel the perceived threat. This view, formulated by the Rivash, R. Aaron ha-Kohen, and Meiri, seems to have been an accepted one. Where the attack is made by an intruder onto private property, the upshot of the talmudic discussion is to dispense with the need for warning, in that it can be assumed that such an intruder will resort to violence, if necessary. Even so, a third party who comes across such a situation should if at all possible issue a warning prior to acting with force.

Thus we can conclude that the intended victim himself can make a subjective judgment on the spur of the moment and act accordingly, without having to ascertain by some objective means (e.g., forewarning) the true intent of the attacker. But a third party cannot intervene without warning, under most circumstances, thereby to establish some objective, reasonable, standard of violent intent.

What kind of violent response is permitted? It is clear from the early rabbinic midrashim that a third party must use only the minimum level of violence available to him to thwart the attacker's intent. If he kills when he need not have, he is himself subject to the death penalty. This too is the point of a pivotal statement in

Sanhedrin by R. Jonathan b. Saul, and codified by the major authorities.

The situation is more complicated, however, when it is the intended victim himself who acts with gratuitous violence, killing the attacker when mere injury would have sufficed. A major debate on this issue seems to have divided the halakhists over the course of generations, based on their respective interpretations of two key scriptural passages, in Genesis 32 (where Jacob confronts Esau) and the Second Book of Samuel (the events surrounding the death of Abner). R. Elijah Mizraḥi derives from the former that the intended victim may indeed resort to homicide even where he can otherwise disable his attacker, and be held guiltless. Others who support his view are the *Tur*, *Mishneh la-Melekh*, Levush, and R. Samuel Alkalai. Yet others are opposed to this dispensation, notably Rashi (in extending the principle of R. Jonathan b. Saul to cover the actions of the intended victim as well), Tosafot, R. Meir Abulafia, and Meiri. The position of Maimonides is somewhat more complex, but (unlike the Ravad) he seems to side with Mizraḥi's viewpoint. Among later authorities, a majority agrees with Rashi, and holds an intended victim liable for gratuitous violence. And Ovadiah Yosef considers the possibility that even Mizraḥi only permits homicide under wartime conditions, where extreme responses are sometimes called for.

Maimonides' ruling that gratuitous violence by an Israelite is not actually punishable by a court leads a number of twentieth-century halakhists to consider his precise understanding of the passage in Samuel detailing the death of Abner, who had acted in self-defense and killed Asahel. Was Abner's death at the hands of Asahel's brother Joab legitimate or not? Rabbi Eliezer Waldenberg considers the latter to have acted as a blood-avenger. Ovadiah Yosef, however, disputes this. Rabbi Meir Simḥah of Dvinsk makes a pertinent distinction between a pursuer who acts with the permission of the court (such as Asahel or Pinḥas) and one who does not act properly (such as Esau). The former cannot be summarily killed, but the latter, according to Maimonides, may.

Yet another difference of opinion surfaces in the context of a pursuer turned pursued: may he defend himself by killing his intended victim who is now his attacker? Rashi seems to feel that he may not, in that once he became a pursuer he forfeited his legal rights to self-defense. Meiri, however, disagrees, and argues that whatever preceded is extraneous to his present predicament, and the fact is that he is now in danger of his life, thus he may defend himself at all costs. Again these respective views are encountered in later times (the *Mareh Panim* vs. the *Or Sameaḥ*).

Similar differences surface when we consider the appropriate response to nonmurderous assault. The Rosh joins the Meiri in requiring a minimalist reaction wherever possible, but R. Jacob Weil, R. Solomon Luria, and the Taz hold a murderous response blameless, even in the absence of a murderous assault, given the exigencies and intense emotions of the moment.

The final question is that of unintended or indirect threat to life. To qualify as a *rodef*, must a person intend the harm of the one so endangered? Maimonides, it would appear, answers in the positive, and thus codifies the law that once the fetus has emerged, it is a person who intends no harm, and thus cannot be killed. In so doing, Maimonides seems to be following the view of Rav Ḥisda in *Sanhedrin*, which disqualifies all minors from the category of *rodef*. But others, indeed a majority, follow the view of Rav Huna: intent is not required, hence a minor can be considered a *rodef*. As explained by the *Noda bi-Yehudah*, what is at stake here is whether we consider the principle of *rodef* to be intended primarily as rescue or as punishment. If it is punishment, then punishment requires intent to harm on the part of the perpetrator; if it is rescue, then intent is irrelevant, just so long as the threatened life or limb can be saved.

Similar considerations lead to the related issue of indirect cause: where a person sets up a chain of events leading to the death of his intended victim, a majority of halakhic authorities consider him a *rodef* in the fullest sense, even though a court cannot execute him on technical grounds. This principle in turn leads to the question of the surrender of one person to save a threatened group; can that person be classified as a pursuer, and be handed over to be killed, in that his life poses a threat to theirs? The Tosefta records several views, and in the Jerusalem Talmud Resh Lakish and R. Yoḥanan differ: the former requires that the named individual be guilty of a capital crime, while the latter does not. Here again, the authorities divide on the issue: Maimonides for once sides with Resh Lakish (consistently, it would appear, in requiring a measure of guilt as part of the criteria of *rodef*), whereas Meiri, the Ran, and R. Moses Isserles prefer the view of R. Yoḥanan.

In this century, two parallel views emerged. The Ḥazon Ish, agreeing with R. Yoḥanan, sees no point in requiring guilt or intent to harm; more important is the calculus of saving lives. Thus an individual is to be sacrificed under such circumstances. Rabbi Unterman dissents sharply, siding with Resh Lakish and Maimonides, against R. Yoḥanan. Similar divisions are encountered in the Holocaust responsa literature: Rabbi Efrati found reason to endorse the sacrifice of a baby posing a threat to the survival of a group of adults in hiding, absent all intent to harm on its part, while Rabbi Oshry (and on another occasion Rabbi Meisels) cannot give his assent to those who saved some Jews (themselves included) and thereby condemned others to almost certain death.

What are the conclusions of all this, in the context of the questions with which we started this chapter? In the first place, it is clear that a violent response to the threat of violence is permitted, and often required. Secondly, the intended victim is entitled to make a subjective judgment as to the intent of the assailant, especially where there is more than one such pursuer. But bystanders must be more careful in attempting to establish objective intent before they may act. Thirdly, while it is clear that a third party must without question attempt to intervene if at all possible without taking the attacker's life, there is a genuine difference of opinion as to whether that requirement is germane to the intended victim himself; i.e., while it is certainly preferable to avoid homicide, if he kills anyway there are opposing views as to any guilt he might bear.

Accordingly, if the man in question did not aim to kill he would be exonerated by most halakhic authorities. If he did aim to kill, even though he was quite capable at that moment of merely disabling his attackers, then many halakhic authorities would hold him liable on charges of manslaughter, while others would dissent.

5

Child Custody

Introduction

In recent years a number of changes have taken place in child custody awards in many American courtrooms. Whereas in the past it was the mother who invariably got custody upon termination of a marriage, more and more states have moved in the direction of legislation that would allow fathers to sue successfully for such guardianship.

Divorced fathers have for many years felt that theirs is an uphill battle against a system which tends by and large to place children with their mothers after divorce, on the unwritten assumption that mothers are as a rule more fit to play the role of homemaker, caretaker, and nurturer of the young. Such men claim that the stereotype of the father who does not wish to care for his youngsters, and in any case is incapable of doing so, unfairly discriminates against fathers who do care deeply about their children and could well provide a positive home environment for them subsequent to divorce. As a result, rather than get involved with expensive court battles, many fathers agree to give up custody to their ex-wives, and consequently experience a whole range of frustrations in maintaining any semblance of a close relationship with their children subsequent to divorce. This in turn is one cause for some fathers to be delinquent in living up to their child-support commitments.

Yet, on the other hand, a good number of women now claim that it is they who are being discriminated against. Perhaps as a result of changing perceptions of the role of men and women in our society, both in the family and beyond it, many women now feel that the pendulum has swung the other way; i.e., that women are unfairly losing custody of their children to their ex-husbands. This, they argue, is because courts, claiming to act in the best interest of the child, penalize mothers whether they stay home to care for the child (hence are not as able to provide for the child financially) or go out to work to secure financial independence (in which case the judge may decide that the children are better off with the father and his second wife, who will stay home to care for them).

In confronting these arguments, American courts have tried to balance conflicting considerations involving the respective rights of the parents, while at the same time pursuing what is referred to as the welfare of the child. And different courts have come to opposing conclusions as to the relative weight to be attached to the "rights" of each of these parties.

Nonetheless the resolution of the issue of child custody depends in no small measure on larger social attitudes and values, relative to the changing roles of men and women, evolving patterns of family life, and questions as to the willingness of individuals to conform to widely held social expectations. One rather extreme example should suffice to illustrate: some courts have gone so far as to award custody to homosexual or lesbian parents, in spite of the opposition of the other parent, and notwithstanding the open practice of such deviant behavior in the custodial house. Clearly such decisions are a function of changing societal attitudes towards homosexuality.

For Jewish law too the issues involved in custody cases involve a delicate balance of competing considerations. The sanctity of the family, the safety and education of the young, adherence to traditional patterns of behavior, and the fair treatment of parents as individuals before the law, are all high priorities of the Halakhah. And while much of the problem is not new or radically different from early precedent as encountered in talmudic literature, nonetheless contemporary halakhists must be cognizant of certain changing realities in the modern world.

Thus it is that child custody represents a fascinating case

history, as yet unfinished, on the response of Jewish law to a challenge that is both old and new, demanding careful consideration and sensitivity on a case-by-case basis.

The Question

A couple agrees to be divorced after thirteen years of marriage. They have three children: a girl aged eleven, a boy aged nine, and a boy aged five. Each parent claims custody of the children, asserting that he or she can benefit the children in one way or another. The father argues for custody on the grounds that he can be a role model for his sons, and provide a better education and material benefits for all the children. The mother maintains that she can spend more time with them than can their father, who is away all day, and that the children need a mother's love and guidance at this stage of their development. Two of the children themselves do have a preference: the girl to be with her mother, and the nine-year-old boy to be with his father. The mother plans to be remarried within the year. To whom should custody of the children, together or separately, be awarded?

This case presents the following questions:

1. What are the classic halakhic principles that determine custody of children in case of divorce or death, where the child is under the age of six?
2. What if the child is of school-going age (i.e., six or over) but not yet an adult (i.e., a girl not yet twelve or a boy not yet thirteen years old)?
3. To what extent does the Halakhah allow for overriding such formal rules as there might be, so as to implement broader considerations or principles? What might such principles be?

Sources

A. Eruvin 82a

Said Rav Assi, a minor till the age of six is automatically included in the domicile [*eruv*] of his mother. How is this possible, for we have learned that only a minor who cannot be without his mother is included in her *eruv*, but not otherwise?

Similarly we have learned that a minor must be educated regarding the *sukkah* as soon as he can be without his mother. The school of Yannai is of the opinion that this occurs when a child no longer needs his mother to wipe him. R. Simon b. Lakish says that it is when he no longer cries out for her if he wakes up at night. At what age is this generally? At approximately four or five years. [If so, how does Rav Assi assert that even a six year old is automatically included in his mother's *eruv?*]

R. Joshua b. Idi answers as follows: Rav Assi describes a case where the mother had consciously included her six-year-old in her *eruv* extending southward, while the father did likewise to the north, in which case even a six-year-old follows the mother, for we presume that it is better for him to be with his mother [*be'ẓavta de'imei niḥa lei*].

B. Ketuvot 65b

R. Ulla taught . . . : Even though the sages have said that a man is not obligated to feed his sons and daughters all the time that they are minors, he is required to feed them while they are young minors, till the age of six. As Rav Assi said (A), a minor till the age of six is automatically included in the domicile [*eruv*] of his mother. (*Rashi:* if for instance the mother extended her Sabbath domicile northward, while the father's was southward, the child can be taken to the mother's northerly domicile, but not to the father's, for the child is still in need of his mother, and the sages gave her custody. Thus till the age of six he is in need of his mother, and just as a husband must feed his wife, so must he feed his son while in her custody.)

C. Ketuvot 102b

Mishnah: A man who marries and agrees to feed his wife's daughter [from an earlier marriage] for a period of five years is obligated accordingly. If [their marriage ends and] she marries another who agrees to feed her daughter for five years, he too is obligated. And the former husband cannot say that he will feed her only so long as she lives with him for he is obligated to provide her food wherever her mother resides.

Gemara: Said Rav Ḥisda, this means that a daughter [whether she be a minor or already an adult] always stays with her mother. (*Rashi:* in that the phrase is "wherever her mother resides," and not "to the house of her brothers." This teaches us the law that a daughter is to grow up under the custody of her mother, and if the daughter is provided food by her brothers they are to provide it at the home of her mother, for she is not required to live with them.)

But how can you say that the Mishnah means to include a daughter who is already an adult—is it not possible that it is only while she is a minor [till she turns twelve years old] that it is assumed that she remains in her mother's custody? For that would be consistent with the case that is on record in the following Beraita: "If a man should die and be survived by a minor son, and his widow requests that the child remain with her, while others who inherit his estate wish to have the boy in their custody, the boy is to remain with his mother, and not with the legatees of the estate. For it once happened that the legatees who had custody of a minor killed him prior to Pesaḥ."

[The answer is that if a daughter does not remain in her mother's custody even if in the interim she becomes an adult] it would have said in the Mishnah "wherever she resides." By stating "wherever her mother resides," we must conclude that the daughter stays with her mother, irrespective of whether she is an adult or a minor (*Rashi:* for the Mishnah makes it quite clear [*milta pesikta*] and thereby implies that every daughter is to stay with her mother).

D. Ketuvot 59b

If a mother takes an oath not to breast-feed her child, the house of Shammai say her oath is upheld, while the house of Hillel say she is forced to breast-feed nonetheless. If she is divorced she is not forced to breast-feed, unless the infant recognizes her already, in which case she is required to feed him at a salary, so that his health not be endangered.

E. Oẓar ha-Geonim, Ketuvot 434

[Where the mother is deceased, and the father abroad, and the respective grandparents fight over custody,] it is apparent that we should act to benefit the child himself; if the child is accustomed to one grandparent, and familiar with him, and happy when with him, he should take custody, for it is with him that the child will find peace of mind.

F. F. Toldot Adam ve'Ḥavah 23:3 (197a)

"A daughter always stays with her mother" . . . but the geonim have written that while this is the case with a daughter, a son stays with his father even under the age of six. For the father can force the mother to permit the son to stay with him, in that just as the mother teaches her daughter the way of young women, so should the father teach his son what is appropriate for him.

G. Responsa of Isaac of Molena, Kiryat Sefer 44:557

I found the following responsum of the geonim, of blessed memory: If a divorced woman with custody of her small children wishes to remarry . . . and their father says that it is unacceptable to him that his children should be raised in the house of another man, his view is upheld, [and he may assume custody of the children] as long as he has a mother or sister to care for them, for it is women who care for small children.

H. Joseph Gaon, Ginzei Kedem 3:62 (6)

The leaders of the Academy conclude that as a matter of course a daughter should remain with her mother until the mother remarries, at which time, if her father opposes her being raised in the house of another man, the following applies: if the father has a female relative such as a mother or sister, then the daughter is sent to live with one of them; but if not, then the daughter remains with her mother until the daughter herself marries. . . . Thus it has been communicated in the name of R. Amram Gaon of Maḥsa and R. Ẓemaḥ Gaon of Pumpedita.

I. Responsa of Rabbeinu Joseph Ibn Migash 71

[A man divorces his wife, leaving his four-year-old daughter with her, while himself moving to another town, without providing support for the girl. After two years he returns and requests custody, claiming that his father had undertaken to support his daughter in his absence. The mother, in turn, claims continued custody, citing his negligence, and the girl's wish to remain with her.]

Such a question was already posed to R. Sherira Gaon, who indicated that the girl should stay with her mother, not father. The Baal Halakhot Gedolot came to the same conclusion. Without doubt they perceive the statement that the daughter always stays with her mother (C) to apply to custody disputes between a father and mother. And even though my own view is that this statement speaks specifically of a case where the father is deceased, and the dispute is between the mother and the brothers of the girl, nonetheless as a practical matter I would follow the footsteps and reasoning of these geonim. Thus because it is evident to us that the interests of the daughter are served by staying with her mother who can care for her better than her father, teaching her and showing her what girls need to know . . . the father should not be permitted to remove the daughter from her mother. This is especially true in that the mother undertakes to provide an appropriate wedding and dowry, whereas the father, who comes and goes, is unreliable.

J. Maimonides, M. T. Hil. Ishut 12:14–15

Just as a man is obligated to feed his wife, so is he obligated to feed his sons and daughters who are minors, till the age of six. From that point and on he feeds them till they are adults, by reason of rabbinic decree. If he is unwilling, he is urged, publicly denounced, and excoriated. . . . But he is not forced to feed them if they are over the age of six.

That is true only if he has no financial means, or it is unclear if he is in a position to give charity. But if he has the assets, such that he can give charity in sufficient degree to cover their needs, then the money is taken against his will, as with a charity, to feed them till they become adult.

K. Maimonides, M. T. Hil. Ishut 21:16–18

A divorced mother is not obligated to breast-feed, but if she is willing to do so, her ex-husband should pay her [as a wetnurse would be paid]. And if she refuses to breast-feed, the ex-husband should take custody and care for the child. But this is only if the infant does not yet recognize her; if he does recognize her, even if he be blind, he is not removed from his mother, for that would pose a danger to the infant. Thus she is forced to breast-feed, as a paid service, till he is twenty-four months of age.

A divorced woman is not entitled to support [by her ex-husband], even though she is breast-feeding her son. But the ex-husband must provide additional payments for those things which the child needs, such as clothing, food and drink, or bathing ointments. But if she is pregnant she receives nothing. If she weans the boy at his proper time, and she wishes to keep her son with her, he is not to be removed from her custody until he has completed his sixth year. (*Ravad:* It makes no sense to separate a father from his son until he is six; after all, the father is obligated to teach him Torah from the age of four and five, so how can he teach him while he is growing up amongst women?) During that time the father is forced to provide his food while he is in the mother's custody.

After the sixth year, the father is entitled to claim that he will provide sustenance only if the boy is in his custody, but not in her custody. A daughter remains in her mother's custody at all times, even past the age of six.

How so? As long as the father has the means to give charity he must provide for his daughter according to his ability, even against his will, feeding her while she is with her mother. And even if the mother remarries, if the daughter remains with her the father must feed her as a charitable act. . . . And if the mother, after weaning, wishes not to have custody of the children, whether male or female, that is her right, and she may give them to their father or to the care of the community if there is no father, for them to be cared for.

L. Maimonides, M. T. Hil. Ishut 23:17

If a man marries and agrees to feed his wife's daughter for a specified number of years, he is obligated accordingly. If they then divorce within that time, and she remarries, with her new husband agreeing to feed her daughter for a specified time, the original husband may not declare that he will only feed her if she lives under his roof, for he is obligated to provide her food wherever she dwells with her mother. Furthermore the two husbands are not to share the cost of her food; rather the one should provide all her food while the other provides the financial equivalent of her food.

M. Responsa of Rashba, Attributed to Naḥmanides, no. 38
[Where the father dies] the daughter, whether a minor or an adult, should stay with her mother, even if the mother remarries, so that the mother can train the daughter, teaching her the ways of women, to avoid immoral behavior. But a son is more correctly placed with male relatives, to train and teach him the ways of men, more effectively than his mother could, for the sons raised by their widowed mothers follow strange paths. . . . and what we learn from the Beraita (C) is that where the boy is not a minor, or even where he is a minor but there is no reason to suspect that his relatives will attack him, he should be placed in their custody, and not that of the mother. As a rule [in matters of custody] it is necessary that the rabbinical court examine each case very carefully to determine what is in the best interests of the orphaned children, for the court is the "father of orphans" to seek out their best interests.

N. Responsa of Rosh 82:2
You ask regarding a man who has quarreled with [and separated from] his wife, but does not want to divorce her, and the wife too no longer wishes to live with him because he is an inveterate gambler. They have a son under the age of six, and both father and mother desire custody of the boy. With whom is the law in agreement? It is my view that the father gets custody. For while according to Rav Ḥisda (C) a daughter always stays with her mother, and some authorities say that this is even if her father is still alive, this is only because the mother can spend more time with her in the house than her working father can, and her mother supervises and teaches her modesty and the ways of women. But in the case of a son, the father must teach him Torah, and in order to educate him to the commandments, he must be living with him.

O. Shulḥan Arukh, Even ha-Ezer 82:7
After a child is properly weaned, if the divorced mother requests custody we do not remove the child until it has completed its

sixth year, during which time the father is required to provide its food. After the sixth year, the father can say that he will not provide food unless the child is with him. A daughter always stays with her mother, even after the age of six. And so if the father is in a position to give charity, monies are taken from him, even against his will, to feed her while she is in her mother's household. This remains so even if the mother remarries . . .

Rema: But this is true only if in the opinion of the court it is good for the daughter to remain with her mother. But if it appears to them that it is better for her to be in the house of her father, the mother cannot force the daughter to remain with her. And if the mother should die, the grandmother cannot insist that the children be with her.

Discussion

1. CUSTODIAL PRINCIPLES FOR CHILDREN UNDER AGE SIX

Prior to Weaning

From the discussion in *Eruvin* 82a (A), it is quite clear that the talmudic tradition assumes that in the first years of life, an infant has a primary need for his or her mother, more than for any other individual. Thus this Gemara speaks in terms of "a minor who cannot be without his mother," or of one who "cries out for his mother when he wakes up at night," and of an infant for whom "it is better for him to be with his mother." And while, as we shall see, there is some disagreement among the amoraim as to when these needs are no longer present, all are agreed that they are real at least till the age of two.

On the other hand, the Gemara in *Ketuvot* 59b (D) establishes the principle whereby a divorced mother is not required to breast-feed her child out of maternal duty—as long as another woman can be hired by the father to perform this task. For breast-feeding is defined as a marital obligation that ceases with divorce, whereas the paternal duty to provide sustenance remains intact even following divorce. But this principle is overruled in cases where the infant's well-being is threatened, as where the infant recognizes or yearns for the mother, hence the mother is obligated to continue until the infant is properly weaned, usually at the age of twenty-four months.

As the Tosefta puts it, a woman is the primary caretaker of her child, and certainly during the first twenty-four months of life, until the infant is weaned, her child-rearing responsibilities should take priority, if need be to the exclusion of other activities or employment.[1] This principle was accepted by subsequent authorities, including the Rashba, Radbaz, and R. Samuel de Medini (known as the Maharashdam).[2]

Maimonides in particular codified this law, making it quite clear (K) that parents are to act in the best interests of their infant, which usually means that the child is to remain in close physical proximity to his or her mother. Thus he rules that if she were to stop breast-feeding and thereby compromise her child's well-being, she is forced (albeit at a salary) to continue, unless another woman can be contracted to act in her place without negative effects upon the child.

A parallel ruling from the geonic period (E) (i.e., the ninth through the eleventh century) involved an infant (the term used in the responsum is *tinok*) where the mother had died, the father was abroad, and each set of grandparents petitioned for custody. The gaon in this case determined custody on the basis of the best interests of the child, specifically by giving consideration to where the child felt more comfortable, contented, and tranquil, in addition to the more objective criteria of material substance and ability to care for basic needs.

In another case presented to the Radbaz,[3] the mother of an infant had died, and the child was placed in the care of the mother's mother, whereas the father petitioned for custody citing his paternal rights. Radbaz ruled in this case that if indeed the maternal grandmother can provide superior loving care for the infant, the father is to be denied custody, unless he remarries and his new wife can provide the needed home environment for the child. Here too, the Radbaz invokes the right and duty of the court to consider only the best interest of the child in determining custody.

But as a rule in cases of divorce, all things being equal, it appears clear that the Halakhah would consider the place of a child under the age of two, whether male or female, to be with the mother.

---

1. Tosefta *Niddah* 2:4. For a general review of halakhic and secular approaches to custody, see the insightful article of Dr. Sylvan Schaeffer, "Child Custody: Halakhah and the Secular Approach," *Journal of Halakhah and Contemporary Society* 6 (Fall 1983): 33–45.

2. *Responsa Rashba* 7:492; *Responsa Radbaz* 1:429; *Responsa Maharashdam, E.H.* 123—on which see below.

3. *Responsa Radbaz* 123.

Subsequent to Weaning

Once the child has passed the twenty-four-month stage, and until the end of his sixth year, other principles come into play. A major source of discussion is the passage in *Eruvin* 82a (A), where Rav Assi expresses the view that until the age of six a child naturally gravitates toward his or her mother, and is therefore presumed to be incorporated in her legal actions. Thus if each parent establishes a separate Shabbat *eruv* (enlarging their respective domiciles) for themselves and the child, that child will be considered included in the *eruv* of the mother, and not in the one established by the father. The reason that he offers for such maternal priority is his belief that "it is better for him to be with his mother." In addition, the Gemara establishes (A) that younger children aged four or five are certainly included with the mother, even without her consciously including them—their dependence on her (whether for daily care or emotional security) being all the more obvious.

Once this principle was established, it was echoed in other contexts. Thus Ulla, quoting Rav Assi, extrapolates in *Ketuvot* 65b (B) that even though the Torah does not require a father to support his children till they reach adulthood, nonetheless he is obligated till they are six years of age.[4] Rashi, commenting on this passage, makes it clear that this applies equally where the child is no longer with the father and lives with the mother, for till that age "the child is still in need of his mother, hence she has custody."

Accordingly, Maimonides (K) rules that if she so wishes the mother is entitled to custody of her son till the age of six, and

4. An analysis of the halakhic principles involved in child support is beyond the scope of this chapter. For a detailed discussion of the material obligations of a father to provide food, clothing, shelter, and education for his children, see Rabbi Gideon Perel, "Ḥovat ha-Av li-Yeladav," *Torah she-be-Al Peh* (5730) 12: 152–160. In the Talmud (*Ketuvot* 49b), by decree of the town of Usha, a father is obliged to provide support till his children reach puberty, but over the age of six this cannot be enforced beyond moral exhortation. For a discussion of paternal responsibilities as decreed and updated by the Israeli Chief Rabbinate in light of modern socioeconomic realities, see Freiman in *Sinai* 14 (1943): 254 ff., as well as Z. Warhaftig, "li-Mekorot ha-Ḥovah li-Mezonot Yeladim," *Teḥumin* 1 (5740): 255–272. See also R. Moshe Feinstein, *Iggerot Moshe*, *E.H.* 1:106, *Y.D.* 1:143, extending the father's obligation to the point that the children are capable of supporting themselves.

custody of her daughter even beyond that age. He further echoes Rashi, and says (J) that until the child reaches six the father is forced to provide support even though the child no longer lives with him. And in a printed responsum of Maimonides involving a divorced mother who claimed that her estranged husband should continue to provide for their child while in her custody, he likewise ruled in favor of the mother.[5] Such a position seems to be based on the view of Rabbeinu Joseph Ibn Migash who, quoting several geonic sources and precedents (I), denied a divorced father's request, upon returning from an extended absence, to take over custody of his four-year-old daughter from her mother.[6] This ruling was subsequently accepted by R. Joseph Karo (O).

Yet this opinion was far from unanimous, at least as far as male children were concerned. The discussion in *Eruvin* (A) itself records the views of Yannai and R. Simon b. Lakish that a minor can be without his mother at least a year prior to the sixth year, depending on the maturity of a given child.[7] And from the period of the geonim, there is preserved an anonymous view (F) whereby a father can indeed insist on gaining custody of his son even prior to the boy reaching the age of six, in that the father can claim the need to teach his son those things that are appropriate for him to learn at that tender age.

And whereas Maimonides delineated the dividing line for custody of male children at age six, his view was emphatically rejected by his resident critic, Ravad. The latter, in his gloss (K) to this passage in Maimonides, remarks that Maimonides makes little sense, in that a father is obliged to teach his son Torah starting at the age of four or five, an obligation that can be properly discharged only if he has custody of the boy from that age. Clearly Ravad reflects the view of the geonim quoted earlier. Yet a third view is found in a responsum of the Rosh (N) and one by R. Simon b. Ẓemaḥ Duran (Tashbaẓ), both of whom awarded custody of a

5. *Responsa of Maimonides*, ed. Blau, no. 367.

6. *Responsa Ri Ibn Migash* 71.

7. See the most comprehensive essay by Eliav Shoḥatman, "le-Mahutam shel Klalei Halakhah be-Sugyat Haḥzakat Yeladim," *Shenaton ha-Mishpat ha-Ivri*, 5:285–320, especially p. 293, n. 35. This quotes the responsum of Maharam Rothenburg, ed. Klein, 4:203, that accepts the notion that already at the age of four or five he is no longer in need of his mother's presence.

boy under the age of six to his father. It would appear that these authorities both favor the father's claim for custody any time after the youngster reaches the age of two.[8] Interestingly enough, the *Tur* implicitly rejects the Rosh's (i.e., his father's) position and sides instead with Maimonides.[9] Significantly, the *Tur* quotes the concurring view of R. Meir Abulafia, who in turn had invoked an anonymous geonic opinion that the mother retains custody of such a child till six, whether she be divorced or widowed.

What is the basis of this three-way disagreement? Following the Maggid Mishnah it would appear that Maimonides feels that because most boys are introduced to consistent textual study at the age of six, and not before,[10] prior to that point it is not necessary for the father to have the constant supervision that custody provides. Those general principles of faith and practice that are to be taught during the earlier years can be accomplished simply by regular visitations. Yet the Ravad begs to differ: it is his view that the obligation devolving upon the father to teach his son Torah at the age of four or five,[11] no matter how "general," cannot be effectively carried out when the boy is "growing up among the women." Apparently the Ravad believes that the basics to be conveyed are more than theoretical formulations, they are rather such as to require constant reinforcement and consistent paternal teaching. The Rosh and the Tashbaẓ, it would appear, consider the son's place to be with his father as soon as he has been weaned, for a father is needed not only to teach him Torah in the formal sense, but in addition, as the Rosh puts it, "to educate him to the commandments" (*le'lamdo torah u-le'ḥankho le'miẓvot*).

What if by awarding sole custody to the mother, the father will be substantially prevented from communicating religious teach-

8. *Responsa Tashbaẓ* 1:40 and *Responsa Mabit* 1:165, in referring to and explicating this responsum. See Rabbi H. D. Gulevsky, "Ba'ayot al Ba'alut ha-Yeladim," *Sefer Kevod ha-Rav*, pp. 110–111, and a similar view in *Mishneh La-Melekh* to *M.T. Hil. Ishut* 21:17.

9. See *Tur E.H.* 82:7, and the comments of the *Drishah* ad loc.

10. This is reflected in Maimonides' statement in *M.T. Hil. Talmud Torah* 2:2, based on *Ketuvot* 50a, that prior to the age of six or seven a child is not to be brought to the study hall, depending on his physical maturity.

11. In the fifth chapter of the *Ethics of the Fathers* we find the statement that at the age of five a child is to be taught Scripture (*ben ḥamesh le-mikra*). See the *Kesef Mishnah* to *M.T. Hil. Talmud Torah* 2:2.

ings to his five-year-old son? In a case involving a divorced custodial mother who wished to relocate to a distant city, the *Noda bi-Yehudah*, quoting Maimonides, ruled that the father should then take custody.[12] And in modern times, a rabbinical court in Israel ruled that where the mother effectively negates the religious education attempted by the father during occasional visitations, she can be deprived of custody on such grounds.[13]

Precisely such a case came before Rabbi Eliezer Waldenberg, as described in a responsum of his published in 1985.[14] The case involved the disputed custody of two boys, aged four and seven, wherein the mother had proven unfaithful to her husband, stopped taking proper care of the children, and in numerous ways stood opposed to their ongoing religious education and observant way of life. Rabbi Waldenberg ruled that the father should indeed assume custody of the younger boy (putting aside for the moment the older one). He does so on the strength of the Ravad's position that advances the age of "transfer" to the father at approximately four—not to speak of the even earlier age mandated by the Rosh. He further quotes the Maharit, as well as the Maharashdam and the *Noda bi-Yehudah*, who explain that even Maimonides would agree to such paternal custody where the mother intentionally frustrates the father's religious and educational responsibilities (as would be the case if she moved to another town). Thus Rabbi Waldenberg concludes that in this case, as a result of her behavior and impact upon the children, the father cannot effectively carry out his paternal duties as long as the children are under her roof, hence she must forfeit custody. This is not to say, however, that under other circumstances Rabbi Waldenberg would award custody of a four-year-old to the father. For in the next responsum he clearly accepts the position of Maimonides, ratified by the *Shulḥan Arukh*, that the correct age at which custody as a rule passes to the father is indeed at six years.[15]

An area of significant debate is encountered in cases where the

---

12. *Responsa Noda bi-Yehudah, Mahadura Tinyana* 89.

13. See Shoḥatman, p. 295, n. 11, quoting the Jerusalem rabbinical court. On the question of consideration of the religiosity of either parent in determining a custody award, see Shoḥatman, pp. 316–319, and below.

14. *Responsa Ẓiẓ Eliezer* 15:50.

15. Ibid. 15:51.

father has died, leaving a child between the ages of two and six. Here the key text is a Beraita quoted in *Ketuvot* 102b (C), stating that in such an instance the child is to remain with his mother, and not with relatives of the deceased father who have inherited the rest of the estate.[16] The reason offered is that those relatives are liable to harm the youngster (possibly so as to prevent him from inheriting his share of his father's estate at some future time), as once happened when such a youth was killed by his custodial relatives. The problem is that none of the major codifiers (Maimonides included) quote this ruling. In point of fact, where such specific concerns of safety are not present (i.e., where the boy is old enough to defend himself if attacked), the Rashba explicitly rules in favor of the paternal relatives—against the mother.[17] What is the reason? The Tashbaẓ explains that it is because as a rule male relatives can educate the child in ways generally not available to the mother.[18]

Likewise reflecting this view, in a case where a widowed mother of two small boys wishes to relocate to another city, and the paternal grandfather opposes such a move on the grounds that he wishes to ensure their proper education, R. Moses of Trani ruled in the sixteenth century that the grandfather can indeed prevent her leaving with the children (or, alternatively, can assume custody if she leaves). The reason he offers is that where there is no father present, the grandfather assumes all responsibility to educate the child. Thus, he writes, if the child is already six, even Maimonides would agree to the request of the grandfather; if he is only four or five years old, then according to the Ravad the paternal obligation passes to the grandfather, whose custodial claim may prevail over that of the mother.[19]

---

16. The laws of inheritance that come into play here are somewhat complex. A comprehensive description is found in Maimonides' *M.T. Hil. Naḥalot*, chap. 1, in which it is made clear that the wife does not inherit her husband's estate, which should pass to the male and then female children (and their descendants), followed by the deceased husband's father and brothers. As to orphans who are minors, their affairs are to be handled by an appointed *apotropos* (guardian) until such time as they are of an age sufficient to assume responsibility for their own affairs. See *M.T. Hil. Naḥalot*, chap. 11.

17. This is a position that is echoed by subsequent halakhists, including the *Responsa Ramah* 290, *Or Zarua* 1:746, *Responsa Mabit* 1:165, and other sources found in Shoḥatman, n. 51.

18. *Responsa Tashbaẓ* 2:216, 292; *Responsa Radbaz* 1:429.

19. *Responsa Mabit* 1:165.

And in yet another case, where a widow wished to retain custody of her three sons, aged two, three, and six, expending the inheritance that had accrued to the children upon the death of their father, whereas the brothers of her deceased husband contested such custody, requesting that the children be brought up their homes, Rabbi Yomtov Ẓahalon ruled in favor of the brothers. He explained that unless the mother was prepared to support the children from her own funds, the paternal uncles could assume custody and thereby assure the financial as well as educational well-being of the children.[20]

What of the Beraita in *Ketuvot* (C) that seems to favor maternal custody? Ẓahalon answers that Maimonides understands the Mishnah (and R. Ḥisda) to differ with the Beraita, and to hold that maternal custody takes precedence only in cases of divorce; but where the father is deceased, the mother does not get automatic custody, for custody will depend on other factors, including considerations as to where the children will be the more secure, comfortable, or liable to benefit from the positive role modeling that would result from living with male relatives of good character. In other words, says Ẓahalon, Maimonides considers the Beraita in *Ketuvot* (C) to be non-normative, and not accepted by subsequent halakhists, and thus he can dispense with its provisos, and allow the orphaned children to be in the custody of the father's relatives. Accordingly, Rabbi Ḥayyim Dubber Gulevsky rules that a court can properly remove children from their widowed mother's custody in order to enable them to live with financial security in proximity to their late father's assets. Certainly this is the case where the mother agrees to relinquish custody to her husband's relatives.[21]

Yet others do differ. Thus R. Moses Alshikh rules definitively that the mother does retain custody, even where the paternal relatives pose no danger to the child's life whatsoever. For in a case brought before him, in which the father had died, and the mother wished to take her minor son to live in the Holy Land with her father, while the paternal grandmother wished to exercise the custodial right of a paternal relative, Alshikh ruled in favor of the mother, in that the grandmother was not capable of educating

---

20. *Responsa Maharit Ẓahalon* 1:16, 2:232.
21. Gulevsky (see above at n. 8), p. 114.

the boy, whereas the maternal grandfather in the land of Israel could. And he adds that even the Ravad would agree in this case, insofar as his stated concern was for the proper Torah education of the child at this tender age.[22] Nonetheless this remained a minority view.

2. WHEN THE CHILD IS BETWEEN SIX AND PUBERTY

At this point it is necessary to examine the rules involving male and female children separately.

Male Children Aged Six to Twelve

From the foregoing discussion it is apparent that all authorities would agree that once a boy has reached an age where he can benefit significantly from regular Torah textual study, i.e., six years of age and above, he should in fact be placed with his father. Yet even here there are competing considerations that come into play. Thus in the sixteenth century we find recorded in the writings of R. Isaac of Molena a responsum preserved from the geonic period (G) in which constraints are placed upon a divorced father, denying him custody of his son (where the divorced mother is about to remarry) unless there is some female relative of the father who can adequately care for the youngster in question. In other words, the father by himself is deemed inadequate to the task of raising a minor child, in the absence of an appropriate maternal or nurturing female figure. And more specifically, the responsum, in referring to the father's mother or sister, excludes from this role the father's second wife, if in the interim he has remarried. This exclusion reflects a talmudic assumption that there is a likely tension between stepmothers and stepchildren. For the Gemara in *Berakhot* and *Yevamot* sees an allusion to such strains in the scriptural verse "thy sons and thy daughters shall be given to another people."[23]

A similar ambiguity is encountered in Maimonides' formulation of this principle. He states (K) that a father may properly refuse to

22. See *Responsa Alshikh* 38.

23. Deut. 28:32, as interpreted in *Berakhot* 56a, *Yevamot* 63b. See below, p. 199 for further discussion of this point.

support his son over the age of six if the boy remains in the mother's custody. This can be read to imply that if the mother is prepared to forgo such child-support, she may indeed retain full charge of the youngster even at that stage. A number of later halakhists understood Maimonides in precisely this way, including Mahari ben Lev, Alshikh, and R. Isaac of Molena.[24] And on this basis Alshikh ruled that where the father is deceased, and the son is over the age of six, the mother and her relatives can insist on retaining custody as long as they are prepared to forgo all child support from the father's relatives.[25] But others understand Maimonides differently. Thus R. Moses of Trani (himself orphaned at a young age, to be raised by an uncle who was also his primary teacher)[26] interprets him as referring only to the case where the father has freely elected to leave his son with the mother, in which case he may say that he is absolved of the need to provide any and all support.[27] He points to the immediately preceding statement of Maimonides in which he states that "he is not to be removed from her custody until he has completed his sixth year" (K), i.e., prior to the seventh year he is not to be removed, but thereafter he is to be removed by the father. And R. Moses b. Isaac Lima (the *Ḥelkat Meḥokek*) strenuously opposes the position of the Alshikh and would not grant custody of a son to his mother beyond the age of six.[28] In addition, as we saw earlier,[29] the *Noda bi-Yehudah* awards custody of a boy under six years of age to the father (again on educational grounds), where the mother wishes to move permanently to another town. Finally Rabbi Waldenberg too takes a restrictive view of this Maimonidean passage, quoting R. Moses Trani and *Ḥelkat Meḥokek* approvingly, to allow the father to assume custody of a seven-year-old against the wishes of the mother.[30] He adds furthermore that were the boy to express a clear preference to stay with his mother,

24. *Responsa Mahari ben Lev* 1:12, 74; *Responsa Alshikh* 38; *Responsa Isaac of Molena*, recorded in Abraham David, *Kiryat Sefer* 44 (5729): 557. See Shoḥatman, n. 68, as well as R. Gulevsky, *Sefer Kevod ha-Rav*, pp. 127 ff.

25. Alshikh, loc. cit.

26. See *Encyclopaedia Judaica*, s.v. "Trani, Moses b. Joseph."

27. *Responsa Mabit* 1:165.

28. *Ḥelkat Meḥokek, Sh.A. E.H.* 82:7 (9). See Gulevsky, op. cit., p. 127.

29. Above, p. 192 .

30. *Responsa Ẓiẓ Eliezer* 15:50.

the father would thereby be absolved of any responsibility to support him.

But how does the former interpretation of Maimonides square with the immediately preceding statement of Maimonides (K) that a boy is not to be forcibly removed from the custody of his mother until his sixth year, which implies that from that point and on he *is* to be removed at the father's insistence? R. Isaac of Molena answers that the critical purpose of transferring the boy to his father is that of furthering his formal education, so that if that education is accomplished by sending him to an appropriate teacher or school, it is no longer necessary for the father to take custody. On the contrary, as the Gemara *Berakhot* 17a records, it is the custom for mothers, not fathers, to bring small children for their study lessons.[31] Thus where the mother can reliably ensure the appropriate education (to be paid for by the father, insofar as imparting Torah to the child is ultimately *his* responsibility),[32] the boy can well remain with her, with the father making his regular visitations to supplement that education, albeit without his having to provide the boy's sustenance, as Maimonides explains. On the basis of this, Molena rules in a case before him[33] that where the father is deceased and the mother with custody of a six-year-old boy wishes to remarry (and the new husband is prepared to educate the boy), the paternal relatives are to be denied their petition for custody of the youngster. After all, he says, the father himself would be denied custody under such circumstances, whereas the mother's claim would be upheld.

As opposed to all of this, Trani and those in his camp would argue that a father's responsibility to educate his son is more than just a question of textual or intellectual pursuits, for like the mother-daughter relationship, it involves the father functioning as a role model, confidant, as well as primary purveyor of personal values and marketable skills. In their view, these desid-

31. For a discussion of the parameters of a mother's obligation to impart, or at least provide the framework for, the Torah education of her children, relative to the role of a father, see Rabbi Y. M. Charlop, "ha-Av ve'ha-Aim be'Ḥinukh ha-Banim ve'ha-Banot," *Or ha-Mizraḥ* 18 (5729): 71

32. See Maimonides, *M.T. Hil. Talmud Torah* 1:6–7; *Hagahot Maimoniyyot, Hil. Talmud Torah* 1:1; Rema, *Y.D.* 145:4.

33. See *Kiryat Sefer* ad loc.

erata cannot be disposed of without strong ongoing paternal supervision, necessitating the father's physical custody.

In the twentieth century, in a number of rulings, several additional considerations were added, in support of the contention that custody of a son over age six can, under certain circumstances, be entrusted to his mother. Thus Rabbi Ben Ẓion Uziel writes that when a boy is over the age of six he is not to be forcibly removed from his mother, insofar as there is a presumed bond between them that would make such separation particularly difficult for a mother.[34] He then quotes Maimonides' *Guide of the Perplexed*, which speaks of the special maternal bonding that occurs in the animal world, a product of the so-called imaginative faculty common to all animate life, and extrapolates this principle to human mothers as well.[35]

Likewise, an Israeli rabbinical court introduced a novel twist in interpreting the Ravad. In its opinion, Ravad requires paternal custody *only* for sons between the ages of four and six, but not beyond that age, in that during this interim period the child is too young for the schooling to be gained in an educational institution in lieu of his father's teaching him. Thus he is in need of his father's custody when under six. But once he can be schooled in an academic setting, he can indeed spend the balance of his time in his mother's custody, insofar as the time spent in parental supervision is largely limited to taking care of his basic physical needs.[36]

A further responsum is that of Rabbi Ovadiah Hadaya,[37] in which he argues that the spouse who initiates divorce proceedings is at a disadvantage when it comes to child custody, insofar as the one responsible for breaking up the home should not be rewarded with custody. This is true whether it is the husband or wife who is responsible for the breakup, leaving the other spouse emotionally distraught or vulnerable, and not to be further penalized by the loss of custody over the children.

34. *Responsa Mishpetei Uziel, E.H.* 91.

35. *Guide of the Perplexed* 3:48. For a more detailed discussion of Maimonides' and ha-Halevi's respective positions on this point, and animal mental processes, see my "Speaking of Man and Beast," *Judaism* 28, no. 2 (Spring 1979): 169–176.

36. See Shoḥatman, n. 73, discussing a case before a rabbinical appeals court, in a decision handed down in 1964.

37. *Responsa Yaskil Avdi*, vol 2, *E.H.* 2.

Furthermore, where the father is clearly incapable (for health or other reasons) of caring for his son, the boy is indeed entrusted to the care of the mother, even beyond the age of six. Such a conclusion is based on the opinion of R. Judah b. ha-Rosh and the Ritva, and has been subsequently confirmed by the Israeli rabbinical courts.[38]

But on the other hand, Rabbi Waldenberg does award custody of a boy to his remarried father in a case where the father, having initially agreed to the mother's custody, then requested custody upon the boy's reaching the age of six.[39] His reasoning is as follows: one can assume that the initial agreement was intended to conform to the conventional custodial arrangements by which a boy is to live with his father after the age of six. But, he says, even if this was not the case, the father is still entitled to change his mind and assume custody as per the usually determined arrangements, i.e., at the age of six. Precedent for this argument is found in the Mabit, who, as we shall see,[40] in very similar terms grants a mother custody of her daughter after having given it up.

It is thus apparent that the question of custody of minor boys is a complex one, not simply following a set formula, i.e., for fathers to be awarded custody. A number of other factors enter into the analysis, so that in effect there are a number of scenarios in which a mother could well retain custody of a son beyond the conventional age of six.

Daughters Over the Age of Six

The Mishnah in *Ketuvot* (C) posits the law that a husband who undertakes to provide for the daughter of his wife is required to furnish such support "wherever her mother resides." Commenting on this Mishnah, Rav Ḥisda in the Gemara (C) concludes that an unmarried daughter, whether minor or adult, is to remain with her mother, for were this not the case, the Mishnah would instead have required the support to be furnished to the daughter's place of residence, i.e., it would have said "wherever she resides." This statement of Rav Ḥisda consequently became piv-

38. *Responsa Zikhron Yehudah* 35, *Bet Yosef* to *Tur H.M.* 290; *Piskei Din Rabbani* 2:162, 170, 171; 4:97, 108.
39. *Responsa Ẓiẓ Eliezer* 15:51.
40. See below, p. 202.

otal to the question of placement of such a daughter upon the death of the father or divorce of the parents.

There is some difference of opinion as to whether Rav Ḥisda meant to include divorce in this principle. From Rashi's comments (C) it appears that divorce is not included (the only alternative he refers to is her staying with her brothers, inheritors of the father's estate). In this he seems to follow the view of Rabbeinu Joseph Ibn Migash (I). But most halakhists take Rav Ḥisda to refer equally to divorce—including the geonim (as quoted by the Rosh), Maimonides (K), R. Meir Abulafia, R. Joseph Karo (O), and R. Mordecai b. Judah ha-Levi, known as the *Darkhei Noam.*[41]

To what extent is the principle of Rav Ḥisda universally binding? Are there other factors that might come into play to vitiate the presumption that a daughter always goes with her mother? A number of sources would appear to introduce other factors and considerations.

Thus as early as the geonic period there was a widespread view (H) that upon remarriage of the mother, the father can sue for custody on the grounds that he is opposed to his daughter being raised in the house of another man. This in turn requires that the father not himself be remarried, given the presumption[42] that his new wife and daughter will not have an easy relationship. Thus, to ensure the daughter's proper development and education, the father would need to arrange for her to be housed with an appropriate female relative, such as his mother or sister. But where both divorced parents are remarried, the geonic position is that preference is given to the mother, in that the daughter is more in need of her maternal guidance and nurturing, while the father's objection to the stepfather is weakened in light of his own remarriage.[43]

In later centuries the question of the mother's remarrying was considered again, with the majority of authorities, including the Tur and the Radbaz, of the view that the daughter can well stay

41. *Responsa Darkhei Noam, E.H.* 26; *Responsa Maharival* 1:59. See Gulevsky, pp. 111–112.

42. See above, p. 196.

43. See *Ginzei Kedem* 3:62 (6); *Oẓar ha-Geonim, Ketuvot* 496, in the name of Sherira Gaon. The latter does make an exception to this rule where the stepfather is suspected of immoral or improper behavior, to which the father objects as inappropriate for his daughter.

with her mother, the father's protestations notwithstanding.[44] One such case involved the following question posed to R. Moses of Trani.[45] The parents of two young daughters had divorced, with the mother taking custody. After remarriage and consequently encountering difficulties with her new husband, the mother released the girls to their father's custody (he having remarried in the interim), only later to petition once again for renewed custody, once her second husband had left her. He ruled in favor of the mother, saying, pointedly, that the notion that a daughter's place is with her mother is not predicated upon the idea of a mother's special or constant love for her daughter, but rather on the very prosaic goal of maternal guidance and teaching, which in this case would be resumed and furthered by the now contrite mother.

The question of exclusive maternal custody of daughters came to the fore in the mid-sixteenth century, in a controversy that split the rabbinic community of Salonika and its two leading authorities, R. Samuel de Medini (Maharashdam) and R. Joseph Ibn Lev (Maharival). The case involved a young widow whose daughter was not yet weaned. The widow wished to return to her hometown, taking her daughter with her, in opposition to her brother-in-law's wishes, the latter having been appointed guardian (*apotropos*) of the child by the father before his death. The brother-in-law argued that such a long-distance trip would be injurious to the delicate health of the baby, and that he would not be able to carry out his custodial responsibilities toward the youngster from afar.

In dealing with this question, Maharival decides, primarily on the basis of Rav Ḥisda, that the mother is unquestionably within her rights to move away together with her baby daughter.[46] His major consideration is the fact that the daughter is, in the first place, in need of her mother's guidance and teaching in the ways of women. The only circumstance that would prevent the mother exercising that prerogative would be where she demonstrates immoral and licentious behavior that would be a negative influence on her daughter, if the latter were over the age of six. But other than that, he argues, a rabbinical court cannot intercede

44. *Tur E.H.* 82:9, *Responsa Radbaz* 1:429. See, however, *Responsa Halakhah le'Moshe, E.H.* 6–7.

45. *Responsa Mabit* 2:62.

46. *Responsa Maharival* 1:58.

with or oppose her intent to move away with her child. As further proof, Maharival points to the Rashba (M), who places a daughter with her widowed mother, as opposed to the treatment of a son, who, at the discretion of the rabbinical court, can be placed with the father's relatives.

Yet Maharashdam (who was himself orphaned at a young age) disagrees vigorously with his colleague, and insists that the mother not be permitted to take the infant with her.[47] He argues that while R. Ḥisda (C) mandates that a daughter is to stay with her mother, it must be in a place where the girl can be supported properly by her father (if he be alive) or her brothers or stepfather, something which would be impossible were she to be removed to another town altogether. And when Maimonides states (L) that a husband sworn to support his wife's daughter must carry out his obligations "wherever she dwells with her mother" (i.e., even in another town), that is only because he is not her father, has no paternal or familial bond, and is merely obligated by virtue of his financial undertaking, an obligation that can be honored even from a considerable distance.

He argues as well, quoting the comments of the Ravad (K) and the Maggid Mishnah, that it is necessary to provide regular visiting privileges for the noncustodial relative, something which is surely precluded by a move to a distant locale. Maharashdam sees any suggestion to the contrary, while based on the Mishnah, to be quite incompatible with the Torah's legislation that allocates to the father his daughter's earnings and marital arrangements. Thus he concludes that the intent of R. Ḥisda is simply to benefit the child, that she be supported while in her mother's custody, without any suggestion that the mother is entitled to remove the girl to another city. And so, in the case at hand, he rules that the court can well prevent the mother from removing the child when it judges that such a trip is not in the child's best interest. He quotes a number of authorities (including Rashba [M] and Rashi) all of whom, under varying circumstances, consider a rabbinical court to be charged with the responsibility of acting in the best interests of orphaned minors—generalized principles (such as that of R. Ḥisda) to the contrary.

---

47. *Responsa Maharashdam, E.H.* 123. Other related responsa by Maharashdam include *H.M.* 308, 405.

When the same case was presented to the other great authority of the generation, the Radbaz, he sided with Maharashdam.[48] In the first place he refers to Rashi (C, at the end), who says that "every daughter is to stay with her mother," pointedly not saying "a daughter is to stay with her mother in any place." He further reasons that just as the mother can prevent the relatives from removing the infant to another locale, so, in reciprocal fashion, can she be thwarted. After all, the other relatives still retain the obligation to support and protect the child, something which is made vastly more difficult when separated by large distances, rendering it exceedingly difficult to keep fully informed of the child's material and spiritual well-being.

Radbaz also invokes Scripture, in reference to the biblical phrase "according to their families, and the house of their fathers,"[49] deriving therefrom the notion of the patriarchal extended-family structure. And finally he quotes the Rashba (M), whereby the court is charged with the full responsibility of protecting the orphan, hence to act in whichever way it sees fit in the circumstances at hand. Unlike Maharival, he takes the Rashba to include a daughter as well as a son in the prerogative of a rabbinical court to place her with the father's relatives. Elsewhere the Radbaz in similar fashion awards custody of a seven-year-old daughter to her father, even against the girl's wishes, where the mother is guilty of immoral behavior[50]—a situation in which, as we saw earlier, Maharival himself would likely concur. This is quite consistent with his ruling, seen above, allowing a mother to retain custody even after she has remarried in legitimate fashion.

This latter situation finds a contemporary echo in several custody decisions in Israeli rabbinical courts involving divorced mothers who subsequently enter into nonsanctioned or immoral living arrangements while claiming custody of minor children.[51] In all such cases the courts accept the argument that ongoing negative behavioral models are sufficient to deny a mother custody of her daughter.

One other factor that has been invoked to remove a daughter from her mother's custody is consideration of material comforts.

---

48. *Responsa Radbaz* 1:360.
49. Numbers 4:34, 38, 46.
50. *Responsa Radbaz* 1:263.
51. See Shoḥatman, n. 102, dealing with a number of such cases.

Thus another sixteenth-century halakhist, the Maharam of Padua, favored a request by a young girl to be placed with her brothers, as opposed to her mother, insofar as the brothers could provide for her needs in abundance. As long as there was appropriate female supervision, and the mother was in a state of poverty, he saw no reason not to honor such a request. After all, he argues, the thrust of Rav Ḥisda's phrasing must be understood as intended for the benefit of the child, not that of the mother per se, thus "it is obvious that one can overturn the proverbial plate to benefit her."[52] Yet at the same time R. Samuel b. Moses, author of the *Mishpetei Shmuel*, rules that if a divorced mother wishes to retain custody of her daughter and can only support her by going out to work during the daytime, she may still have custody, given the presumption of a special mother-daughter relationship.[53]

Where the mother is deceased, the Rosh indicates that custody of the daughter is assumed to pass to the father.[54] Others, however, such as Maharashdam, allow for the possibility that a maternal grandmother might provide a better home and learning environment for the young girl, if such an arrangement is consistent with local custom.[55] Where both mother and father are deceased, and there is a conflict between the maternal grandmother and the paternal relatives over custody, the prevailing view (as represented by the *Ḥelkat Meḥokek* and Tashbaẓ)[56] is to favor the maternal grandmother as a rule, *in loco parentis*, "given that the compassion of a woman for her child's child is like that for her own child." The Radbaz evinces the same preference when the mother is deceased and the father cannot properly care for his child.[57]

Even here, however, there was some debate, where there is some question as to the fitness of the father to assume custody over his daughter. Thus the *Mishpetei Shmuel* emphatically for-

52. *Responsa Maharam of Padua* 53.
53. *Responsa Mishpetei Shmuel* 80; *Piskei Din Rabbani* 1:113, 118.
54. *Responsa Rosh* 82:2, on the grounds that a daughter will benefit from "peace of mind" (*korat ruaḥ*) in being with her father, more than with anyone else.
55. *Responsa Maharashdam, H.M.* 308. See Shoḥatman, n. 112, who refers to a number of similar views, including R. Moshe Ḥanin.
56. See *Ḥelkat Meḥokek* to *Sh.A. E.H.* 82:11; *Responsa Tashbaẓ* 1:40.
57. *Responsa Radbaz* 1:123.

bids a father's custody where there is any possibility that he might use violence against his daughter, in that one should always fear for the girl's life.[58] But the *Darkhei Noam* disagrees, saying that the Gemara in *Ketuvot* (C) only raises that possibility in the context of her brothers or other relatives, but not the father.[59] Indeed the Maharashdam too discounts such a possibility of paternal violence, unless there is concrete evidence to the contrary.[60] Thus the majority view would prefer to remove such a daughter from her maternal grandmother's custody, in favor of her father's claim. The *Darkhei Noam* concludes that a father can assume custody of his daughter in place of the deceased mother's mother, as long as there is a qualified woman to care for her.[61] He also asserts that both Maharival and Maharashdam would concur with this ruling, even to transfer the girl to a different town, just as long as there is no likely danger in such travel.

Finally we can look at one further case recorded by the *Darkhei Noam*, involving a custody conflict between a widowed father and the maternal family.[62] The case involved a man twice married: the first terminated in divorce, while the second ended with the death of his wife. Rather than give up custody of the children from the second marriage to his in-laws (from whom he was estranged and in whose house he could not visit his children), he arranged to have them properly cared for by his first wife, to the chagrin of his second wife's family, who then sued for custody. Here, too, the ruling went in favor of the father, conditional upon every safeguard being in place to assure the physical and emotional well-being of the children in question. The successive views of the Rosh, Tashbaẓ, Radbaz, and Maharashdam, combined to strengthen the claim of the father to be the primary determinant of the disposition of his children. Nonetheless, the *Darkhei Noam* makes the point repeatedly in this responsum that this ruling is predicated upon the general assumption that it is in the best interests of the children involved; if for some reason, or in similar cases, the rabbinical court perceives certain children's interests

58. *Responsa Mishpetei Shmuel* 96.
59. *Responsa Darkhei Noam, E.H.* 38.
60. *Responsa Maharashdam* 308.
61. *Responsa Darkhei Noam*, loc. cit.
62. Ibid., *E.H.* 26.

to be otherwise, then the court is obliged to award custody to the other side. Here then is concrete evidence that it is the court, and not the parents, that ultimately determines custodial arrangements.

C. FOLLOWING THE RULES, AND THE PREROGATIVE TO IMPLEMENT UNDERLYING PRINCIPLES

Our discussion thus far has attempted to identify the various and sundry rules formulated and invoked by halakhic authorities over the ages as they attempted to resolve child custody issues for children of various age levels. The question that is raised by all of this, however, is whether these rules are cast in concrete, to be followed perforce in any given situation, or whether, as the *Darkhei Noam* would have it, there is some higher principle which can be invoked at any given time to supersede these particular rules, so that a court or rabbinic leader would not need to feel constrained by these formal rules in resolving a custody dispute.

Reviewing the material, it would appear that there is indeed such an inclusive principle in child custody, and it is the principle that the court (or halakhic authority) must always seek what is in the best interests of the child at hand. As opposed, for instance, to the American system of law, the Halakhah is not overly concerned with the so-called parental rights that a father or mother might claim over children. This reflects the general attitude of the Halakhah as a duty-oriented system of law, as opposed to a rights-oriented system such as the American one.[63]

Again and again the halakhists qualify their discussions of child custody by saying that in spite of any specific rules found in the rabbinic literature, what ultimately counts is what the court perceives to be in the best interest of the child. Thus it could fairly be said that the various rules formulated for different sexes and age groups should be seen more as guidelines than as binding obligations in any given case. It is entirely within the prerogative of a court or rabbinic ruling to make an alternative determination based on its perception of the specific case at hand, and the particular interests and needs of the child.

63. *Piskei Din Rabbani* 1:145, 147. See R. Warburg, "Child Custody: A Comparative Analysis," *Israel Law Review* 14, no. 4 (October 1979): 480–503, esp. pp. 480–485, 490–492.

Thus, in some of the examples we have seen, a mother can be required to breast feed her infant who recognizes her, overriding her own "rights" following on divorce. As early as the geonim (E) we encounter statements to the effect that "we always act to benefit the child himself" where there is a parental dispute. Similarly the Rashba writes (M), "it is necessary that the rabbinical court examine each case very carefully to determine what is in the best interests of the orphaned children, for the court is [quoting *Gittin* 52b] 'the father of orphans' to seek out their best interests." Likewise R. Moses of Trani derives from the Rosh (who had spoken of the child's *korat ruaḥ*, or peace of mind) that "it all depends on the judgment of the court as to the best interest of the orphans."[64]

A good illustration is likewise found in the fact that the Halakhah does not link paternal child-support obligations to the father's gaining custody. For even though the father may lose custody of his minor children, still he is obliged to maintain them and provide for their basic needs.[65] In other words there is no doctrine of reciprocity which would effectively make the child hostage to either parent's custodial demands. For the Halakhah is not concerned to safeguard or preserve the parent's rights as much as it is determined to see to it that the parent fulfills all of his or her obligations toward the child. As Warburg argues, in Jewish law the child's right (to have his best interests served) is actually derived from, and the result of, this parental duty to provide proper care of the child.

It is in this light that we can perhaps understand the majority view (Rashba, Tashbaẓ, Mabit, and R. Yomtov Ẓahalon) encountered earlier, which upon the death of the father favors transfer of the minor children away from their mother and to the paternal relatives. Such separation from the mother clearly underscores their view that it is not the well-being or interests of the mother that is important here, but rather those of the children. They clearly believe that such a transfer of custody is indeed in the children's own best interest.

It is further apparent that the obligation of the court to safe-

64. *Responsa Mabit* 1:165, 2:62.

65. See *Shittah Mekubbeẓet, Ketuvot* 35b, *Responsa Maharam Rothenburg* 244, *Mishpetei Uziel, E.H.* 4. Warburg, "Child Custody," n. 36, provides a full listing of sources.

guard the interests of the child is not limited to orphans in the literal sense, for even if both parents are alive, and the child is in their custody, still the court would intercede in the interests of the child as if he or she were an orphan.[66] And both Maharashdam and Maharam Padua explicitly place the interests of the child before that of the mother in interpreting the pivotal statement of Rav Ḥisda (C). Rabbi Gulevsky extends this principle on both sides, i.e., that even in those instances where in principle the father has the upper hand in getting custody, if he is patently unfit to act as a custodial parent the child is to be placed with other relatives more fit than he.[67]

This is true even where both parents agree on a particular provision for their child. Thus the Mabit writes that if the court perceives the terms of their agreement to be against the interests of the child, the court is in no way bound by parental arrangements.[68] In another responsum, where townspeople appealed to the local court on behalf of small children whose parents were about to take them on a dangerous trip to the Holy Land, R. Jonah Landsofer allowed the court to interfere in such parental decisions, expressing his doubts as to the safety of the children involved.[69] Similar conclusions are supported by the rabbinical courts of Israel.[70]

At the basis of such decisions lies the fact that the Halakhah does not accept the Roman notion of *patria potestas.* This latter concept underlay the Roman practice by which children were considered the legal property of their father, who was empowered by law to mete out to them corporal punishment, slavery, or even death, not to speak of owning all property and services performed by a son or daughter.[71] As opposed to such notions, and rather than speak of parental rights with respect to their children, Jewish law prefers to speak of parents' and children's obligations

66. *Responsa Sha'arei Uziel* 1, introduction, and p. 126. See Shoḥatman, n. 132.

67. Gulevsky, pp. 122–123.

68. *Responsa Mabit* 2:62.

69. *Responsa Me'il Ẓedakah* 26, as quoted in Shoḥatman, n. 134.

70. See Shareshevsky, *Dinei Mishpaḥah,* p. 380, n. 27, and Shohatman, n. 115. See also E. Sheftelowitz, *Dinei Mishpaḥah ve'Shifutam li-Yehudei Yisrael,* pp. 133–136.

71. See G. Blidstein, *Honor Thy Father and Mother,* pp. 175–176. The volume provides a general discussion of parental-child obligations and relationships.

and duties towards each other. As to such parental obligations, a good description is that of Rabbi Ben Ẓion Uziel when he writes that "sons and daughters are not the possessions of a person, as are his material assets . . . they are in fact a legacy bestowed upon parents, so that they should raise them, educate them in Torah and *miẓvot*, and in life's ways."[72]

In fact, parents are viewed in the first place as playing the role of *apotropos*, or guardian of the child's interests. As explained by Shareshevsky, parents are the natural embodiment of such a protective role, yet because they are viewed as guardians, the *bet din* can overrule their actions, as it does with any *apotropos*, if it judges such actions to be inimical to the interests of the child.[73] And both the *Shulḥan Arukh* and the Rema make it clear that parents are fully accountable to the court for the well-being of their minor children, in that all children remain ultimately the wards of the court, the guarantor of last resort.[74] The implications of such a doctrine in matters of parental child abuse are such that at the very least the Halakhah would consider it a primary communal responsibility to preserve and protect every child, no matter the family circumstance.

In custodial arrangements, this attitude is well reflected in the matter of respecting children's wishes. In the above responsum, Maharam Padua quotes Rashi's words ("she is not *required* to live with them") (C) as warrant to conclude that where a daughter expresses her wishes to be with her mother, and not with her brothers, her wishes are to be respected, as they are when it is the reverse and she wishes to be with her brothers. This ruling, based on the Tosefta,[75] was endorsed by the Rema (O). As explained by the *Ḥelkat Meḥokek* and Vilna Gaon,[76] they reason that Rav Ḥisda intended the daughter to remain with her mother

72. *Responsa Mishpetei Uziel, E.H.* 91.

73. Shareshevsky, *Dinei Mishpaḥah*, pp. 376–380. While at one point mothers were excluded from this role, by reason of their being relatively protected from the marketplace, more recent rulings have included them, given the changing role of women in Western society. See *Responsa Sha'arei Uziel* 1:109 and Shareshevsky, n. 20.

74. *Sh.A. H.M.* 290:1 and Rema ad loc., in the name of Rashba; *Sh.A. E.H.* 82:7, and the comments of Rema, *Ḥelkat Meḥokek*, and *Pitḥei Teshuvah* ad loc.

75. See Rabbi S. Lieberman, *Tosefta ki-Peshuta*, *Ketuvot* 11:4, in reference to a reading of the Tosefta by the *Or Zarua* 1:646.

76. See their comments to the Rema in *Y.D. E.H.* 82:7.

only where the daughter expresses no preference whatsoever. Nonetheless it must be said that Rashi's words are somewhat ambiguous, in that it is quite possible that he is referring not to the daughter's preferences, but rather to the mother's request for custody which is to be honored.[77] A conclusion similar to that of Maharam Padua is reached by Alshikh, when he says (in the above-quoted responsum) that if a boy over the age of six expresses his preference to stay with his mother, as opposed to the decision of his legal guardian (*apotropos*) to place him with the paternal relatives of his deceased father, the boy should have his preference honored.[78] The Israeli rabbinical courts have enforced similar considerations, giving significant weight to a daughter's custodial preferences, but only once the court has determined that such preferences are made without duress or else that placement with the mother would be obviously inappropriate.[79]

More recently the Israeli rabbinical courts have ruled that where a child is old enough to make an intelligent judgment about his own custody (as with a thirteen-year-old boy), his preferences to stay with his mother, as opposed to his father, are to be respected and followed in practice.[80]

An interesting modification of this principle is found in another responsum of the Radbaz, wherein a divorced father sued to regain custody of his seven-year-old daughter because the mother, since the divorce, had fallen pregnant and given birth out of wedlock. Radbaz ruled that even though the daughter herself expressed her wishes to remain with her mother, nonetheless the father is correct in having her removed from the mother's custody, in light of the improper moral influence and climate in the mother's home.[81] He goes even further: if the father is deceased, and it is merely his relatives, or the court itself, that recognizes the untoward influences on the daughter, it is proper that she be removed and placed in a proper environment, she being of an age where she can already begin to understand sexual behavior and its implications.

---

77. For such a reading, see Rabbi H. Gulevsky, "Ba'ayot al Ba'alut ha-Yeladim," *Sefer Kevod ha-Rav*, p. 105.

78. *Responsa Maharam Alshikh* 38.

79. See Sheftelowitz, *Dinei Mishpaḥah*, p. 135, quoting the records of the courts at some length.

80. *Piskei Din Rabbani*, 1:55, 61; 2:298, 300, 301; 4:332–333.

81. *Responsa Radbaz* 1:263. See the *Pitḥei Teshuvah* to *Y.D. E.H.* 82:7 (6).

A contemporary commentator, Rabbi Ḥayyim Dubber Gulevsky, goes one step further, to state that a father does have a proprietary interest in asserting paternal control over his children. Because the father alone carries the obligation of supporting his children, and the Torah refers to offspring as belonging to "their fathers' household," children (once weaned) should in fact be considered to "belong" to, and go with, their father.[82] Rabbi Gulevsky explains that this generalized principle is suspended by R. Ḥisda (C) in the case of daughters, insofar as a young girl needs her mother's guidance. But other than this, says Rabbi Gulevsky, children correctly belong with their father, not mother. By way of proof he invokes the authority of the Rashba (M), who had stated that "a son is more correctly placed with male relatives, to train and teach him the ways of men, more effectively than his mother could." He understands that responsum to imply that in case of divorce or death, male children should indeed remain with their father, or the father's relatives, unless such relatives are disqualified for some other reason.[83] He is also of the opinion that where the mother remarries, it is forbidden to have the children adopted by her new husband, insofar as such a step constitutes "outright theft" (*mamash gezeilat nefashot*) perpetrated against the family of the first husband.[84] It would appear, however, that this is a minority view.

In any case, where personal preference is incompatible with the child's best interest, it is clear that the latter must take preference in the calculations of the court. To do any less would be an abdication of its role as protector of minors and court of last resort in carrying out its primary role of safeguarding the well-being of all Jewish children.

There is, however, one further question that is raised by the foregoing matter of best interest, and that is whether these principles mask a religious "bias" in determining what is or is not in the best interest of a child. The issue is particularly

---

82. Rabbi H. D. Gulevsky, "Ba'ayot al Ba'alut ha-Yeladim," pp. 106 ff. The biblical reference was seen earlier in a responsum of the Radbaz; see above.

83. He also cites the supplementary comments of R. Joseph Karo to the *Tur/Sh.A. E.H.* 82, known as the *Bedek ha-Bayit*, which favors the custody of paternal relatives over the claims of a widowed mother, as long as they are not considered homicidal.

84. See Gulevsky, p. 129.

germane in the context of the need to provide appropriate religious education for a boy—to what extent is this motivated by the desire to act to his benefit, as opposed to the realization of some external religious agenda?

Shoḥatman argues that even this principle is not intended primarily for the narrowly defined "religious education" of the youngster, but rather for his overall preparation to face life as a well-rounded and socially productive adult.[85] This he maintains on the basis of the fact that the father takes custody as a rule only when the youngster is six. Had it been the case that the dominant consideration was religious inculcation, such paternal custody would have occurred at a much younger age, for already at such an early age religious instruction should occur.[86] And so, being deferred to the later age of six, one can conclude that the child's emotional development is primary, until the point that his father can take over and provide the education necessary for him to function as a knowledgeable, adult Jew. This, he argues, is entirely analogous to the rationale offered for a girl's staying with her mother.

Similar conclusions are reached by the Israeli judge Yiẓḥak Kister, who concludes on the basis of these sources that a boy of this age requires the guidance, role modeling, and character-building custodial presence of a father-figure. The practical result of this observation is that such paternal custody is in fact to be awarded even where the father is not particularly religious or qualified to provide a religious education.[87] This, however, is not the view of Rabbi Gulevsky. For he argues that even though he would normally award custody to the paternal relatives even over the child's mother, a more important consideration in his view is that of religious education. Thus he would place the youngster in whichever setting was more conducive to his proper religious development, whether with the mother, the father, or for that matter even a nonrelative.[88]

---

85. See Shoḥatman, pp. 317–318.

86. See Maimonides, *M.T. Hil. Talmud Torah* 1:6, who stipulates that a father should start elementary scriptural lessons as soon as the boy starts to speak.

87. Shoḥatman, pp. 318–319.

88. Gulevsky, p. 109.

SUMMARY AND CONCLUSIONS

In summarizing the many strands of thought encountered in this chapter, a number of salient points emerge with some clarity.

Infants under the age of two years must as a rule be accorded the primary custody of their mother. The Gemara in *Eruvin* 82a assumes that there can no real substitute for such maternal presence, and *Ketuvot* 59b insists that a divorced mother cannot delegate breast-feeding to another if doing so has any negative impact on the infant. This principle was accepted by all subsequent halakhists, most notably Maimonides, Rashba, Radbaz, and Maharashdam.

Where the mother has died, the tendency, starting with the geonim, was to adjudicate each case on its own merits, to be determined by a careful consideration of what would be most beneficial to the infant, whether it be with the father, the maternal grandmother, or other relatives. The Radbaz in particular would not give automatic custody to the father, but would give consideration to such factors as the ability to provide tender care, material subsistence, and a nurturing presence.

Past the age of two, similar sentiments are expressed. Thus the same passage in *Eruvin* records R. Assi as saying that up to the age of six it is better for a child to be with the mother, and that as a rule a child younger than six is presumed to share her domicile. And *Ketuvot* 65b speaks of fathers providing child-support to children of this age as they live with their mothers, in that, as Rashi puts it, such a child "is still in need of his mother." Maimonides codifies this practice into law, in addition to providing an explicit responsum to the same effect—apparently influenced by the views of R. Joseph Ibn Migash.

Yet others disagreed. Amongst the geonim there were some who felt that a father can assume custody even prior to the sixth year if that is necessary to teach his son effectively what should be taught at that age. And the Ravad too took issue with Maimonides' six-year dividing line, saying that even at the age of four or five custody can be switched to the father. Others (the Rosh and Tashbaẓ) advance the age to as early as the two year level. Those who agree with Maimonides include the Tur, R. Moshe Abulafia, and an anonymous gaon.

At the basis of their disagreement are differences in how they perceive the educational role of the father in relation to the young: Maimonides stresses the father as primarily imparting intellectual and rational knowledge. Ravad and, to a greater extent, the Rosh and Tashbaẓ emphasize his function as role model and behavioral reinforcer, matters which come into play at a much earlier age. Where maternal custody effectively precludes a father's educational role, the *Noda bi-Yehudah* favored the father's taking full custody, even below the age of six. And modern Israeli rabbinical courts would similarly penalize a mother to forfeit custody if she deliberately prevents the father from discharging his pedagogical obligations towards his child upon occasional visitations. Rabbi Waldenberg too would have the mother forfeit custody of a four-year-old boy if she effectively precludes the father from fulfilling his paternal responsibilities.

Where the father is deceased, and the mother incapable of providing educational amenities to the child, most major halakhists (including Maimonides, Rashba, Tashbaẓ, and the Mabit) would favor an award of custody to the relatives of the deceased father, on the assumption that they can indeed provide such an educational framework. How soon this might occur would depend on their earlier views regarding transfer to the father's custody. And Rabbi Yomtov Ẓahalon likewise favored the paternal relatives, rather than permit the widowed mother to expend the children's inheritance. Such considerations of financial security remained a valid factor for most halakhists in allocating custody, but a small minority (e.g. Alshikh) did favor the mother, as long as she could provide the educational stimulus to further their proper development.

Once a boy has completed his sixth year, all would agree that as a rule he should live with his father by reason of his further education. Yet R. Isaac of Molena requires in addition that there be a female nurturing presence, whether it be the father's sister, mother, or some other woman (but not his new wife). Maimonides' formulation is ambivalent: some (Mahari b. Lev, Alshikh, R. Isaac of Molena) understand him to allow the mother to retain custody if she is prepared to forgo child support by the father. This view (as explained by R. Isaac of Molena) is predicated on the principle that as long as the mother ensures the proper education of the youngster, to be supplemented by the father's regular visitations, she can retain custody, the major purpose of custody having been achieved. Others (including the Mabit, *Ḥelkat Meḥokek*, the *Noda bi-Yehuda*, and Rabbi Waldenberg) do not read Maimonides as allowing the mother such a prerogative. They, in turn, understand custody as going beyond formal educational considerations, to include the full panoply of fathering activities that cannot be fully passed on to others—hence the father retains the prerogative of custody at all times beyond six years of age. Rabbi Uziel, under similar circumstances, attaches more weight to the mother's role and duties, such that a boy over six should not be forcibly removed from his mother's custody. And Israeli courts have ruled that a father's custodial role can be suspended if a satisfactory formal education for the youngster is guaranteed under the mother's supervision.

With daughters over the age of six, other factors come into consideration. A statement by Rav Ḥisda in *Ketuvot* establishes the presumption that a daughter's place is with her mother. Rashi and Ibn Migash understand that Rav Ḥisda does not include a divorced mother in this rule, but most others (Maimonides, R. Meir Abulafia, R. Joseph Karo, and others) do not make such a distinction. Yet there are other circumstances that are recognized as sufficient to remove a daughter from her mother's custody. The geonim permitted a father to take custody of his daughter where the mother remarries and the father objects to his daughter being raised by a stranger—as long as an appropriate female figure can take the mother's place, and the father is himself not remarried. But in later periods a consensus of sorts emerged to favor a remarried mother, in light of the special guidance and role modeling afforded uniquely by a mother.

A major contretemps burst forth in the sixteenth century over the permissibility of a widowed mother to move back to her hometown with her infant daughter despite the opposition of her husband's family. Maharival ruled in her favor, citing R. Ḥisda and the pivotal role of maternal care and guidance of her daughter. Opposed to him stood the Maharashdam, who insisted that a mother's prerogative cannot be exercised if in so doing the paternal responsibilities are completely frustrated, as would be the case were she to move away completely, thereby precluding all contact with the father or his family. Notable amongst those siding with the Maharashdam on this issue was his contemporary, the Radbaz. Radbaz finds grounds to distinguish this case from R. Ḥisda's general rule favoring the mother's custody, saying that it is the parent who changes location who should properly be at a disadvantage, and in addition it is entirely within the right of the court to ignore such formal rules of placement if in its judgment the daughter would be better off not going with her mother. Such a case would be one involving travel to a distant city or immoral behavior on the part of the mother, which would serve as a negative influence upon her daughter. This latter judgment has been largely accepted by contemporary courts in modern Israel. Similar considerations led Maharam Padua to deny a destitute mother custody of her daughter in light of her inability to provide a secure and comfortable home setting for the girl. The *Mishpetei Shmuel* did not see any problem with a working mother retaining custody, even though in so doing she would be out of the house all day.

When it is the mother who has died, there is some difference of opinion. The Rosh would have the minor daughter live with her father (as opposed to a maternal grandmother), but the Maharashdam disagrees, if better care can be provided by the grandmother. There seems to be a general acceptance of the undoubted benefits of care provided to a girl by her loving grandmother—in any case superior to those of other relatives. Indeed where the father is unfit to care for his daughter, Radbaz is clear that he should not get custody. Where there is some variance in opinion is when a particular father demonstrates marked anger: *Mishpetei Shmuel* would deny his custody on that ground alone, whereas the *Darkhei Noam* and Maharashdam would not, unless there is concrete evidence of violent behavior. In a parallel responsum, the *Darkhei Noam* ruled in favor of a father, widowed in his second marriage, who wished to place his children with his former wife, as opposed to the claims of the children's grandparents. But here again he makes it clear that it is for the court to adjudicate such claims based on considerations of the child's best interest, while being guided in a general way by earlier rules and precedents.

From all this discussion, it is readily apparent that the *Darkhei Noam* is correct in suggesting that the court, or halakhic authority, is not necessarily bound by past rule or precedent. In each case it is the question of the child's best interests that is the determining principle of custodial placement, even if it means going against this or that formal rule. Put differently, it is not a parental right that is at stake, but rather a parental duty to ensure the best possible outcome favoring the child.

Illustrative of this point is the significance attached to ongoing child-support obligations of the father—irrespective of custody. This is also true of the majority view that a widowed mother can be deprived of custody if it is in the child's interest to be raised by the deceased father's relatives. And the rabbinic readiness (exemplified by the Mabit) to ignore an agreement arrived at by both parents, if judged inimical to the child, illustrates the bottom line of all such deliberations, i.e., the child's interest. Clearly the family unit is to be regarded in the legal context as a network of reciprocal duties and obligations, whether from parents to children or in the reverse. This clearly differs from the Roman notion of *patria potestas.* In talmudic terms, the parent can be described as guardian, or *apotropos*, beholden to safeguard and advance the interests of the child as sacred ward. And the *apotropos* of last resort is the rabbinical court, as empowered by the community in discharging its responsibility to protect minors.

Similarly emblematic of this philosophy of protection of the child's interest is the attitude toward the child's own preferences. Maharam Padua, building on Rashi, requires that preferences of a six-year-old girl be respected; and his view was endorsed by the Rema and the Vilna Gaon, inter alia. And Alshikh does the same for a boy, in a manner that was subsequently upheld by the Israeli courts. But the key is that in all these cases the child's preference is not automatically adhered to unless and until the court can satisfy itself that such preferences are not injurious to the child in question, whether it be in terms of its physical safety, moral development (Radbaz), or material comforts. Again it is for the court to make the final determination.

One contemporary authority who does go to great lengths to support the paternal claims to custody is Rabbi Gulevsky. It is his view, albeit a minority one, that almost always are male children to stay with their fathers or father's family, and certainly never to be domiciled in the house of the mother's new husband. He refers back to the Torah's expression "their father's household" as demonstrating the father's proprietary interest in the disposition of his children, and he quotes the Rashba in favoring the father's prior claims.

One final consideration dealt with in this chapter was the matter of religious "bias" in custodial placement. How much weight does the Halakhah attach to the likely religious influences in one or another custodial arrangement? While Rabbi Gulevsky feels that this consideration is a primary motivating factor, Shoḥatman and Kister both argue that this is not at all the case—and that it is rather consideration of normal healthy personality development of the child that motivates the various halakhists to advocate the positions that they do.

We are now in a position to draw conclusions and perhaps answer the questions with which this chapter began.

Putting aside the consideration of keeping all the children together under one roof, and looking at each child separately, it would appear that the younger boy, aged five, should preferably stay with his mother at least until the end of his sixth year, while she ensures a proper religious preschool education, supplemented by regular visitations with his father. After his sixth year he should live with his father, unless such separation from his mother at that point would be traumatic for him. The nine-year-old boy should be placed with his father, but only where there is a suitable woman in the house providing an appropriate nurturing presence—with the mother being assured of regular visitations. This would also accord with the boy's own preferences. Finally the eleven-year-old girl should be placed with her mother, and even though the mother will shortly remarry, such remarriage will provide a stable family environment for the girl, whose preference is in any case to stay with her mother. Here too the father should have regular visiting "privileges." With all three children, irrespective of where they reside, the father should provide child support until they are capable of supporting themselves.

6

The Limits of Truth and Deception in the Marketplace

Introduction

In business, contemporary promotional activities have raised a number of questions as to what constitutes acceptable practice. How may products be aggressively advertised without violating the truth; what constitutes deceptive behavior on the part of the seller or buyer; what disclosure requirements ought to be imposed on merchants at the time of sale; who is responsible after the sale for goods that are defective or unsatisfactory?

Questions such as these, and the apparent failure of government agencies to adequately protect the consumer, have given rise to the movement dedicated to what has become known as "consumer protection." Concerned at the unwillingness or inability of industry or government to police the goods or services provided in the broad marketplace, and in order to protect the "consumer," groups and associations have in recent years proliferated, in a concerted effort to foster the interests of consumers as opposed to those of businessmen. Such efforts include independent testing services, the proliferation of malpractice lawsuits, lobbying for truth in advertising, popular magazines and radio and TV programs devoted to the topic of "better business," and other similar public-interest groups.

These developments have led to a significant change in the way business is carried out. Whereas in the past the philosophy of *caveat emptor* ("let the buyer beware") served to insulate the "seller" from responsibility for goods sold or services provided, the current emphasis on consumer protection seems to have tilted the scale in the opposite direction. As a result advertising is more carefully monitored, the number of lawsuits, and monetary awards therefrom, have mushroomed, disclosure of product information has accelerated, and there are widespread efforts to educate the public to these issues.

Yet there is another side to this issue. While everyone is, as a matter of preference, in favor of truth and high quality, at what cost are these to be achieved? What if demands for ever better quality control result in ever higher costs to the consumer? What if the costs of malpractice awards result in significantly higher costs to the consumer himself, or even a cutback in desired goods or services because of high insurance premiums?

But even assuming that the vendor or manufacturer is indeed responsible for the quality and reliability of all goods and services that he provides, very practical questions still remain: Where precisely does the responsibility of the manufacturer or merchandiser end, and that of the purchaser or patient/client begin? How much are they duty-bound to disclose? What kind of advertising is to be considered misleading? When can they assume that the buying public is sufficiently informed as to the quality or risks involved in the product? What responsibility must the purchaser bear in ascertaining these facts?

But our question can be put in even broader, and more inclusive, terms. In the larger picture of financial transactions, what is the lowest level of disclosure that is to be considered proper? When must analysts, executives, or Wall Street traders and insiders properly divulge information that might cause loss to others? Such considerations of honesty, integrity, and good faith have always been matters of concern, but in recent years they have become even more pronounced, given the violations and fraudulent activities that have come to light. Yet there are opposing considerations that enter into the moral calculus, in that the modern entrepreneurial business model is built on privileged information and at times concealment of value or intent. Where is the line to be drawn?

The issue, it need hardly be said, reaches beyond the world of business. Honesty and integrity are the sine qua non of societal well-being. And everyone pays lip service to these virtues as morally axiomatic and fundamental. Yet even here it is necessary to clarify what precisely constitutes deception or misrepresentation. What if, as a result of one person's misrepresentation, others are not materially harmed? What of students who engage in questionable behavior to improve their grades? Or of people who create social facades so as to benefit themselves in the eyes of others?

On all of these issues the Halakhah contains important ethical and moral principles and concepts that attempt to balance all of these competing claims and considerations, in a manner that combines abstract principles and practical implementation, without losing sight of the realities "on the ground." It is to an examination of some of these fundamental halakhic parameters that the present chapter is devoted.

The Question

The widow of a lung cancer victim sues for damages from the manufacturer of the cigarettes which the victim smoked for over forty years. She claims that even though the company through its research was aware of the health dangers of its product, it failed to provide adequate warning to its customers as to the medical risks involved (until forced to do so by law, at a relatively late juncture). Furthermore, she contends that the company misled the public by advertising that indirectly suggested that it was safe to smoke.

The tobacco company in turn argues that the victim had chosen to continue to smoke despite awareness of the risks, because he enjoyed smoking. In addition it is its contention that the company was not obliged to fully reveal all the results of its own research into the nature of smoking, insofar as its customers are themselves responsible to determine the safety and effects of the products they purchase. In advertising its products, the company claims, it simply attempted to present them in their most favorable light.

Is the company guilty of improper and misleading promotional activities? Did the customer bear any responsibility to establish for himself the dangers of the product purchased?

The following issues are raised in this situation:

1. According to the Halakhah, what is the nature of the prohibition to misrepresent oneself or one's product, and is it forbidden to mislead another party, even where there is no financial loss involved?
2. Are there any circumstances under which the seller or provider is not required to make full divulgence of pertinent facts? Put differently, what responsibilities must a purchaser

or consumer bear in determining the value, the condition, or the risks of the goods or services that are purchased?

3. What are the limits of legitimate promotional and advertising activity, and according to the Halakhah, what kind of claims or statements can be considered to be misleading and improper?

Sources

A. Leviticus 19:11

Ye shall not steal, neither shall a man deal falsely, nor lie to his fellow.

B. Leviticus 19:36

Just balances, just weights, a just ephah, and a just *hin* shall ye have: I am the Lord your God, who brought you out of the land of Egypt.

C. Leviticus 25:17

And ye shall not wrong [*lo tonu*] one another; but thou shalt fear thy God; for I am the Lord your God.

D. Numbers 32:22

And you shall be guiltless [*nekiyyim*] before the Lord and before Israel.

E. Mekhilta, Mishpatim, chap. 13; Tosefta, Bava Kamma 7:3

There are seven categories of fraud [*ganavim*]: the first among them is one who misrepresents himself to others [*gonev da'at ha-beriyot*], one who insincerely invites another to his home, one who plies another with gifts that he knows he will not accept, one who impresses his guest by opening a barrel of wine that is already sold to a vendor, one who has improper measures, one who lies regarding his weights, one who adulterates his merchandise. . . . Whence do we know that misrepresentation is a form of stealing? Because it says, "so Absalom stole the hearts of the men of Israel" [II Sam. 15:6].

F. Mishnah, Bava Meẓia 4:12 (58b)

Just as there is unfair advantage [*ona'ah*] in pricing, so is there unfair verbal exploitation [*ona'at devarim*]. Thus one should not say "how much is this item" when one has no intention of purchasing it.

G. Bava Meẓia 60a–b

Mishnah: R. Judah said: A shopkeeper must not distribute parched corn or nuts to children, because he thereby accustoms them to come to him. The sages permit it. [And R. Judah said:] Nor may he reduce the price. But the sages say such a practice is to be commended. One must not sift pounded beans [to remove the refuse]. This is the view of Abba Saul. But the sages permit it. Yet they admit that he must not pick out the refuse only from the top of the bin, because such activities are like engaging in deceptive appearances. Men, cattle, and utensils may not be painted.

Gemara: The sages have taught: An animal may not be given an appearance of stiffness, entrails may not be inflated, nor may meat be soaked in water. What is meant by "an appearance of stiffness"? Here, in Babylon, it is explained as referring to bran broth [which bloats the animals fed on it]. Ze'iri said in R. Kahana's name: brushing up an animal's hair [to make it look more valuable]. Samuel permitted fringes to be put on a cloak. R. Judah permitted a gloss to be put on fine cloths. Rabbah permitted hemp cloths to be beaten [to appear of finer texture]. Rava permitted arrows to be painted. R. Pappa permitted baskets to be painted. But doesn't our Mishnah say that men, cattle, and utensils may not be painted? The answer is that painting new utensils is permitted, whereas old ones [to make them appear new] is forbidden.

What is the purpose of painting men? It is like the case of the aged slave who dyed his hair and beard. He came before Raba and said, "Buy me." [He refused.] So he went to R. Papa b. Samuel, who bought him. One day he said to him, "Give me some water to drink." Thereupon he went, washed his head and beard white again, and said, "See, I am older than your father [and you should not order me to do such things]!"

H. Bava Meẓia 49a

Where a verbal agreement is reached [and subsequently the price fluctuates, leading one party to revoke the terms as agreed to], it is the view of Rav that this does not constitute improper reneging [*meḥusrei amanah*]. R. Yoḥanan says that this is improper reneging.

The following statement contradicts Rav: R. Yossi b. Judah asked why in (B) does the verse include the requirement of a just *hin* in addition to the requirement of a just *eifah*, when a *hin* is one sixth of an *eifah?* It must refer to the requirement that one's *hain* ["yes"] and one's *lav* ["no"]—i.e., one's word—should be righteous (*Rashi:* live up to your word, and justify it).

Abbaye answers for Rav as follows: This statement forbids only the practice of saying one thing while intending another (*Rashi:* at the time he makes his verbal commitment he should not intend to change the terms, but this does not address the situation where the prices subsequently change).

I. Ḥullin 94a

Samuel has stated that it is forbidden to deceive anyone—even an idolater. And although Samuel never actually made this statement, it can be deduced from his actions. For it once happened that he used a ferry, and instructed Shemaya to pay the Gentile ferryman, but subsequently Samuel rebuked Shemaya. Why was he angry? Abbaye said that it was because Shemaya paid him with an unkosher chicken, which the ferryman presumed to be kosher. Rava said he was angry because he told Shemaya to pay him with [undiluted] wine, whereas he gave diluted wine (*Rashi:* and the ferryman thought it to be undiluted).

R. Meir would say: One should not repeatedly invite one's fellow to one's home knowing full well that he will refuse (*Rashi:* in so doing one receives the undeserved appreciation of the invitee who thinks that one genuinely expects him to accept the invitation). Likewise one should not ply another with gifts knowing full well that they will not be accepted. One should also not honor a guest by opening a new barrel of wine that was already sold to a vendor unless he informs him that it is already sold [in that the guest mistakenly believes that his host has on his account risked a financial loss, given that an open barrel of wine might spoil until such time as a vendor comes along to purchase it]. And if one knows that a person will not accept the offer, one should not present him with an empty container of oil, unless the effect is to bring public honor to the one so approached.

How is this possible—did it not happen that Ulla once visited with R. Judah, who opened a new barrel of wine for him, one that was already sold? There are two answers: either R. Judah so informed him, or even if he did not it was because Ulla was so beloved of R. Judah that even were it not already sold he would have opened the barrel for him.

. . . The sages have taught: a person should not sell shoes of leather from an animal that died of natural causes on the pretense that the leather is from a healthy animal that was slaughtered, for two reasons: because he is deceived, and because it might be dangerous (*Rashi:* perhaps it died of a snakebite, and the leather is poisonous).

. . . For two reasons they said one should not sell unkosher meat to an idolater: firstly because he is thereby deceived, and secondly because he may resell it to another Jew.

J. Ḥullin 94b

How is the public pronouncement [that nonkosher meat has been sold to a Gentile] formulated [to prevent Jews from purchasing it in error]? Said R. Isaac b. Joseph: "It is formulated to say, 'Meat has been sold to Gentiles.' " Why do we not say, "Nonkosher meat has been sold to a Gentile"? Because then the Gentiles will not buy it at all (*Rashi:* they will not want to be shamed by purchasing meat that the Jews do not want). But by not so identifying it as nonkosher, are we not misleading them? The answer is that really they are misleading themselves.

It is similar to the case where Mar Zutra b. Naḥman was once going from Sikara to Maḥoza, while Rava and R. Safra were going to Sikara, and they met on the way. Believing that they had come to meet him, Mar Zutra said: "Why did you take this trouble to come so far to meet me?" R. Safra replied: "We did not know that the master was coming; had we known it we would have put ourselves out even more than this." [Later] Rava said to R. Safra: "Why did you say that, you upset him." Said R. Safra: "We would be deceiving him otherwise." "No," said Rava, "he would be deceiving himself."

K. Pesaḥim 13a

It is stated in a Beraita: where collectors of brass coins for charity have no poor people on hand to whom to distribute the coins, and they must consequently exchange them for silver ones [that do not corrode as easily], they should not use their own silver coins, but those of others. Likewise those who collect food for the poor, and having no poor on hand must sell the food, should not buy the food themselves (*Rashi:* because people might suspect them of paying less than the market price), as it is said (D) "and you shall be guiltless."

L. Maimonides, M. T. Hil. De'ot 2:6

It is forbidden to accustom oneself to smooth speech and flatteries. One must not say one thing and mean another. Inward and outward self should correspond; only what we have in mind should we utter with the mouth. We must deceive no one, not even an idolater. A man, for example, must not do the following: [as in (I)]. . . . Even a single word of flattery or deception is forbidden. A person should always cherish truthful speech, an upright spirit, and a pure heart freed of all pretense and cunning.

M. Maimonides, M. T. Hil. Mekhirah 18:1–4

It is forbidden to mislead [*le'ramot*] people in business or to deceive them [*lignov et da'atam*]. This is equally true whether it involves Gentiles or Jews. Thus when one knows that there is some defect in one's merchandise, one must so inform the purchaser. And it is even forbidden to deceive people in words only.

One may not display old persons, animals, or vessels that are for sale so that they appear young or new. But one may display new ones by polishing, ironing, or beautifying them all they require.

One should not feed a man bran broth or the like to fatten him and thus make his face appear robust; nor should one paint his face with red clay. One should not inflate animal intestines nor soak meat in water. All similar acts are likewise forbidden. One must not sell to a Gentile meat of an animal not slaughtered according to ritual law under the impression that it is meat from an animal slaughtered according to ritual law, though to the heathen the two are the same.

It is permitted to sift pounded beans—but not when the sifting is only at the top of the bin, because the latter serves to deceive the eye into thinking that the whole container is similarly sifted. And a storekeeper may distribute parched corn or nuts to children and maid-servants to accustom them to frequent his store. And he may reduce the price to increase his customer share. And his competitors cannot prevent this, for it does not constitute deception.

N. Rabbeinu Yonah, Sha'arei Teshuvah 3:184

The seventh category [of liars] consists of those who deceive their neighbor by telling him that they have done him a favor or spoken well of him, when in reality they have not done so. Our sages of blessed memory have said, "it is forbidden to deceive others, even Gentiles." The sages of Israel account this sin as more severe than that of robbing a Gentile, because lying lips bear great guilt. We are obliged to remain within, and uphold, the bounds of the truth, because it is one of the foundations of the soul.

O. Tur H.M. 228

Just as it is forbidden to defraud, so it is forbidden to deceive. And deception is a greater transgression than fraud, for the proceeds of fraud can be returned, whereas deception cannot; fraud affects one's possessions, whereas deception affects one's self. . . . It is likewise forbidden to deceive another by making it appear that one acts to his benefit when that is not the case. . . . thus one should not open barrels for one's guest that are already sold, without informing the guest that he does not open them only for him. . . . But this is not the case where it should occur to the other party that this act was not done only for him—in such a case he deceives himself, and one does not have to correct him, e.g., where one meets another en route, and he thinks one has come to meet him.

Discussion

1. PROHIBITIONS INVOLVED IN MISREPRESENTATION BY THE SELLER

Elsewhere we have examined the question whether it is permissible to avoid the truth and even speak an outright lie where the intent is to benefit the person so deceived.[1] Our conclusion was that according to the Halakhah such deception is indeed sometimes permitted. Our present concern is to clarify what precisely is involved in deceptive behavior intended to benefit oneself, in a variety of settings, including business and career advancement.

Where anyone has recourse to an outright lie or false statement, it is quite clear that such behavior is forbidden under the rubric of the biblical exhortation to "keep thee far from a false matter" (Exod. 23:7). But the question is whether this verse applies as well to statements that carefully avoid or conceal the truth. For certain statements can be technically true even while they misrepresent the reality of a situation.

Similarly it is unclear precisely what is involved in deception or misrepresentation that does not cause financial loss for the other party. In other words, while the various prohibitions against stealing (A) or fraudulent behavior of various kinds seem clear enough, it still remains to be clarified whether it is permissible under any circumstances to misrepresent the quality or condition of goods or services, even if the other party receives full value for its money.

---

1. See *Jewish Ethics and Halakhah*, vol. 1, chap. 2, addressed to the question of confronting dying patients with the truth as to their condition. Some recent general halakhic analyses of the topic include Rabbi M. Dratch, "Nothing But the Truth," *Judaism* 37, no. 2 (Spring 1988): 218–229, and Rabbi Gary Lavit, "Truth Telling to Patients with Terminal Diagnoses," *Journal of Halakhah and Contemporary Society* 15 (Spring 1988): 94–125.

Ona'ah

In examining these questions, we can deal first with the prohibition of *ona'ah*, or "exploitation." The prohibition derives from the passage in Leviticus (C) that forbids "wronging one another" (*lo tonu*). As understood by the oral tradition, this prohibition takes two forms. The first involves unjust enrichment in regard to the price paid for goods or services, whether from the point of view of the seller (setting too high a price) or from that of the purchaser (where the price is unconscionably low). Such practices violate the prohibition against brazen stealing (*gezel*), even though not force but a business transaction is involved.[2] Thus a significant body of halakhic discussion and law is devoted to the various aspects of pricing policy, and means of redress on either side.[3]

But the prohibition of *ona'ah* exploitation goes beyond considerations solely of profit margins. Even if the other party receives full value for monies paid, it remains necessary that the seller provide proper disclosure as to the nature of the goods or services provided. As Rabbi Eliav Shoḥatman puts it, the moment one party conceals from the other the precise quality and character of the goods, or by his words and actions creates the impression that they possess a superior quality which they in fact do not have, then the prohibition of *ona'ah* is triggered.

What precisely is involved? The Mishnah in *Bava Meẓia* (F) delineates both kinds of *ona'ah*, referring to the latter as *ona'at devarim*, or verbal exploitation. One example offered by the Mishnah is that of a person who has no intention of purchasing an item from a particular vendor, yet nonetheless inquires as to the sale price involved. Here, as the fourteenth-century R. Menaḥem Meiri points out, what is involved is an insensitivity to the feelings of the vendor, whose emotions are needlessly manipulated in the expectation—and then disappointment at the loss—of a successful sale.[4] Of course where there is a genuine interest on the part

2. See E. Shoḥatman, "Haganat Ẓarkhan Mipnei Te'ur Kozev be'Halakhah," *Dine Israel* 3 (5732): 227–228.

3. See *Encyclopedia Talmudit* 1:328–343. A most comprehensive discussion of the implications of this principle for modern-day economic systems is to be found in I. Warhaftig, "Haganat ha-Ẓarkhan le'Or ha-Halakhah," *Teḥumin* 2 (5741): 444–488.

4. *Beit ha-Beḥirah, Bava Meẓia* 59a.

of the customer to price the article, so as to purchase it if the price is suitable, such an inquiry would be entirely permissible.[5] A second instance in this Mishnah involving economic activity occurs when a person directs a potential customer to a third party, knowing full well that the third party does not deal in such merchandise. Such advice is forbidden, according to R. Joseph Karo, because it will likely compromise the dignity of either the customer or the third party—a blatant case of emotional insensitivity.[6] These instances of *ona'at devarim* are equated in the Mishnah with similar noncommercial circumstances,[7] all of them sharing the characteristic of needless emotional pain inflicted on another human being. As R. Shneur Zalman of Liadi (the eighteenth century author of the *Shulḥan Arukh ha-Rav*) put it, such activities are a source of genuine heartache (*ẓa'ar ha-lev*) to the other party—and are thus forbidden.[8]

A rather revolutionary explanation of the principle of *ona'at devarim* has been suggested by Rabbi J. David Bleich.[9] Rather than the rationale of *ona'at devarim* as inflicting shame or emotional pain, Rabbi Bleich believes that the prohibition should be understood as forbidding behavior that shows disrespect for another, and deprives him of his essential honor and dignity, irrespective of how that other person actually feels. In other words it is not the feelings of the injured party, but rather the insensitivity of the sinner, that is the operative factor. If, for instance, the other party was not even aware of the disrespect intended and hence felt no pain whatsoever, even so, says Rabbi Bleich, *ona'at devarim* is committed. While this explanation is based on a careful analysis of Tosafot and Maimonides, it has little explicit

5. Rabbi A. Levine, *Economics and Jewish Law* (New York, 1987), pp. 8–9 (hereafter cited as *Economics*), concludes from this that consumers who deliberately use the showroom and sales personnel of nondiscount stores in order to select the merchandise that they intend to purchase at a discount store are in flagrant contravention of the biblical prohibition of *ona'ah*. See the same author's treatment of this matter in his *Free Enterprise and Jewish Law* (New York, 1980), pp. 119–120 (hereafter cited as *Free Enterprise*).

6. *Kesef Mishnah* to Maimonides, *M.T. Hil. Mekhirah* 14:12.

7. Other prohibited behaviors listed by this Gemara include references to another's sinful past, raising the matter of a convert's Gentile past, any attempt to justify another's sufferings by imputing that they must be deserved, or referring a questioner to a third party whom one knows to be unable to provide an answer.

8. *Shulḥan Arukh ha-Rav, Hil. Ona'ah u-Geneivat Da'at* 27, 28.

9. *ha-Darom* 35 (Nissan 5733): 140–143.

precedent in halakhic literature, and seems to be contradicted by the above authorities.

The gravity with which the sages viewed this transgression is demonstrated by the fact that while behavior involving *ona'at devarim* is not punishable by the statutory lashes given for a negative commandment (being a transgression of a merely verbal nature), the Gemara here considers it to be even more reprehensible than instances of financial exploitation. For unlike the latter, the emotional trauma of the former cannot be fully undone. In addition, the perpetrator's intention cannot be easily uncovered or proven (hence the verse refers to the fear of God as the primary motivating factor).[10] And, according to Naḥmanides, even though the purchaser may have paid no more than the actual value of what he received, still he can claim that the transaction was conducted under false pretenses, not having received what was contracted for, and be allowed to void the sale altogether.[11]

Subsequent authorities extended the list of *ona'ah* prohibitions: needlessly hurtful criticism, cursing another to his face, the use of shameful nicknames even though the person so named be accustomed to them, and even inflicting an *ayin ha-ra*, or "evil eye."[12] And several early authorities (notably R. Eliezer of Metz and the *Sefer ha-Ḥinukh*) permitted an individual who is thus abused to respond vigorously so as to avoid debasement—but to remain at all times dignified and respectful, "for it is permitted to answer a fool, just as the Torah permits one to kill someone who breaks into one's property before being killed oneself, for there is no doubt that a person is not obliged to suffer at the hand of another, but can rather save oneself."[13]

Geneivat Da'at

In addition to *ona'ah*, there is an even more inclusive prohibition involved in misrepresentation, and it is that referred to in the

---

10. *Bava Meẓia* 58b and Maimonides, *M.T. Hil. Mekhirah* 14:18. Rabbi Zalman Halevi Uri, *ha-Pardes*, 35:5, pp. 21–22, has argued that verbal abuse is a lesser infraction than others because it is "merely" verbal, and hence requires no confession on Yom Kippur. But while the absence of lashes is clearly because of the exclusively oral nature of the transgression, this characteristic by itself does not appear to vitiate the need for divine forgiveness.

11. *Naḥmanides' Commentary to the Torah*, Lev. 25:15. See I. Warhaftig, "Haganat ha-Ẓarkhan le'Or ha-Halakhah," pt. II, *Teḥumin* 3 (5742): 356.

12. See the sources quoted in the *Encyclopedia Talmudit* 1:344.

13. *Sefer Yerayim ha-Shalem* 180; *Sefer ha-Ḥinukh* 338.

expression *geneivat da'at*, literally "stealing another's mind." Under the rubric of this prohibition, it is forbidden to engage in any activity that misrepresents any fact or situation to the mind of another person, Jew or Gentile. The Midrash *Mekhilta*, as well as the Tosefta (E), lists seven categories of theft, and the very first of them is the one by which a person steals the mind of another via misrepresentation—and it goes on to specify several commonly encountered behaviors that do just that. Such illicit activity is described by these early sources not as stealing the mind, but as stealing the heart (in reference to a phrase describing the devious actions of Absalom). But the difference in phraseology is inconsequential. What is forbidden by the term *geneivat da'at* is the very act of concealing the truth to the detriment of another person. The definitive formulation of the prohibition of *geneivat da'at* is that of Samuel, who said (I), "it is forbidden to deceive anyone—even an idolater."

What is the source of the prohibition? According to the Ritva, quoting "certain sages in the name of the Tosafot," it is of biblical origin, and included in the Levitical verse "ye shall not steal, neither shall a man deal falsely, nor lie to his fellow" (A). He explains that the verse prohibiting stealing is intentionally nonspecific, so as to incorporate all forms of stealing, including purloining the mind.[14] Ritva, in referring to Tosafot, is in all likelihood referring to the above-mentioned R. Eliezer of Metz, author of the *Sefer Yerayim ha-Shalem*, who in that work also derives this principle from (A), as do several additional early authorities.[15] A different biblical source is identified by Rabbeinu Yonah of Gerondi (N), in that he perceives *geneivat da'at* to be entirely subsumed under the category of lying. Yet others, notably the *Sefer Miẓvot Katan*, R. Joel Sirkes (the Baḥ), and R. Shneur Zalman of Liadi, see no biblical source or dimension at all, but rather a prohibition of purely rabbinic provenance.[16] As for Maimonides' position on this question, R. Menaḥem Krakowski, author of the *Avodat ha-Melekh*, is of the view that he too considered it merely rabbinic, in that Maimonides omits any

14. *Novellae of the Ritva, Ḥullin* 94a.

15. *Sefer Yerayim ha-Shalem* 124; *Sefer Miẓvot Gadol* (R. Moses of Coucy), Neg. 155; *Kiryat Sefer* (Mabit) to *M.T. Hil. Mekhirah* 18.

16. *Sefer Miẓvot Katan* 261; Baḥ to *Y.D. H.M.* 228; *Shulḥan Arukh ha-Rav, Hil. Ona'ah u-Geneivat Da'at* 12 ("*mi-divrei sofrim*").

mention of such a biblical prohibition in enumerating the commandments in the *Sefer ha-Miẓvot.*[17] It should be noted, however, as we will see below, that Maimonides does mention a prohibition against *geneivat da'at* in the context of the prohibition against the *me'onen.*[18]

Notable in this regard is the inclusive nature of Samuel's formulation, in that even idolaters must not be the victims of Jewish deception (I). The Ritva finds support for such broad inclusion in the very verse in Leviticus (A). As he explains, while a superficial reading of the verse seems to restrict the prohibition of *geneivah* to actions against one's "fellow," i.e., one's fellow Jew, in fact the limiting phrase "to his fellow" (*ba-amito*) qualifies only the latter half of the verse, i.e., dealing falsely or lying—but not stealing. This is so, says the Ritva, for two reasons: (a) the prefix *ba* ("to") cannot be used in conjunction with stealing (*tignovu*); (b) the authoritative rabbinic cantillation notation places a break (*etnaḥta*) under *tignovu* ("stealing") as if to separate it from what follows. Consequently the prohibition against *geneivah* or stealing, unlike the rest of the verse, is not restricted to deceiving a fellow Jew, but prohibits deceiving a Gentile as well. And the Ritva goes one step further than his teachers Naḥmanides and the Rashba when he states that from Samuel one should conclude that the prohibition also applies when giving a Gentile an outright gift—even then absolute candor is required.

Now there are two primary talmudic texts that detail what is, and is not, forbidden in *geneivat da'at.* The first of these occurs in *Ḥullin* 94a (I) in discussing Samuel's aphorism. Samuel himself, according to the Gemara, disapproved of Shemaya's misleading a Gentile ferryman, even though there was no blatant deception (payment in the form of nonkosher chicken instead of kosher; wine diluted in accordance with common practice). And in the name of R. Meir the Gemara goes on to forbid a variety of similar actions: repeatedly inviting a guest in the full knowledge that he will not accept the invitation; offering a gift knowing it will not be accepted; opening a large container of food for a guest to give the mistaken impression that the uneaten balance will constitute a significant financial loss.[19]

17. *Avodat ha-Melekh* to Maimonides, *M.T. Hil. Deot* 2:6.
18. Maimonides, *Sefer ha-Miẓvot,* Negative 32, and see below.
19. It should be noted that the Gemara qualifies these rules by adding that they

Further notable cases of improper deception involve the sale of leather shoes where the purchaser is not informed that the leather is from an animal that had succumbed to natural causes. For even though there is no prohibition against such leather, still the customer is marginally misled, and might have avoided the purchase on the grounds that the animal skin was diseased or poisoned. And likewise it is improper to sell unkosher meat to a Gentile who believes that it is kosher, for even though it should not really make any difference to him, and he pays no more for it than for any nonkosher meat,[20] it is nonetheless morally wrong, in that he may have his own reasons for preferring kosher meat. Hence he should not be deceived into thinking that this vendor benefits him in this fashion.[21]

Similarly R. Isaac Bar Sheshet Perfet (the Rivash) forbade a Jew to sell a Gentile meat from a healthy animal that had been improperly slaughtered, without properly informing the purchaser, so as not to receive unearned gratitude.[22] These examples are quoted and approved by all subsequent codifiers.[23] A similar example of illicit *geneivat da'at* is proffered in the Jerusalem Talmud when a person is forbidden to bring a gift of wine to a house of mourning in a bottle made of colored glass, giving the impression that it is wine of greater value than it is in fact.[24]

The second passage is found in *Bava Meẓia* (G). The Mishnah specifies that one who wishes to sell his slaves, cattle, or utensils may not paint or disguise them so as to make them appear better than they in fact are. In discussing this statement, the Gemara records a number of complementary views, all of which serve to reinforce and provide specific application to this principle: including artificially stuffing, inflating, or fattening animals by feeding or grooming them to give a temporary appearance that

---

may be suspended where the effect is to bring public honor and recognition to the one so treated, or where in fact such treatment reflects a genuine desire to honor him. See the many sources referred to in *Encyclopedia Talmudit* 6:229.

20. Baḥ to *Sh.A. H.M.* 228:6.

21. See Warhaftig, "Ẓarkhan," pt. II, p. 357, n. 134. For a discussion of the rest of this talmudic passage, see below.

22. *Responsa Rivash* 403. See *Encyclopedia Talmudit* 6:226, n. 23.

23. Maimonides, *M.T. Hil. Deot 2:6, Hil. Mekhirah* 18:3; Rosh to *Ḥullin* 7:18; *Tur H.M.* 228:6; *Sh.A. H.M.* 228:6; *Shulḥan Arukh ha-Rav, Hil. Ona'ah* 12; *Arukh ha-Shulḥan, H.M.* 228:3.

24. J.T. *Demai* 4:3, as explained in the comments of R. Elijah of Vilna and the *Pnei Moshe.*

belies their true condition. The Gemara then goes on to list a number of vendor activities that are permissible, even though they change the appearance of the merchandise: fringes on a garment, polishing or rubbing textiles, and even repainting hardware. But does this latter case not contradict the Mishnah that forbids painting an item that is for sale as a deceptive practice? The Gemara answers that what is forbidden is the dressing of old items to appear new; whereas it is permitted to freshen new, unused items so as to give them their finest appearance. This passage was regarded as normative by Maimonides, the *Shulḥan Arukh*, and other codifiers.[25]

The *Shulḥan Arukh* likewise forbids a vendor to mix fruits or vegetables so as to disguise the true condition of some of them—whether it be a minority that are of lower grade among a majority of higher grade, or even to include some higher-grade older specimens in a lower-grade group that is fresh, for perhaps the purchaser wishes to keep his purchase over a longer period, and the higher grade will spoil.[26] The general rule, as expressed by Hai Gaon, is that a vendor may not intentionally conceal the true quality of his merchandise, but he may so display it that its best qualities are most favorably projected.[27] (Later, in section 2, we will take up the question whether a vendor has any responsibility to correct a purchaser's misconceptions, as well as the issue of which facts he may or may not assume to be "known" to the consumer.)

These two talmudic passages formed the basis for the larger application of the principle of *geneivat da'at* as it might apply across the board.

What kinds of activity are included in the prohibition? In its broadest formulation, what *geneivat da'at* forbids is any attempt to foster or allow an impression that one is acting so as to benefit another person when such benefits are either absent or unintended.[28] Among early authorities, several classic formulations of the prohibition are encountered. Maimonides for one, in his

25. Maimonides, *M.T. Hil. Mekhirah* 18:2; *Tur/Sh.A. H.M.* 228:9; *Sh.A. ha-Rav, Hil. Ona'ah* 18. See similar practices in the Tosefta *Bava Meẓia* 3:12.

26. *Tur/Sh.A. H.M.* 228:10.

27. Hai Gaon, *Sefer ha-Mekaḥ ve'ha-Memkar* 59:14. See the summary in Shoḥatman, pp. 230–232.

28. *Encyclopedia Talmudit* 6:225.

Mishneh Torah (L), after quoting these talmudic passages, goes on to forbid all flattering speech, any inconsistency between sentiments that are spoken and those uttered, and any action that diminishes "truthful speech, an upright spirit, and a pure heart freed of all pretense and cunning." Moreover, he says, it makes no difference whether the addressee is Jew or Gentile. And Rabbeinu Yonah of Gerondi (N) includes any behavior by which one allows the impression that one has done a neighbor a favor, or spoken well of him, when in fact this has not been the case. He likewise extends the prohibition to Gentiles, and adds that this sin is even worse, and bears greater guilt, than robbery, in that truth is one of the "foundations of the soul." In other words, it is not only injury to the other party that is of concern, but also damage to the deceiver himself, whose soul is compromised. Similar sentiments are put forth by R. Judah he-Ḥasid in the *Sefer Ḥasidim* in forbidding anything less than the truth. He specifically forbids a Jew to secretly curse a Gentile when he greets him while pretending otherwise (as he puts it, "for there is no deception greater than this"), and he also excoriates those who show external signs of piety to impress others, knowing full well, as they do, that their spirituality is less than appearances would suggest.[29] These demands for absolute truthfulness do not, however, prevent the *Sefer Ḥasidim* from permitting a righteous man (he refers to a *ẓaddik*) to purchase a Torah scroll or some other religious item from a corrupt person (referred to as a *rasha*), using subterfuge so as to acquire it from him.[30] Apparently such deception is warranted in that it is not intended to benefit the purchaser personally, but rather to safeguard the honor or safety of the religious item itself.[31]

Such formulations of the prohibition of *geneivat da'at* were subsequently applied in concrete fashion by these and later authorities. We can examine three such areas.

---

29. *Sefer Ḥasidim* 51, 7.

30. This is quoted in the *Da'at Zekeinim mi-Ba'alei ha-Tosafot* to Gen. 25:34.

31. In referring to this quotation, Levine (*Economics*, p. 21) understands it as permitting one to pay less than the commercial fair market value for such religious items, and Levine consequently has difficulty understanding such a ruling. But the text does not speak of a price below market value, it merely permits deceptive means to ensure that the item is transferred to more honorable ownership. It is quite possible that *Sefer Ḥasidim* does, even under these circumstances, require payment of full market value.

Sleight of hand. In his *Sefer ha-Miẓvot,*[32] Maimonides refers to the scriptural prohibition against the *me'onen* (Lev. 19:26, Deut. 18:10) and takes it refer to two practices: one is astrological speculation devoted to giving practical advice, and the other is the practice of "beguiling the eyes" *(ha-oḥez et ha-einayim).*[33] In the latter sense, *me'onen* is etymologically related to *ayin,* or "eye" (in the former sense it is related to *onah,* or "time period/ phase"). Maimonides explains that this latter group includes practitioners of sleight of hand, who through manual dexterity lead people to believe that they have performed magic, whereas in fact they merely deceive them (the examples he gives are ropes allegedly transformed into snakes, and coins that seem to disappear into thin air and then reappear). Such a person, says Maimonides, in contravening the prohibition of *me'onen,* is guilty of *geneivat da'at ha-beriyot,* i.e., deceiving his fellow men. By thus extending the principle of *geneivat da'at,* Maimonides takes this principle far beyond the merely commercial sphere.

This view of Maimonides was reinforced by one of his descendants, known as R. Joshua b. Abraham Maimoni ha-Nagid, a leader of Egyptian Jewry in the fourteenth century.[34] In answering a question regarding an apparent inconsistency in the *Mishneh Torah,* R. Joshua discusses the Maimonidean view of the *me'onen.* Maimonides in the *Mishneh Torah* writes that any person who "beguiles the eyes" *(ha-oḥez et ha-einayim)* is considered a *me'onen* who is punished with the biblical lashes.[35] R. Joshua defines this act of beguiling by referring to the Arabic term *al-no'argi,*[36] which probably refers to the medieval doctrine (associated with the Moslem Avicenna and with Ibn Ezra) by which certain men claim to be able to perform miracles and unnatural feats through the interaction of their souls with higher

32. *Sefer ha-Miẓvot,* Neg. 32.
33. For a good summary of the various definitions of the concept of *aḥizat einayim,* see the entry in the *Encyclopedia Talmudit* 1:460–463.
34. See "Teshuvot ha-Rav Yehoshua ha-Nagid," *Kobeẓ al Yad* (5700): 85–86. The responsum is also mentioned in the *Kesef Mishnah* to M.T. Hil. *Avodah Zarah* 11:15.
35. *M.T. Hil. Avodah Zarah* 11:9.
36. Interestingly, this same term appears in the original Arabic text of the *Sefer ha-Miẓvot* quoted above, as the act that is prohibited under the rubric of *me'onen.* See the *Sefer ha-Miẓvot,* ed. R. Ḥayyim Heller, loc. cit., n. 23.

supernatural forces.[37] It is clear from the *Sefer ha-Miẓvot* that Maimonides himself considers all such acts to be pure deception, without any real spiritual substance or standing, and he nowhere accepts the Avicennian doctrine as true.[38] R. Joshua then goes on to refer to the Mishnah and Gemara in *Sanhedrin* 67a that speak of witchcraft (*kishuf*) as opposed to beguiling (*ha-oḥez et ha-einayim*). He also quotes Maimonides' own nonextant commentary to *Sanhedrin*, in which witchcraft is punishable by death, while beguilement is that in which "a person makes it appear that he has performed some outcome but in fact has done nothing." The punishment for the latter is lashes. Clearly, according to Maimonides, the actions of *me'onenim* are biblically prohibited, not because there is any reality to what they purport to show, but rather because it essentially violates the prohibition against *geneivat da'at*, being deceptive and misrepresentative of the truth. It is worthwhile noting that such a "naturalism" on the part of Maimonides is consistent with his overall opposition toward astrology, magic, and all similar recourse to supernaturalism. Thus it is to be expected that Maimonides would consider such practitioners to be charlatans, guilty in principle of pure deception.

In a lengthy responsum dealing with the subject, R. David b. Abu Zimra (the Radbaz) discussed Maimonides' approach.[39] Radbaz does indeed accept the possibility of real supernatural effects (as opposed to mere deception), and he takes issue emphatically with Maimonides' refusal to accept such a possibility. The very prohibition against sorcery, he argues, is proof positive that there is some reality to the claims of its practitioners. And the Torah would not punish with lashes the mere sleight of hand practiced in order to deceive. Nonetheless, he too recognizes that, besides the concern for illegitimate supernaturalism, part of the reason for the Torah's prohibition against the actions of the *me'onen* is indeed *geneivat da'at*.[40]

---

37. *Kobeẓ al Yad*, n. 6, as stated by Prof. D. Z. Baneth. For a comprehensive treatment of this subject in medieval Jewish philosophy, see Aviezer Ravitsky, "The Anthropological Theory of Miracles in Medieval Jewish Philosophy," *Studies in Medieval Jewish History and Literature*, vol. 2, ed. I. Twersky (Cambridge, 1984), pp. 231–251, esp. n. 14.

38. Ravitsky, p. 241.

39. *Responsa Radbaz* 1695.

40. For a discussion of this responsum, and some of the problems it raises, see R. Ḥayyim Heller's comments to his edition of the *Sefer ha-Miẓvot*, ad loc.

Self-evaluation in offsetting discrimination. The passage in *Ḥullin* 94a (I) includes, among the list of improper deceptive practices, the case of a host who opens a new barrel of wine for his guest without informing him that the balance of the barrel is already sold. The act is forbidden because the guest, believing that the remainder represents a real financial loss incurred on his behalf, is misled and unduly indebted to his host. The Gemara then records that R. Judah once entertained Ulla under such circumstances but did not so inform him, in spite of this disclosure requirement. The Gemara provides one answer to the effect that R. Judah did not have to inform him because R. Judah felt that he would have opened the barrel under any circumstances for his honored guest. In other words, a person is capable of judging his own motives in his dealings with others, so that he can legitimately behave in ways that under other circumstances would be deceptive.

Yet while Maimonides (L) and the *Tur* (O) both codify the prohibition against opening a wine barrel without such disclosure, neither of them includes this leniency that relies on honest self-evaluation. Why the omission? One answer is provided in the nineteenth century by R. Aryeh Judah b. Akiva.[41] He feels that Maimonides and the *Tur* consider R. Judah's character and ability to practice honest self-evaluation to be exceptional. It is simply not applicable to most people, who cannot be expected to demonstrate such moral fiber and objective self-knowledge, and are likely to confuse self-serving gestures with true selflessness. If the story of R. Judah and Ulla is included in the Gemara, it is merely to illustrate their moral greatness, but not in order to make such behavior universally permissible. Thus the law requires a host to disclose the prior sale of the wine. Indeed the Gemara itself provides a second explanation of R. Judah's behavior, saying that he did actually make full disclosure to his honored guest and correct any false impressions that he might have had.[42]

Yet in spite of the views of Maimonides and the *Tur*, later authorities seem to take a more lenient position, at least regarding self-evaluation to offset job discrimination. A case in point involves a man who wishes to gain employment in a particular

41. *Lev Aryeh*, *Ḥullin* 94a.
42. See the analysis of this question in Levine, *Economics*, pp. 23–24.

position and is certain that he is fully able to discharge all the duties involved. Yet he feels that he might encounter age discrimination on account of his graying beard, in that such beards generally give a man the appearance of being advanced in years. May this man, to offset such potential discrimination, dye his beard? More specifically, does the Halakhah consider him capable of honestly evaluating his ability to fulfill the job requirements, so that he does not improperly deceive his potential employer? Or do we say that he cannot be expected to show such high moral judgment concerning his own motivations, and therefore must present himself as he is, i.e., with full disclosure?

In the twentieth century several authorities considered this question. R. Moshe Mordecai Epstein of Slabodka considered an average man capable of objective self-evaluation as to his ability to perform a given job, and he thus gave permission to dye one's beard under such circumstances.[43] Similarly permissive is a responsum by R. Eliezer Meir Preil.[44] Both of these views are mentioned by Rabbi Moshe Feinstein, and he too concurs, permitting self-evaluation and the dying of one's beard under such circumstances.[45]

Rabbi Aaron Levine attempts to reconcile these latter views with the more stringent rulings of Maimonides, the *Tur*, and R. Aryeh.[46] In his opinion it all depends upon the situation: thus even Maimonides and the *Tur* can agree that self-assessment can be considered sufficiently reliable in ordinary, predictable life-situations, such as the ability to function on a given job on a day-to-day basis. This is not the case for circumstances that are extraordinary, in that most people cannot extrapolate with any degree of certainty how they would react to special or rare situations; in such cases even these modern authorities would concur with the more restrictive view, and require the fullest disclosure.

This discussion would appear to dovetail with the express position found in the Gemara in *Bava Meẓia* 60a–b (G). There the Mishnah forbids dying of a beard to give a mistaken impression of youthfulness, and the Gemara explains that such improper actions are sometimes carried out in marketing a slave, so

43. *Levush Mordecai* 24.
44. R. Eliezer Meir Preil, *ha-Maor* 1:26–27.
45. *Responsa Iggerot Moshe, Y.D.* 2:61.
46. Levine, *Economics*, p. 25.

as to give the appearance of youth. The Gemara illustrates the point by referring to R. Papa, who purchased an elderly slave, misled by his appearance, and subsequently was ill-served by him. Clearly what is forbidden is intentional misleading of the potential buyer, whose expectations will not be met. It does not, however, forbid honest self-evaluation as to one's ability, or readiness, to perform expected work, and then acting in good faith.

The written word: Publishing and academic liberties. In 1980, Rabbi Eliezer Waldenberg wrote a responsum to a young doctor who had inquired whether it is halakhically permissible to alter details of medical research when it comes to publication, so as to further the career of the author—without, however, endangering the life of others.[47]

Rabbi Waldenberg finds that such activity violates the prohibition against *geneivat da'at.* It makes no difference, he says, that the vast majority of the readers are Gentiles—and he refers to Maimonides' formulation of the prohibition (L). He also quotes Rabbeinu Yonah (N), who extends the prohibition to a concern beyond the intended audience to the effect on the inner life of the person responsible for an act of deception. Such reflexive concern, says Rabbi Waldenberg, is similar to Maimonides' novel interpretation of the prohibition against cursing another, i.e., not that the curse has some supernatural effect, but that it undermines the wholesome character of the curser.[48] This is certainly true of written material, in that any modification of the truth "uproots the parameters of truth from foundations of the soul." Thus any alteration in the data or presentation of such a paper violates *geneivat da'at.*

In addition, Rabbi Waldenberg considers such "tampering" to be prohibited under the rubric of the prohibition against lying ("keep thee far from a falsehood," Exod. 23:7). Based on another passage in Rabbeinu Yonah, he concludes that it is prohibited to "embellish the truth" to benefit oneself, even where it does not lead to financial loss for someone else. He further quotes the twentieth-century Ḥafeẓ Ḥayyim, who included under the rubric of forbidden lying, loose talk that takes liberties with truth in

47. *Responsa Ẓiẓ Eliezer* 15:12.
48. *Sefer ha-Miẓvot,* neg. 317. For further discussion of this aspect of Maimonides' philosophy, see my *Joseph Ibn Kaspi's "Gevia Kesef"* (New York, 1982), pp. 119 ff.

order to enhance the social standing of its speaker.[49] This, says Waldenberg, is essentially identical with the case of a researcher who publishes a "doctored" paper to advance his career. Moreover, hiding one's rationale in this fashion is quite analogous to the case of a man who faithfully reports events as they happened, but conceals his own motivation and intent for reasons of his own (he might get pleasure from keeping his own counsel.) This latter situation is prohibited by the *Sefer Yad ha-Ketanah.*[50]

There is, however, one early view that appears to differ with this negative conclusion. The *Sefer Yerayim* of R. Eliezer of Metz, quoted earlier, states that the lying that is prohibited refers to lying that causes damages to another person, "whereas falsehood that causes no injury to others is not forbidden by the Torah."[51] As explained by the To'afot Re'eim in commenting on this passage, this distinction serves to explain the well-known view of Beit Hillel, found in *Ketuvot* 17a, that it is permitted to lie in describing a bride at her wedding, just as one may falsely praise a friend's new purchase.[52] Beit Hillel apparently considers a lie forbidden only where it causes definite loss (financial or otherwise) or material misrepresentation, but not where it serves merely to set another's mind at rest. Beit Shammai, on the other hand, considers *any* lie *geneivat da'at,* constituting an act of forbidden deception. According to the *Sefer Yerayim,* therefore, if we accept Beit Hillel's view, it is permissible to tamper with nonessential information, if as a result there is no measurable harm to others.

Yet, as Rabbi Waldenberg points out, it is likely that even this minority view speaks only of the absence of a Torah prohibition. On a rabbinic level, as suggested by the To'afot Re'eim, such activity represents improper behavior.

A somewhat different, although essentially similar, question is posed by the common practice of students who cheat in one form or another, so as to inflate their grades, albeit without apparent "damage" to either their fellow students or their teachers. Is this too *geneivat da'at?*

---

49. *Sha'arei Teshuvah* 3:186, *Sefer Shemirat ha-Lashon,* chap. 6.
50. *Sefer Yad ha-Ketanah, Deot* 10:9, as quoted in *Ẓiẓ Eliezer* 15:12.
51. *Sefer Yerayim ha-Shalem* 235.
52. For a discussion of this Gemara and some of its ramifications, see *Jewish Ethics and Halakhah,* vol. 1, pp. 55–56.

R. Menasheh Klein was asked this question, and he answered that such actions are definitely forbidden.[53] Which prohibition is involved? It depends on the purpose of the studies undertaken. Where they are intended to be used to gain subsequent employment, such cheating constitutes outright theft against a future employer, who is misled into a mistaken evaluation of this employee, including payment of salary beyond his or her actual qualifications or expertise. But where the purpose of the studies is merely to become a diplomate or for self-enrichment, and the grades are fraudulently manipulated by means of such cheating, while this is not theft per se, it is deceptive, and therefore constitutes *geneivat da'at*, according to Rabbi Klein.

Very similar thoughts were expressed in a short essay authored by a young Israeli yeshivah student, dismayed at the incidence of cheating by her classmates in school examinations.[54] Pointing to the ramifications of *geneivat da'at*, she also holds teachers and proctors who tolerate such behavior equally guilty of unacceptable indulgence. Rabbi David Bleich, reviewing this issue, adds the further consideration of *ḥillul Hashem*, by which a religious student who cheats in this fashion can bring dishonor to the Torah and religious life, and ultimately to the God who commanded the *miẓvot*. Widespread cheating in religious institutions would certainly discredit all these, and for this additional reason be prohibited.[55]

It might be added that the halakhic concerns relative to the problem of plagiarism and infringement of copyright are also of significance to this issue. Beside the specific prohibitions involving theft or unauthorized use of material belonging to another—bans that are not within our present purview[56]—it would appear that considerations of deception should come into play. After all, when one person gains unearned and unwarranted respect or other rewards by passing off the work of others as his own, he has surely committed an act of deception upon his fellows, whether or not there is a financial cost to them. Such considerations are raised by a number of halakhists in dealing with the question of Torah scholars who repeat the scholarship or creative

53. *Responsa Mishneh Halakhot* 7:275.
54. Zipporah Wieder, *Shma'atin* (Tammuz 5736): 80–81.
55. Bleich, *Contemporary Halakhic Problems*, 2:109–111.
56. For a good summary, see ibid., 2:121–130.

thought of other scholars whom they have heard, or whose work they have read, but without proper attribution. The Maharam Schick considers this an infringement of *geneivat da'at*,[57] and a number of others, including the Magen Avraham (R. Abraham Gombiner) and the *Noda bi-Yehudah*, largely concur.[58]

Before concluding this section, we can examine two other principles that occur in the context of deceptive behavior. Besides considerations of *ona'ah* and *geneivat da'at*, principles that are essentially negative and prohibitive, there are two positive exhortations that are derived from the Torah.

Hain Ẓedek

In Leviticus (B) the Torah requires that commercial transactions be carried out with honest weights and balances. The prohibition, as the Torah formulates it, even extends to the mere possession of inaccurate weights. Now the Gemara in *Bava Meẓia* (H) contains the following discussion, pertinent to this scriptural verse:

Where there is a verbal agreement as to the terms of a commercial transaction, and prior to the formal consummation of the deal, the market value of the goods fluctuates, may either party renege on its oral obligations? The Gemara records two views: Rav permits such action and perceives no real lack of good faith, whereas R. Yoḥanan considers such action reprehensible in that it indicates an improper failure to live up to one's word. In questioning the lenient view of Rav, the Gemara quotes R. Yossi b. Judah in the *Torat Kohanim* to *Kedoshim*. R. Yossi notes that in (B) there is an apparent redundancy—if the Torah requires precise weights in the case of an *eifah*, why must it repeat the requirement in the case of a *hin*, which is merely one-sixth the size of an *eifah*? He answers that the term *hin* in this context has an additional connotation, notably as it is etymologically related to *hain*, meaning "yes" or "agreed." Hence *hin ẓedek* in this context teaches the obligation of treating one's "word," or verbal agreement, with utmost seriousness, i.e., as binding and sacred,

---

57. *Responsa Maharam Shick, Y.D.* 156.

58. *Magen Avraham* to *O.H.* 156; *Noda bi-Yehudah, Mahadura Tinyana O.H.* 20. These and other sources are quoted by R. Shelomoh Zalman Braun, *She'arim ha-Meẓuyyanim be'Halakhah*, vol. 4, p. 200, n. 4.

even in the absence of a written agreement. If so, says the Gemara, how can Rav permit a man to renege on his solemn word or agreement?

Abbaye answers on behalf of Rav that a distinction is to be made. What R. Yossi refers to is the obligation to remain true to one's word, so that one does not agree or commit to a transaction without every intention of living up to the terms agreed upon. R. Yossi requires solemn consistency between one's word and one's heart. But he does not, according to Rav, insist that a man must honor his word even if in the interim (prior to formalization of the transaction) the market fluctuates and new conditions prevail. Pulling out of a verbal agreement under such conditions does not automatically qualify as bad faith.

Even so, it is not the view of Rav which became normative, but that of R. Yoḥanan.[59] Thus even where circumstances change, a man should feel obligated to honor his word and his verbal undertakings. And even Rav agrees that where circumstances remain constant, the Halakhah requires complete consistency between the spoken word and one's inner intentions.[60] And Maimonides makes it quite clear that this standard is certainly applicable to the dealings of a *talmid ḥakham*, a student of the law, as he comports himself with "truth and good faith."[61]

The obligation to live up to one's word emerges in yet another context. The Mishnah in *Bava Meẓia*,[62] in discussing various forms of acquisition, states that one party to a transaction can renege up until the moment that actual possession of the goods is taken. This is true even where payment has been made, insofar as it is not the payment per se which renders the transaction final, but possession alone. But having said this, the Mishnah then adds, quoting what is apparently a tannaitic consensus, that "they said that the God who punished [*mi she-para*] the

59. *M.T. Hil. Mekhirah* 7:8. See *Shulḥan Arukh ha-Rav, Hil. Mekhirah* 2.

60. In the subsequent literature, two views emerged as to the primary sense of the verse in Leviticus, whether it be the principle of consistency between one's words and one's heart (Naḥmanides, Rashba, and Rosh), or the importance of sticking by a verbal commitment (Baal ha-Ma'or, Ittur, Sema, and the Shelah). For a full treatment of these various views in the halakhic literature relative to the sources, biblical status, and application of *hain ẓedek*, see the entry in the *Encyclopedia Talmudit* 9:463–466.

61. *M.T. Hil De'ot* 5:13.

62. *Bava Meẓia* 4:1 (44a).

generation of the great flood and the generation of those who built the tower to heaven, will likewise punish anyone who is not true to his word." In other words, while in the strictly legal sense it is quite permissible to renege on one's verbal commitment of purchase or sale, even up to the last moment, nonetheless it is wrong and morally reprehensible to act in such a fashion.

With this Mishnah as the foundation, the Halakhah subsequently incorporated the so-called *mi she-para* curse to be invoked upon any Jew who reneged on his verbal commitment, whether as buyer or seller. Indeed the one guilty of such a moral offense is obliged to "accept" the malediction at the hands of the rabbinical court. As Maimonides put it, such behavior is unworthy of a Jew, for in so doing "he has not acted in the way that a Jew should act [*lo asah ma'aseh Yisrael*]." In Maimonides' version, the curse includes additional references to the divine punishment of Sodom and Gomorrah, and of Egypt at the Red Sea.[63]

Clearly, the Halakhah in this prescription demands fealty to one's solemn undertakings well beyond the letter of the law, and takes great care to instill the fear of heaven in favor of honesty and fairness.

From these passages it is clear that not merely honesty, but good faith too, is required in one's business dealings. Again we can refer to Maimonides' inclusive statement (L) that the Halakhah requires that "one must not say one thing and mean another . . . only what we have in mind should we utter with the mouth."[64]

vi'Heyitem Nekiyyim

When the Torah in Numbers (D) exhorts one to be held guiltless (*nekiyyim*) before God *and* Israel, the Halakhah took this as an obligation not only to do the right thing, but also to *be seen* as doing the right thing.[65] Sometimes known as *mar'it ayin*, or "mistaken appearance," this refers to situations in which one is likely to be suspected or perceived by others as acting improperly.

---

63. Maimonides, *M.T. Hil. Mekhirah* 7:1.

64. Regarding the relationship of this passage in *Hil. De'ot* to the concept of *hain ẓedek*, see the respective views of *Minḥat Ḥinukh* to 259 and the *Or Sameaḥ* to *Hil. De'ot* 2:6.

65. An exhaustive treatment of the entire topic, known as *ḥashad*, can be found in *Encyclopedia Talmudit* 17:567 ff.

Now in the realm of commerce and finances, this principle of *vi'heyitem nekiyyim* has some very specific applications. A case in point, found in *Pesaḥim* (K), affects collectors of charity. For such collectors, it is not sufficient that they be scrupulously honest in handling and disposing of charity funds. This Gemara requires them to invite outside participants to ensure that no questions can be raised by others. Thus they may not exchange their own coins for those in the charity fund, and they may not themselves purchase charitable perishables, even at market price, lest they be suspected of taking advantage of such funds.[66] According to *Responsa Beit Ya'akov*, the only exception involves very small quantities, where it is unlikely that people will harbor such suspicions.[67]

Other situations where the Halakhah specifically calls for avoiding all appearances of impropriety include the use of monies, goods, or food in one's possession as security on loans;[68] a widow who disposes of her children's assets to ensure her own *ketubah* rights; the proper disposal of lost and found property to ensure that the value of the goods is preserved in case the owner is located;[69] and the proper payment of money pledged to charity and payable in a distant city.[70]

In all such cases, it is not merely suggested, but required, that a Jew make every effort to treat the property and person of others with complete fairness, openness, and integrity. Only in that way can one be held guiltless and irreproachable, as the verse puts it, both in the eyes of God (for the objective reality of one's actions) and in the eyes of men (who can, after all, only judge based on subjective reactions to a given situation).

2. THE RESPONSIBILITIES AND ONUS DEVOLVING UPON THE PURCHASER

The discussion to this point has concentrated exclusively upon the halakhic expectations that relate to the seller, or vendor, in

66. *Encyclopedia Talmudit* 17:596–597. See also Levine, *Economics*, p. 16. See Maimonides, *M.T. Hil. Matanot Aniyyim* 9:11.
67. *Responsa Beit Ya'akov* 70, as quoted in *Pitḥei Teshuvah*, *Sh.A. Y.D.* 257:1.
68. *Bava Meẓia* 38a.
69. *Bava Meẓia* 28b.
70. *Megillah* 27a.

commercial transactions. Clearly, these standards are considerable. Yet there are also limitations on these duties and responsibilities, as will soon become clear, insofar as the consumer must assume certain responsibilities for ascertaining the condition of the goods involved in the transaction.

The passage in *Ḥullin* 94a (I) that formed the basis for our discussion of *geneivat da'at* lists, inter alia, the prohibition against the sale of nonkosher meat to a Gentile, for the reason that he is thereby deceived, and furthermore that he might resell it to a Jew as kosher meat. Thus, as Rashi explains, the Gentile must be informed at the time of sale, so that there is no deception, and furthermore such meat can only be sold to him in a community where Jews know not to purchase any meat from Gentiles (and in such a community it is unnecessary to alert other Jews to this sale by public pronouncement). The Gemara (J) then asks as follows: in those communities where Jews do indeed purchase kosher meat from Gentiles, and in so doing rely on their fellow Jews to make a public announcement in cases where nonkosher has been sold to Gentile suppliers, how is that announcement to be made? R. Isaac b. Joseph permits a nonspecific statement that "meat" has been sold to Gentiles, without specifying "nonkosher meat," for we can presume that the Gentile only buys it because he believes it to be kosher, hence a more specific announcement will result in his not purchasing the meat altogether.

But, the Gemara asks, does this not constitute *geneivat da'at* and deception? The Gemara answers that in such a case, the purchaser is not misled by the seller—rather he misleads himself (which is but another way of saying that he has been negligent). Rashi explains this answer as saying that it was his responsibility to inquire whether the meat be kosher or not, and not to assume it to be kosher. This, says Rashi, is to be distinguished from the earlier-mentioned sale of nonkosher meat forbidden by the Gemara, for in the earlier case the seller intimated clearly that the meat was kosher (*be'ḥezkat kesheirah*). Likewise, says Rashi, the earlier-quoted case of a host opening wine barrels for his guest forbids the host to say, "I am opening these specifically for you." Thus, according to Rashi, *geneivat da'at* occurs when one party falsely describes the nature of the goods or states in so many words that he is acting to benefit the other party. To Rashi, mere silence is not *geneivat da'at*. Tosafot, however, finds this explanation of Rashi problematic.[71] In the case of the wine barrels, the Gemara (I) had said that the host acts improperly "unless he so informs him that it is already sold." Apparently, says Tosafot, the host practices deception when he does not fully inform his guest, and he violates *geneivat da'at* by passively permitting his guest to get the wrong impression. Furthermore, says Tosafot, R. Judah would never have lied to his honored guest; thus the Gemara must mean that R. Judah disclosed all the facts fully to him. From this we can learn, says Tosafot, that even silence in such a case is forbidden, for "a guest should not be expected to know that the barrels are already sold." This is to be distinguished from the case of selling meat to a Gentile, for there it should indeed occur to the purchaser that the meat might not be kosher.

It would appear that Rashi and Tosafot differ as to the essential definition of forbidden deception. According to Rashi, the vendor should not make a false statement, but he does not have to correct an unwarranted misconception on the part of the purchaser, where the vendor did not deliberately create the misunderstanding. Tosafot, on the other hand, requires that the seller actively disabuse his customer of any such error, whenever he recognizes the purchaser (or guest) as likely to be laboring under some misconception, either as to the circumstances or the quality of the goods.

The Gemara goes on to record an incident in which Mar Zutra mistakenly believed that Rava and R. Safra had set out in his honor to welcome him as he approached their town. R. Safra hastened to correct Mar Zutra's wrong impression, telling him that they were indeed on their way elsewhere, and their meeting had been entirely fortuitous. Rava, on the other hand, disagreed with R. Safra, saying that it had not been necessary to correct Mar Zutra's error. R. Safra claimed that to have acted otherwise would have constituted *geneivat da'at*. "No," said Rava, "he would be deceiving himself." Here, too, Rashi says, "we did not tell him

71. Tosafot, *Ḥullin* 94b, s.v. *inhu*. In the preceding Tosafot (s.v. *amar*) Rabbeinu Tam seems to agree with Rashi, and a similar view is attributed to Rabbeinu Tam by the Rosh (to *Ḥullin* 7:18.). It also appears that Rashi is in agreement with his teacher, Rabbeinu Gershom ("*Me'or ha-Golah*"). Tosafot is quoted verbatim in the *Beit Yosef* to the *Tur H.M.* 228.

'we have come to meet you,'" i.e., for Rashi they would be blameless for remaining silent, just as long as they did not make a false statement to mislead him. Whereas Tosafot explains, "It should have occurred to Mar Zutra that they might not be journeying to meet him," i.e., in this case there was no need for them to correct his mistaken impression, for he should have known better. But under other circumstances, it is implied by Tosafot, they would have had to set the record straight, in word or in deed. Among later medieval authorities, Nahmanides and the Rashba side with Rashi,[72] while the Rosh,[73] R. Joseph Karo (in the *Beit Yosef*),[74] and the Sema agree with Tosafot.[75]

Maimonides' position in this regard is not quite clear. In *Hilkhot De'ot* (L), in forbidding various kinds of *geneivat da'at*, he does not expressly include the concept of self-deception that emerges from the talmudic discussion. This alone would indicate that there is a categorical obligation, à la Tosafot, to correct a wrong impression, no matter that it was unwarranted in the circumstances.[76] Maimonides' all-inclusive formulation of the need to embrace complete honesty would also lead to this conclusion. This, at any rate, is how Maimonides was understood by a number of interpreters, including the *Knesset ha-Gedolah*.[77] R. Abraham de Boton (the *Leḥem Mishneh*), however, feels that Maimonides agrees with Rashi, based on Maimonides' terminology that "even a single *word* of . . . deception is forbidden," i.e., what is forbidden are explicit words that mislead, but in the absence of any such misleading words, where it is self-deception by the other party that is involved, then one can conclude that the first party is not obligated to correct him.[78] Even so, as the *Leḥem Mishneh* himself admits, the problem with this interpretation of Maimonides' text is that Maimonides should have made the distinction more explicit than it appears in his formulation.

In any case, this dispute between Rashi and Tosafot, involving

72. See their Novellae to *Ḥullin* 94b.
73. Rosh, *Ḥullin* 7:18, explicitly differs with Rashi.
74. *Beit Yosef* to *Tur H.M.* 228.
75. *Sefer Me'rat Einayim* (Sema), *Sh.A. H.M.* 228:9.
76. See *Encyclopedia Talmudit* 6:230.
77. *Knesset ha-Gedolah* to *Sh.A. H.M.* 228:3. Likewise R. Masud Hai Rekaḥ (the Ma'aseh Rokeaḥ) understood Maimonides in similar terms, in his *Ma'aseh Rokeaḥ, M.T. Hil. Mekhirah* 18:4 (4). See Shoḥatman, pp. 232–233.
78. *Leḥem Mishnah, M.T. Hil. Deot* 2:6. See also the *Kesef Mishnah* ad loc.

the issue of the purchaser who comes to mistaken conclusions for lack of his own careful consideration, seems to be decided in favor of Tosafot. Thus the *Tur* (O), in formulating the law of *geneivat da'at*, starts out by emphasizing the gravity of the transgression, due to the difficulty of undoing the negative effects that follow such tactics. He then goes on to refer to the case of the wine barrels, and states that it is necessary for the host to make it quite clear to his guest that the barrels are already sold; i.e., mere silence is not sufficient, in that the guest might well assume the barrels to be opened exclusively for him. Clearly this position reflects the view of Tosafot. A similar position is codified by the *Shulḥan Arukh*, as well as the *Shulhan Arukh ha-Rav*.[79] The *Arukh ha-Shulḥan*, however, sides with Rashi's minority view.[80]

Related to this question of the responsibility of the purchaser to exercise care in making certain assumptions regarding goods or services purchased is another issue: where the goods are defective, how specific must the seller be in describing the condition of the goods in question? Does the purchaser bear any responsibility to clarify the condition of the goods at the time of purchase?

R. Vidal Yomtov of Tolosa, the *Maggid Mishnah*, is of the opinion that where the purchaser could have checked the condition of the goods at the time but did not, he has no further claim on the vendor.[81] Other authorities, however, differ with him. Thus the *Mishneh la-Melekh* disagrees, in view of the fact that the major codifiers do not include such a law. And R. Jacob Moses Lorberbaum (the *Netivot ha-Mishpat*) assigns such responsibility only where the purchaser uses the goods, in that such usage can be taken as a readiness to overlook the defect.[82] The view of the Radbaz is that the purchaser does not have to check if the seller assured him that the goods were free of all defects.[83] Regarding the purchase of a building, two views are expressed. R. Joshua Falk in his *Prishah* is of the opinion that if the purchaser does not check the facility at the time of purchase, he cannot claim to

79. *Sh.A. H.M.* 228:6; *Shulḥan Arukh ha-Rav, Hil. Ona'ah* 13.
80. *Arukh ha-Shulḥan, H.M.* 228:3.
81. *Maggid Mishnah, M.T. Hil. Mekhirah* 15:3. The section that follows here is based on the article by Warhaftig, pp. 350 ff.
82. *Netivot ha-Mishpat* to *Sh.A. H.M.* 232:1.
83. *Responsa Radbaz* 4:1206.

be misled if he subsequently discovers obvious defects.[84] But the twelfth-century R. Joseph Ibn Migash has an opposing view.[85]

If the defect was obvious to the purchaser at the time of purchase, he cannot subsequently claim to have been misled. Thus the Gemara *Ketuvot* 57b states that when a man purchases a slave with an obvious blemish, it can be assumed that he purchased him knowing, and accepting, the defect. And where it is common for purchasers of wine or other foods to taste prior to purchase, they cannot subsequently claim to be misled, for they should have tasted it at the time.[86] The same is true, says the Rema, where the nature of the goods is obvious to the purchaser, even though the seller describes them in a manner that is clearly incorrect (e.g., describing wood as gold).[87] When the purchaser continues to use the goods even after the defective nature of the item is known to him, this can be taken as clear indication that he has accepted such defects in their entirety, and cannot subsequently return the goods in question.[88] Once the purchaser informs the seller of the problem, he remains responsible for the item until it is returned.[89]

If the seller does indeed point out defects or possible problems with the item in question, the purchaser cannot subsequently return the goods with a claim to have been misled.[90] Maimonides in particular requires not simply a general disclaimer as to possible defects, but a detailed enumeration of every defect known to the seller—otherwise the purchaser may claim to have been misled, and in any case could not have waived his rights, given such a vague disavowal.[91] The *Tur* differs with Maimonides on this point, and does not require a detailed disclaimer on the part of the seller.[92]

A further consideration occurs where there are certain widespread assumptions as to the condition of goods purchased. Thus, it is permissible, according to the *Shulḥan Arukh*, for a

84. *Prishah* to *Tur H.M.* 232:5.
85. *Responsa Ri Migash* 51.
86. *Bava Meẓia* 60a.
87. Rema, *Y.D. H.M.* 232:7.
88. Maimonides, *M.T. Hil. Mekhirah* 15:3; *Tur/Sh.A. H.M.* 232:3.
89. Warhaftig, p. 352.
90. *Sh.A. H.M.* 232:19.
91. Maimonides, *M.T. Hil. Mekhirah* 15:6.
92. *Tur/Sh.A. H.M.* 232:7.

distributor of grain to mix the product using various types and qualities, without explicitly informing his customers of such mixing, because it is generally understood by buyers that this is the usual procedure.[93] The fact that a given customer may not be aware of this conventional practice does not require the seller to assume the responsibility of informing him. Furthermore, says Warhaftig, where the quality of the product is likely to be doubtful or ambiguous, it is the responsibility of the purchaser to take the initiative and ask the appropriate questions.[94] This can be deduced from *Ḥullin* (J), where the Gemara permits the ambiguous announcement that "meat" has been sold, putting the onus on the purchaser to clarify the precise nature of the meat, because he should realize that there is a reasonable possibility that what is being sold is nonkosher meat. Thus, if the purchaser does not question or seek to establish its status, the seller has no obligation to inform him.

The responsibilities of clarification devolving upon the purchaser emerge in yet another area, treated earlier, where the seller presents the goods in the best possible light, using a variety of nonverbal promotional techniques. Thus we have seen, based on *Bava Meẓia* (G), that the seller may indeed resort to a number of strategies to put the best appearance on new goods. It is understood by purchasers that the merchandise is deliberately spruced up to promote its sale. What is forbidden, as we saw, is the deliberate attempt to mislead or to cover up defects of one kind or another.

A discussion, and difference of opinion, involving precisely such a case arose in the twentieth century, in a way that served to reflect the respective opinions of Rashi and Tosafot (and possibly even of Rava and R. Safra in [J], or for that matter Samuel and Shemaya themselves in [I]), as well as the later discussants, seen above. In 1937 Rabbi Yehoshua Baumol was asked to rule whether it be permissible for kosher butchers to soak liver in blood, which in its congealed state serves to preserve the appearance of freshness.[95] A number of kashrut considerations are raised by this practice, but in addition a key concern is whether this action

93. *Sh.A. H.M.* 228:16.
94. Warhaftig, p. 358.
95. *Responsa Emek Halakhah* 2:4, 5, 6.

improperly misleads customers, who might think that the meat is fresher than it is. Rabbi Baumol refers to the Gemara *Bava Meẓia* (G) that forbids a vendor from soaking meat in water, the reason being, as Rashi explains, that the meat thereby appears fatter and more succulent—hence more valuable. Maimonides (M) accepts this stricture as normative. This, says Rabbi Baumol, is clearly analogous to blood-soaked liver, in that both intend to conceal the true state or quality of the meat. Furthermore, he argues, it makes no difference whether the selling price for fresh liver is higher than for preserved liver or not; even if the price is identical, *geneivat da'at* is involved.

This responsum generated an exchange of views among some of the leading authorities of the day. Rabbi Moshe Feinstein authored two responsa on the topic.[96] In the first, he dismisses the kashrut concerns, but does concede that where the customer is unaware of the butcher's conserving tactic, the prohibition of *ona'ah* is triggered. While Rabbi Feinstein does not explain precisely, it would appear that the *ona'ah* is of the nature of deceptive and misleading business practices. A short while later, in his second responsum, Reb Moshe returned to the topic, this time at greater length. Again he dismisses the kashrut questions raised (in the interim several other rabbis had added their concerns). Furthermore, in this responsum he pulls back from his earlier concession with regard to *ona'ah*. Thus he refers to the Gemara *Ḥullin* 8b, in which Rav Pappa forbids a butcher to display his meat in such a way that forbidden fats (*ḥelev*) lie on top of the permitted cuts of meat, because (as Rashi explains) some of the fat might be absorbed into the meat beneath it. Now Maimonides, in accepting this rule, adds one word of clarification—*le'na'oto*, "to make it appear attractive."[97] Rabbi Feinstein concludes from this that what is forbidden is not the attractive display or presentation per se, but rather any action that might mix nonkosher fat with kosher. Apparently, says Rabbi Feinstein, this case is to be distinguished from the sale of nonkosher meat to a Gentile (I), otherwise Maimonides would certainly have forbidden the activity on the grounds of it being a deceptive business practice as well.

96. *Responsa Iggerot Moshe, Y.D.* 30, 31. The second of these appeared originally in *ha-Pardes*, Elul 5697.
97. Maimonides, *M.T. Hil. Ma'akhalot Asurot* 7:19.

But what of the prohibition in *Bava Meẓia* (G) that forbids soaking meat so as to make it appear more desirable? Reb Moshe answers that there is a difference: soaking meat to fatten it, as with painting old merchandise to look new, is forbidden on grounds of *ona'ah* because "the purchaser has no reason at all to suspect" such a tactic, "and there is no reason for him to have to ask" if the product be fat or fresh. The customer, says Reb Moshe, properly relies on his eyes in judging the quality or freshness of the meat, which the butcher in so displaying implies to be consistent with its appearance. This is to be distinguished from the case of blood-soaked liver, which is like the case in *Ḥullin* 8b of meat displayed to best advantage: in both instances the customer should consider the possibility that the meat is not as fresh or tasty as it appears, insofar as it is common for liver to be soaked or meat to be displayed (in the absence of kashrut considerations) in this fashion, and the butcher merely presents it to its best advantage. In this latter case the onus is on the customer to consider the possibility that it has been so soaked, and thus to ask the appropriate questions. And if he does not ask at the time, then it is apparent that he is not particular in this regard, or if he is particular but omitted to ask, then he has in fact misled himself (or at any rate has been negligent). The seller, says Rabbi Feinstein, does not have to prompt such a question, when it is a question that the customer himself should be asking, given the common occurrence of such merchandising practices.[98]

Proof for this contention, says Rabbi Feinstein, is the Gemara in *Ḥullin* (J), where it is quite permissible for the butcher to sell nonkosher meat to a Gentile under the pretense that it is kosher, without alerting him as to its real status. For it should have occurred to the Gentile purchaser that he was getting nonkosher meat, and by not asking he was negligent and remiss in his own interest. The butcher, in that case, is no more than an indirect cause of self-deception by the purchaser, as is made clear by the analogous case in the Gemara, whereby Mar Zutra deceived himself too.

Thus, says R. Moshe, in the case of the liver the soaking does

98. The *Arukh ha-Shulḥan*, *H.M.* 228:5, seems to support such a position too, in that he indicates that the prohibition against soaking meat does not apply where butchers resort to such procedures and "everyone knows that they do this."

not establish its freshness, it merely preserves or establishes a neutral appearance, on the basis of which it is for the customer to establish the facts. By not inquiring, it is the customer who is at fault, and the butcher is not guilty of any misleading behavior. Rabbi Feinstein concludes that butchers do nothing wrong in so displaying their merchandise.

In his second responsum, Rabbi Baumol set out to further clarify his views. It is clear, he says, that fresh liver is more desirable, and therefore more costly, than liver that is even a few days old. Hence any activity that has the effect of concealing the age of liver, so that a customer might unwittingly pay for fresh liver while getting the preserved variety, must be considered deceptive, and an infraction not only of *ona'ah*, but of real theft (*gezel*). Rabbi Baumol also questions Reb Moshe's proof from Maimonides' formulation of the law in *Ḥullin* 8b. For he takes Rabbi Feinstein to understand Maimonides as saying that the butcher in this case acts with the intention of taking advantage of the customer (*ona'ah*), and thus Rabbi Baumol takes issue with him, saying that Maimonides means only that the butcher intends to display his wares in the best fashion.[99] In any case, he states, even if the responsibility devolves upon the customer to ask pertinent questions, still that does not permit the butcher himself to exploit such negligence and charge more than the market price of the liver.

In considering these two views, they appear to correspond in rough measure to the views of Rashi and Tosafot in commenting on *Ḥullin* 94a–b (I, J). Reb Moshe, like Rashi, finds room to permit the seller a passive response to a mistaken impression on the part of the purchaser, just as long as the seller does not resort to outright lies or deception. Rabbi Baumol, on the other hand, is closer to the view of Tosafot, in requiring a more activist stance to dispel any misconception, whether the result of negligence on the part of the purchaser or not. For Reb Moshe the key criterion is to establish what is the common and accepted practice in the case at hand, and then to require that each party conform to such expectations. But for Rabbi Baumol what is prohibited is

99. Frankly, however, a careful reading of Rabbi Feinstein's responsum (reflected in our presentation of his views above) yields the conclusion that he too understands Maimonides to be describing the butcher's action as *le'na'oto* ("to make it attractive"), and not as *le'honoto* ("to take advantage of him").

any misleading presentation that contributes to a misunderstanding of the true nature of the goods in question; and it makes no difference that accepted practice requires one party to satisfy certain criteria before it can claim to have been misled. Apropos of these two views, it would appear that R. Shneur Zalman of Liadi offers a hybrid solution: he says that if indeed it is the case that local butchers commonly soak meat to make it appear fatter, and their customers generally are aware of this, then there are those who permit such soaking;[100] nonetheless, he adds, one who is careful will not do such a thing, for certain purchasers might actually believe that what they see is in fact the higher-grade meat when it is not.[101]

Parenthetically, this view of Reb Moshe, with its overtones of halakhic sensitivity to common practice and assumptions, is fully reflective of his position on the presence—or absence—of a prohibition against cigarette smoking and nonmedical drugs.[102] There too it is at least partially a question of what is socially understood, practiced, or sanctioned that heavily influences the halakhic attitude to such activities.

There is one further situation that should be examined, but this time involving a lack of knowledge on the part of the seller and not the buyer. This is the case where the purchaser conceals not the objective condition or value of the item at hand, but rather its potential or subjective value to him. Must he disclose to the other party all the circumstances that motivate him to enter into this transaction, or may he conceal them as long as the seller gets fair market value? One such situation occurs where an entrepreneur wishes to purchase land for development; were he to disclose all pertinent information regarding his intentions, or the subsequent value of the real estate as a result of the implementation of his plans, he would be at a distinct disadvantage in negotiations with the seller, or sellers, of various parcels of the land in question. May he mislead the seller as to his intentions?

Rabbi Aaron Levine answers that in cases such as this, concealment of information can only be viewed as improperly deceptive if it in some way misrepresents the nature of the property

100. He is probably referring to the Sema, *Sh.A. H.M.* 228:16. See Warhaftig, p. 359.

101. *Shulḥan Arukh ha-Rav, Hil. Ona'ah* 19.

102. See *Jewish Ethics and Halakhah*, vol. 1, chap. 9, esp. pp. 232–235.

right being transferred. But the purchaser is under no obligation to reveal his motives or entrepreneurial intent unless the other party explicitly requests its disclosure.[103] Even so, the purchaser should not lie, but he is permitted to distract the other party.

Rabbi Levine finds support for his view in the rabbinic understanding of two incidents in Genesis. In the first, when Abraham purchased the cave of Makhpelah for a burial plot (Gen. 23) he was careful not to reveal to the seller the special significance of that particular parcel of land for himself and his family, it being the ancestral burial ground, according to his family tradition, of Adam and Eve. Had the seller known this fact, he would have demanded vastly more for the land in question. The second incident involved Jacob in his purchase of the birthright from his brother Esau (in Gen. 25). Taking advantage of Esau's hunger, Jacob gets Esau to agree to sell the birthright for a mess of pottage, surely less than what its value to Jacob would subsequently be. Is this not deception or exploitation? The answer, according to Rabbi Levine, is no, in that Esau felt that he was likely to die before his father anyway (as explained by Naḥmanides), hence to him the offer by Jacob represented a fair exchange given his needs and expectations, and in any case he could sell the birthright to no one other than Jacob. Thus Jacob was fully entitled to make his low offer, and even to reinforce in subtle (but not false) fashion Esau's anticipation of his own early death.[104]

Thus it would be similarly permissible for a purchaser to conceal the eventual value to him of the transaction involved, just as long as he (a) pays the current market value to avoid the prohibition of *ona'ah*, (b) does not make a false statement, and (c) if asked directly does in fact disclose all the pertinent facts or motives.

A variation on this theme, leading to a similar conclusion, occurs when one party (e.g., a day laborer) contracts to perform certain work, (i.e., "sells" his services) for his employer, but then is guilty of a breach of contract that would lead to a financial loss for the employer. While as a general rule it is forbidden for either to engage in bluffing or deceptive behavior (for reasons of *ona'ah* and *hain ẓedek*, as above), in this case the Halakhah does permit

103. Levine, *Economics*, p. 17.
104. Ibid., pp. 19–20.

the employer to promise the worker the additional salary to induce him to complete the terms of the contract, but then to withhold the promised differential once the work is actually completed.[105] This is yet another instance in which the "purchaser" may conceal his intentions, given the breach of contract and lack of good faith of the "seller," in order to complete the terms of their agreement and avoid improper financial loss.

3. THE LIMITS OF LEGITIMATE ADVERTISING

The preceding discussion raises many fundamental questions regarding the ethics of mass advertising and promotion as these activities are carried out in the modern consumer society. Given the strict rules and guidelines that we have thus far encountered, we may well ask what be the limits on claims and statements made in support of one product as opposed to another. When may misleading or ambiguous advertising be undertaken? Is it at all proper to allure and entice others to purchase items or services which they had originally no intention to purchase?

In addressing these questions, it seems clear from our foregoing analysis that in merchandising and promoting products it is forbidden to make false claims—both on the grounds of *ona'ah*, insofar as the customer will be disappointed once the purchase is made and claims made on its behalf are proven wrong, as well as on the grounds of *geneivat da'at*, the very act of deception and misrepresentation, whether or not the purchaser gets full value for money paid.

But little, if any, advertising makes blatantly false claims or statements, if for no other reason than that such outright deception would backfire over the long run, in customer dissatisfaction and loss of product credibility. Thus our real question occurs in the context of advertising ploys or statements that (a) are misleading or insincere, or (b) use subtle means to motivate and persuade potential customers to purchase any given product.

We have seen already that the Mishnah (G) forbids painting or disguising old products to appear new. But the Gemara to that

105. *Bava Meẓia* 75b; Maimonides, *M.T. Hil. Sekhirut* 9:4; *Sh.A. H.M.* 333:18–22; Levine, *Economics*, p. 22. For a fuller treatment of this case, see Levine, *Free Enterprise*, pp. 44–49.

Mishnah *does* permit sprucing up new products to project their finest, most appealing image. And the Mishnah in *Arakhin*, as understood by Rashi, states explicitly that it is permitted to dress slaves in their finest clothing prior to their being sold, in order to maximize their salability and market price.[106] In commenting on this Mishnah, R. Israel Lipschutz, the Tiferet Yisrael, makes the pointed observation that while such activity would be forbidden when intended to disguise defects such as aging, it *is* permitted "in order to heighten the desire of customers to make a purchase."[107]

A pertinent passage is encountered in the Mishnah and Gemara in *Bava Meẓia* 60a–b (G). The Mishnah records several tannaitic disputes. In the first, R. Judah forbids storekeepers from promoting sales either by giving away promotional samples to minors or by discounting the price, whereas the sages permit both ploys. In the second, Abba Saul forbids any sifting of a mixture to improve its appearance by more than the value of the refuse removed, whereas the sages permit it as long as the entire mixture (and not just the visible exterior) is sifted. In both cases, the sages favor what might be called "creative merchandising," just as long as no customer is deliberately misled so as to harbor a mistaken impression. Apparently it is permitted, in their view, to promote one's product, but not at the expense of the truth. Significantly, this permissive view of the sages became normative, as codified almost verbatim by Maimonides (M), the *Tur*, and the *Shulḥan Arukh*.[108] In his formulation of the law, Maimonides explains that such activities are simply not considered *geneivat ayin* or visual deception of the customer. It would appear that even though the customer may not be fully conscious of the psychological means used to get him to purchase particular goods at a particular time and place, nonetheless the customer is not improperly misled as to the nature of the product under consideration. One can therefore draw the conclusion that there is nothing improper per se in resorting to subtle yet effective strategies to encourage a purchase, even those that take advantage of any emotional vulnerability on the part of the consumer, just as long as there is neither

106. *Arakhin* 6:5 (24b).
107. *Tiferet Yisrael* to *Arakhin* 6:5. See Warhaftig, p. 359, n. 145.
108. *Tur/Sh.A. H.M.* 228:15–17, *Sh.A. H.M.* 228:17–18.

an intent nor a result of concealing the true nature of the item at hand. Indeed the *Shulḥan Arukh ha-Rav* expressly permits a storekeeper to inflate the price of his spruced-up and attractive products beyond the cost differential involved in the product improvement, because, as he puts it, "someone who is prepared to pay more for attractive items can be considered to have intentionally forgone the additional cost."[109] Likewise the *Arukh ha-Shulḥan* permits a slight additional premium for produce that is sifted or polished, on the assumption that certain purchasers will gladly pay a little extra to avoid additional work for themselves.[110]

Yet even here, there are those who see a clear limit as to the boundary of such motivating strategies. Thus Warhaftig quotes the *Tosafot Yomtov* to this Mishnah, who states that when the sages forbid a seller to sift beans unless the entire mixture is consistent, this applies even where the seller informs the purchaser that it is only the exterior that is sifted.[111] This is based on the mishnaic phrase *ke-gonev et ha'ayin*, "like deceptive appearances"; were the Mishnah describing a case where the purchaser had no idea that the rest of the produce was not of this quality, it would not merely be "like" deception, it would *be* deception, plain and simple. He concludes therefore that the case under discussion involves full intellectual awareness by the customer, but still a lack of customer self-control, given the visual appeal of the item. In other words, the purchaser may be "seduced" by what he sees, and end up purchasing what he knows to be inappropriate or of inferior quality, at a price beyond its market value, and it is this which the sages forbid. If this be the intent of the sages, then clearly an advertiser or promoter must take into consideration that certain consumers or customers will be unfairly exploited, and he is therefore forbidden to promote his product under such circumstances, even though he is, in the narrow sense, quite truthful in his claims or statements.

As outlined by Rabbi Levine, several common promotional strategies fall into this category of halakhically questionable tactics.[112] Thus the so-called weasel-word stratagem, which deliberately creates false or exaggerated claims (e.g., "cleans like a white

109. *Shulḥan Arukh ha-Rav, Hil. Ona'ah* 18.
110. *Arukh ha-Shulḥan, H.M.* 228:13.
111. Warhaftig, p. 364.
112. Levine, *Economics*, pp. 46 ff.

tornado"), would be forbidden where it creates impressions or expectations that cannot be fulfilled by the product. The same is true of any claim that improperly implies that the sale price is a genuine bargain. While, as we have seen, the sages consider price-cutting to be quite permitted, and even to be encouraged, it is forbidden to misrepresent the circumstances surrounding the lower prices.[113] Such a case involves a merchandiser who has dated or overstocked products, and wishes to dispose of such inventory at clearance prices. In advertising the lower prices, he may not characterize them as "discounted" or "in the public interest," implying thereby that he is selling them for less than what is available elsewhere. In short one should not imply that one offers a bargain (defined as a price below "fair market value") when in fact the price merely reflects changed market conditions.

In the realm of advertising a "bargain," similar dishonesty can occur when a retailer claims to be selling an item below the "manufacturer's suggested list price." For if indeed that suggested price is so inflated that hardly any retail stores can charge that amount while remaining competitive, then the "bargain" is no bargain at all, but merely the "going" rate. Hence the advertiser is guilty of seeking to garner undeserved good will by misrepresenting his merchandise or the conditions surrounding its sale.[114] This would not be the case, however, where it is generally understood that the "suggested list price" is merely for reference purposes.

Another common advertising ploy is "puffery," by which the qualities of a product are exaggerated out of proportion to reality. Levine finds that where such claims relate to the realm of subjective feelings or purely aesthetic judgment (e.g., that a certain product evokes a mood of romance, serenity, or glamour), they are not forbidden, as long as they do not misrepresent the extent of popularity of the item in question.[115] But where such puffery occurs in the performance domain, promising results that are

113. A curious caveat is made by the *Arukh ha-Shulḥan, H.M.* 228:14, when he states that price-cutting is permitted only in the case of produce (*tevuah*), for it will lead to a general marketwide reduction of the price, but not in the case of merchandise (*seḥorah*), insofar as it will lead to economic breakdown and financial ruination. The *Arukh ha-Shulḥan* likewise forbids any deliberate deception intended to cause additional purchases by the customer.

114. Levine, *Free Enterprise*, p. 123.

115. Levine, *Economics*, pp. 53–54.

objectively measurable, the law of *ona'ah* requires that such promises or implied benefits must be consistent with what the purchaser can expect to enjoy as a result of the advertising.

Rabbi Levine also finds grounds to object to the tactic known as "bait and switch," by which stores advertise a product which they do not have in stock (or do have, but do not disclose that it is in very limited quantity). By pricing that article at an extraordinarily low price, they hope to attract customers, who, upon being informed that the item is no longer available, might be convinced to purchase some other, more expensive, product. Such activity can be classified as *ona'ah*, in that the seller deliberately intends the customer to experience disappointment, followed by intentional manipulation to purchase other merchandise at more normal prices. Hence "bait and switch" activities are clearly forbidden. It is not, however, forbidden to feature a "loss leader" to attract customers who might subsequently purchase other goods at normal prices, as long as the underpriced item is available in ample quantity and presented in good faith.[116] In this case, the discounted item represents a true bargain, available for less than what it might cost elsewhere.

One final advertising tactic that we can examine is the use of testimonials or statistics. Here, too, Levine points out that use of such data in promoting sales can trigger the *geneivat da'at* prohibition if the source being used is less than absolutely objective, and the advertising fails to reveal that fact. The situation is similar to the halakhic demand for absolute neutrality on the part of a judge in cases that come before him. Thus, for instance, when the effectiveness of a product is measured and attested to by a source that is retained and supported by the marketer itself, and such a relationship is not revealed in advertising the product, then the public has been effectively misled.

In all such cases, according to Levine, it is necessary to clarify how specific advertising or presentations are perceived by the target group. Thus it would be necessary to pilot-test and measure the impressions and inferences the consumer draws; and should the product or the advertised price differential fail to fulfill the benefits stated or implied in the advertising, such promotional activity must be said to be forbidden as *ona'ah* (exploita-

---

116. See ibid., pp. 45–47; Levine, *Free Enterprise*, pp. 120–121.

tion, leading to disappointment) as well as *geneivat da'at* (deceptive business practices).[117]

SUMMARY AND CONCLUSIONS

In examining the issues involved in possible misrepresentation in the business setting, we have examined a number of prohibitions. The first of these is *ona'ah*, or exploitation, involving not so much price fraud as insensitivity to the emotions and feelings of others. As explained by the Meiri, any pretense that necessarily leads to disappointment in the business sphere is forbidden insofar as it needlessly manipulates the feelings of the other party. And insensitivity to the emotional pain thus inflicted is likewise condemned as redundant *ẓa'ar ha-lev*, or heartache, by the *Shulḥan Arukh ha-Rav*.

The second prohibition is *geneivat da'at*, or the intentional misrepresentation of the facts of a situation. According to the *Mekhilta* this behavior is the highest form of thievery, and it was given its definitive formulation by the amora Samuel, to include deception of even a Gentile victim. While there is some disagreement as to the source of the prohibition (the Ritva finds a biblical source that forbids stealing, Rabbeinu Yonah derives it from the biblical prohibition against lying, while the Semak, the Baḥ, and R. Shneur Zalman consider it purely rabbinic in origin), all agree, following Samuel's dictum, that the prohibition applies equally to the treatment of Jew or Gentile.

From the Gemara *Ḥullin* 94a–b are derived the major parameters of forbidden deception: e.g., offering favors or gifts that one knows will not be accepted; allowing a guest the mistaken impression of expenses incurred on his behalf; the failure to reveal to a purchaser the true source of shoe leather; and the sale to a Gentile of nonkosher meat as if kosher—all improper actions because they give the false impression of favors proffered. And from *Bava*

---

117. There are other halakhic concerns raised by modern promotional activities, as discussed by Levine (including providing inappropriate advice, disparagement of competitors or their products, incitement of envy, price gouging, the dissuasion responsibility, and the like) or by Warhaftig (improper value formation, consumerism, and creating artificial needs). But these concerns are extraneous to the specific issues of deception, misrepresentation, and integrity that are the concerns of this chapter.

Meẓia 60 a–b are derived several other facets of *geneivat da'at:* e.g., the impropriety of disguising aging products to appear young or new, and the prohibition against dressing meat to appear of higher quality. On the other hand, it is permissible to spruce up items to their best appearance, as long as there is no deliberate attempt to conceal their true age or defective condition. Such forbidden activity was extended to include mixing of various qualities of merchandise, where done in such a way as to mislead the customer.

Among the medieval authorities, a few formulations of *geneivat da'at* stand out as comprehensive and repercussive. The first is Maimonides, who in *Hilkhot De'ot* of the *Mishneh Torah* requires at all times "truthful speech, an upright spirit, and a pure heart freed of all pretense and cunning." The second is Rabbeinu Yonah of Gerondi, who emphasizes the psychological damage of misrepresentation, in that, as he puts it, truth is one of the "foundations of the soul." Another notable passage is encountered in the *Sefer Ḥasidim*, which decries those who knowingly pretend to false piety.

The principle of *geneivat da'at* finds expression in a number of areas: one, according to Maimonides, and his descendant Joshua ha-Nagid, is the biblical prohibition against the *me'onen*, or "beguiler," which is based on his deceptive sleight of hand that fools his audience, i.e., *geneivat da'at*. The Radbaz echoes this rationale for the prohibition. A second application of *geneivat da'at* is in the realm of self-evaluation. The Gemara in *Ḥullin* records that a certain amora (R. Judah) honored an important guest without informing him of all the circumstances surrounding his generosity in opening a barrel of wine, and the Gemara indicates that evaluation of his motivations could be left to himself. Yet both Maimonides and the Tur, as explained by R. Aryeh Judah b. Akiva, do not consider such self-knowledge and evaluation possible for most people, whose motives, whether they recognize it or not, can be considered to include a measure of deception. Thus complete disclosure of intent and circumstance to one's guests is, as a rule, necessary. Yet in other circumstances, later authorities (R. Moshe Mordecai Epstein of Slabodka, R. Eliezer Meir Preil, R. Moshe Feinstein) were more lenient, permitting a man to evaluate his own ability to perform certain work given his age, and as a result to resort to some deception (dyeing his beard) to offset possible age discrimination against him. A third area in which we saw the principle of *geneivat da'at* implemented was that of publishing and academic grading. Rabbi Waldenberg thus prohibits any alteration of research findings in order to advance the author's career, both on grounds of *geneivat da'at* and of falsehood, whether or not others incur financial loss as a result. A minority view (R. Eliezer of Metz) sees no biblical prohibition as long as no other people are harmed by such tampering, although Rabbi Waldenberg feels that even this view would agree that there is a rabbinic ordinance against it. A related concern is that of students who cheat on examinations; according to Rabbi Menasheh Klein this too is forbidden under the rubric of *geneivat da'at,* whether or not the student subsequently uses those grades to obtain employment. The same is true, according to the Maharam Schick, of those who do not properly acknowledge the sources of creative scholarship which they pass off as their own.

In addition to *ona'ah* and *geneivat da'at,* we also saw that the principle of *hain ẓedek* (to treat one's word as binding) requires good faith and complete consistency between intent, verbal assurance, and fulfillment of even verbal commitments. The Halakhah also curses the man who reneges on a deal at the last moment, after verbal agreement has been reached, considering such behavior unbefitting a Jew. The same is true of the principle of *vi'heyitem nekiyyim,* which requires that one not only do what is right, but also ensure that one is perceived by others as doing it, as for instance in properly disposing of charitable funds, taking proper care in safeguarding items one held either on deposit or as security, protecting lost property, and making full payment of charitable pledges. In all these cases it is important to be held guiltless both in the eyes of God and of man.

Yet the Halakhah does not overlook the responsibilities of the purchaser either. Clearly the purchaser bears a certain onus of inquiring as to the nature of the goods purchased. The major text for this duty is the passage in *Ḥullin* that speaks of self-deception, the case in point being the Gentile who purchases meat without inquiring whether it be kosher or not. Here the Gemara implies that it should occur to him that the meat is not kosher, insofar as the laws of kashrut do not apply to him, and therefore it is up to him to inquire; and the Jew is not obliged to inform him that it is not kosher. In examining this passage, we encountered the opposing views of Rashi and Tosafot. Rashi's view is that while the seller is not permitted to make a false statement at the time of sale, he is also not required to actively correct the purchaser's unwarranted misconception. Tosafot, on the other hand, requires of the seller that he completely disabuse the purchaser of any erroneous notion. All are agreed that where the other party had no reason at all to assume a certain intent (e.g., thinking that a fortuitous meeting with others was planned in his honor), there is no need to correct such a mistaken impression. Maimonides' view is debatable: most understand him to agree with Tosafot, but a minority view (the *Leḥem Mishneh*) takes him to agree with Rashi. The majority of subsequent halakhists (e.g., *Tur*, *Shulḥan Arukh*) side with Tosafot in requiring that the seller actively correct the purchaser's unwarranted misconceptions.

On the matter of defective goods, we encountered a number of views. The *Maggid Mishnah* holds the purchaser responsible for not checking the condition at the time of purchase, but the *Mishneh la-Melekh* disagrees. The Radbaz indicates that the purchaser can rely upon the seller's assurances and does not have to check himself. From the Gemara *Ketuvot* it is clear that where the defect was fully evident at the time of purchase, it must be assumed that the buyer accepted the goods "as is," and has no subsequent claim on the vendor. This is equally true where it is common for purchasers to taste (or test) the product at the point of purchase and obvious defects are present. Likewise, continued use of the goods is clear indication of the purchaser's readiness to overlook such defects, and invalidates any subsequent claim. And once it is clear that the seller did inform the buyer of the presence of defects at the time of sale, the buyer has no further claim in their regard. How detailed must such disclosure be? Maimonides requires complete specificity, whereas the *Tur* is more flexible.

A much-discussed question occurs where there are certain broad assumptions made by the market or purchasers as a class. The *Shulḥan Arukh* permits a distributor to mix grains from various sources, because such recourse is widespread and generally known. This is analogous to the sale of nonkosher meat to the Gentile, who is expected to inquire under such circumstances. Implicit herein, as explained by Warhaftig, is that it is up to the purchaser to inquire whenever the quality is likely to be ambiguous or in doubt, and the seller is not required to inform him if he happens to be ignorant of what is widely known. This is certainly the case where vendors customarily display their goods to best advantage, seeking to paint or spruce up the merchandise in question—as indicated in *Bava Meẓia*—just as long as they do not intentionally mislead or hide defects or aged items.

Just such a situation led to an exchange of views in the twentieth century regarding the practice of butchers who soak livers in blood to preserve a fresh appearance. While Rabbi Yehoshua Baumol and several others were categorically opposed to such practices, on the ground that they improperly disguised meat to hide its age, causing the customer to pay more than its worth, or at any rate to be misinformed, Rabbi Moshe Feinstein saw no reason to forbid it. While the stricter view saw this case as analogous to the talmudic prohibition against soaking meat to make it appear fatter, the lenient view of Rabbi Feinstein refers to the talmudic dispensation, as understood by Maimonides, to display meat "to make it appear attractive." What is permitted, says Rabbi Feinstein, is visual improvement and display that is undertaken with the general knowledge of purchasers at large, whereas what is forbidden is where customers as a rule are not aware of such steps, and have no reason to question the condition or freshness of the item at hand. Thus the butcher is not duty-bound to explicitly notify the customer on each occasion of purchase, insofar as the customer bears the responsibility to inquire whether the meat be fresh or not, given the pervasive custom among butchers. On this issue, it would appear that Rabbi Feinstein takes a position that largely reflects the view of Rashi, whereas Rabbi Baumol seems closer to the position of Tosafot.

Where it is not the purchaser, but the seller, who may be ignorant of the subjective or entrepreneurial value of an item being negotiated, it is the view of Rabbi Levine that the purchaser is not required to disclose that subjective value or intent (unless specifically questioned by the seller), just as long as he does not in some way misrepresent the nature of the property right being transferred, and the seller receives fair market value for his goods. Levine draws support for this position from Abraham's purchase of the Cave of Makhpelah (in which he hid from the seller its subjective value to him), and from Jacob's bargain purchase of the birthright from Esau (given Esau's anticipation of his own early death, and the relatively low value of the birthright to Esau). One further instance involving concealment of intent by the "purchaser" occurs where a day laborer reneges on his work commitment, and the employer deceptively promises to pay a premium to the worker to get him to finish the job. In this case, Rabbi Levine argues, the employer is fully within his rights to conceal his intentions, as long as he pays the original figure, given the breach of contract on the other side.

The implications of the foregoing for product advertising are considerable. Certainly it is true that misleading or false claims would be prohibited by the Halakhah. But what of more subtle means to motivate the purchase of a given product? The Mishnah in several places permits putting the best appearance on products that are for sale (e.g., slaves, produce, clothing), to make them as attractive as possible. It likewise records the majority view allowing the use of promotional samples and price discounting, as well as careful, and consistent, sifting of one product, as long as there is no deliberate deception. This view became normative, and even Maimonides, otherwise so careful, allows such subtle motivating tactics that utilize psychological incentives leading to such sales. Similar dispensations are offered (by the *Shulḥan Arukh ha-Rav* and the *Arukh ha-Shulḥan*) to require a premium for specially packaged or treated goods.

Yet here too there are limits, and competing views. *Tosafot Yomtov* interprets the sages as forbidding any selective sifting that belies the true nature of the mixture, even where the purchaser is fully informed of the practice, because the purchaser will be emotionally vulnerable to the attractive appearance. The effect of this prohibition is to curtail promotional activities that strictly speaking are truthful, but nonetheless are insincere and exploitative. This includes so-called weasel-word tactics, improperly implying a bargain or discount price, when the asking price actually reflects no discount from fair market value. Other forbidden tactics include puffery in the performance domain that promises more than the purchaser can expect to receive by purchasing the product; "bait and switch" that entices a customer under false pretenses, while deliberately steering him to more profitable items (whereas the use of a loss-leader strategy is itself permitted); and the use of testimonials or statistics that are either not fully disinterested or measurable by the purchaser. In all these cases, it is necessary to establish (by pilot-testing advertising or the relevant copy) whether in fact customers or consumers draw inaccurate or unwarranted inferences from the advertising. If this is in fact the case, such advertising must be seen as deceptive, and therefore forbidden.

To answer the questions with which we began this chapter, one would have to say that if indeed the cigarette manufacturer knew, or had good reason to suspect, that its products were faulty or posed a risk, while at the same time there was no widespread public knowledge of such a risk, then the company acted improperly—and deceptively—by misrepresenting the nature of its product. But once it was publicly known that this product was at the very least suspected of causing health problems, the company can properly claim that it was under no special obligation to inform the consumer of what was already widely known. Of course, even at that point, if the company advertised (either explicitly or implicitly) that its product was safe even while it knew the hazards involved, it would certainly be guilty of improper deception. If, on the other hand, the company had no idea as to the hazards involved, it would not be guilty of misrepresentation or deception, but it could be held responsible for damages caused by its product.

In advertising, while the vendor is permitted to project its product in the best light, and even to make it appear as alluring and attractive as possible, nonetheless the company is duty-bound to avoid any implication that the product is safe or without peril, contrary to what it knows to be true. Failure to do so would make the company guilty of irresponsibility, misrepresentation, and deceptive business practices.

Epilogue

Before concluding this volume, a number of comments and conclusions are in order, so as to highlight and crystalize certain underlying realities relevant to the present and future halakhic response to the ethical issues of our time.

At the outset of this book it was stated that the Halakhah is a living, growing, and expanding entity, one that has always been open to a variety of interpretations and viewpoints. Now that we have had an opportunity to examine in some detail the Halakhah's own treatment of, and reaction to, a fair number of issues that are currently debated in our society, it is possible to evaluate that characterization of the halakhic process.

In the first place it should be quite clear that the Halakhah was never as insulated from its larger surroundings as popular misconceptions about medieval Jewish life or the "shtetl" assume. The leading halakhic authorities of each generation and place were always fully conversant with the issues and debates of their time, and moreover strove to articulate responses that were both faithful to tradition and open to innovative approach. As found in the talmudic debates, as well as halakhic commentaries, codes, responsa, and more recently Torah journals and articles, these discussions and conclusions served at all times to provide the Jew with a ready and practical path of action in responding to the challenges of the larger, often non-Jewish, environment, in a manner consistent with Jewish tradition.

Secondly, it should be apparent from the discussions in this book that the leading halakhic authorites were, and are, at all times completely loyal to talmudic precedent. Thus it is inconceivable that new positions could be taken in contradiction to all talmudic discussion of the matter. It was not always necessary to adopt the majority talmudic view, and it is sometimes the case that a particular halakhist will interpret the talmudic discussion in a novel fashion—but the ultimate arbiter of halakhic respectability has always been the degree of fealty to talmudic discussion.

On the other hand, it is clear that there is development and expansion of halakhic thought. That is to say, the major halakhists did not see their role as merely one of interpretation and explanation of accepted, authoritative texts. They saw themselves in addition as finding new precedents in the Talmud, and incorporating additional insights gleaned from their own experiences and environment. This is especially true when it comes to evaluating and accepting physical and scientific information, in place of earlier halakhic assumptions based on erroneous data provided by less developed scientific methods and knowledge. Even so, such innovation is always related to, and supported by, an underlying consistency with the relevant halakhic texts and precedents. Hardly any post-talmudic authority would claim some special dispensation or general "halakhic sense" (sometimes referred to as *da'at torah*) to justify his conclusions on a given issue.

Furthermore, it is abundantly clear that minority dissent was always tolerated and accepted. Absent the central authority of the Sanhedrin or subsequent embodiments of centralized authority (e.g., the Gaonate), individual authorities were always allowed the latitude of disagreement and contradiction, not only in theory but in practice, and not only for themselves but for their followers. Again, such dissent did have to be justified by precedent or acceptable interpretation of prior texts; nonetheless minority views often took hold and flourished, occasionally with the passage of time becoming normative. Nonetheless for the most part the Halakhah tended to coagulate in the direction of consensus and majority view, whereby schism and divisiveness were minimized.

In considering the broad thrust of the views we have encountered, certain fundamental moral principles, values, and assumptions emerge. Of course there is the principle of the sanctity of human life, which the Torah commands and the Talmud confirms is to be saved and prolonged wherever possible. There is the axiomatic notion that we are all responsible for each other's welfare, and duty-bound to exert ourselves and expend our means to safeguard our fellow's life and well-being, even though we are not required to endanger our own lives in that cause. Furthermore there is the unspoken activist principle that it is for man to subdue nature, pushing back the frontiers of scientific knowledge, to ameliorate human suffering. But even so, man is not the measure of all things, in that it is not man, but God's will as inscribed in the Torah, that determines man's proper path in this world.

In the realm of social relations, a number of basic principles are clear. Aggressive behavior that poses a danger to life is to be thwarted at all costs, even if it means taking the law in one's own hands, where no alternative exists. Self-defense, and to a lesser degree defense of others, is mandatory. In this regard, as in the area of bioethics, the Halakhah does not require or tolerate a passive reliance on divine intercession.

In family matters, we encountered the principle of mutual responsibility as it relates to the young. The best-interest-of-the-child doctrine is the foundation for all the discussions surrounding child custody, and it is this which provides strong evidence of the duty-oriented (as opposed to rights-oriented) value system of the Halakhah. Accordingly, it is not so much what one person can demand of another, but rather what one is duty-bound to provide for one's fellow.

In financial affairs, the moral dictates of the Halakhah clearly forbid intentionally misleading behavior. Honesty, integrity, and good faith are essential values in halakhic business and professional relationships. Even so, there are limitations as to the disclosure requirements on the parties involved in various transactions, insofar as every individual is responsible to safeguard his own interests.

Clearly these principles reveal what has been referred to as "the dialectic of the Halakhah," a phrase that describes the manner in which the Halakhah balances often competing norms and goals, keeping them in mutually reinforcing perspective, even while preserving a healthy tension between them. Examples of this tension, among the many that we have seen, include the prolongation of life vs. the acceptance of God's will; subduing nature vs. the acknowledgment of natural processes; respect for the dead vs. the use of cadaver organs for the living; the recognition of scientific progress vs. a deep suspicion of technological arrogance; the demands of due process vs. the need for precipitous action; parental prerogative vs. judicial intervention; child preferences vs. superior adult experience; free market forces vs. the need to protect the weak; and personal responsibility vs. communal protection. In each instance, the halakhists of each generation have attempted to give each "pole" of the spectrum its due consideration and weight, somehow accommodating these conflicting desiderata to create internally consistent models of ethically desirable behavior.

Is there room in this system for independent thought and moral reasoning? Insofar as the fundamental principles are concerned, the answer must be "very little." The principles as given, and as received, are for the most part accepted by the halakhist, and by the halakhically observant Jew. Where moral reasoning does enter the picture is in evaluating and applying various principles and precedents at the point that they coincide. Thus an individual can and should weigh and consider the applicability and weight of one principle over another, being influenced in turn by the relevant judgments and opinions of preceding authorities. Even so, there are many specific situations, each with its own circumstances, that require nuanced and sensitive decisions that may well part company with a general ruling. In such instances, the halakhist, or individual qualified to make a decision, is surely expected to examine all the pertinent legal sources and then to give careful attention to his or her own independent moral considerations in arriving at a final decision. It is for this reason that the halakhic process is so sensitive to the notion of "local rabbinic authority," whereby particular circumstances and conditions can be factored into the eventual ruling.

One final observation needs to be made. It is to the everlasting credit of the rabbis responsible for the halakhic process of every generation that over the centuries, and unlike other religions, the Halakhah never became divorced from real life, but rather found in itself the resources to organize and articulate a way of life in which there would be neither denial nor rejection of ordinary human desires and aspirations, but rather their acceptance, regulation, and sanctification. The Halakhah was at all times anchored in the real world, challenged by the human predicament to help the ordinary man and woman as they grappled with "*la condition humaine*" in all its vagaries.

In so doing Jewish law rejected the cynical notion that the world or society was inherently evil or beyond redemption. In place of such a cynical attitude, the law cultivated the idea that through his daily actions, the Jew can transform an oftentimes harsh and uncaring world, and through adherence to the Halakhah sanctify his life, and that of the people around him. In the process, the halakhically sensitive Jew himself became one more link in the long chain of tradition, joining past to future, and history to redemption.

The challenge of our time, the age of secular man, is for the Halakhah, and those loyal to it, to find that same inner strength and substance, to transcend the twin allures of withdrawal from the real world, on the one hand, and an uncritical embrace of popular yet ultimately un-Jewish values, on the other. To chart a path that is both authentic and enlightened, uncompromising yet sensitive, theoretically coherent yet practically viable. Of such challenges and tensions is the halakhic process made, today more than ever.